D1469142

OXFORD MEDICAL PUBLICATIONS

Closed head injury

Closed head injury

Psychological, social, and family consequences

Edited by Neil Brooks

Oxford   New York   Toronto

OXFORD UNIVERSITY PRESS

Oxford University Press, Walton Street, Oxford OX2 6DP

Oxford New York Toronto
Delhi Bombay Calcutta Madras Karachi
Petaling Jaya Singapore Hong Kong Tokyo
Nairobi Dar es Salaam Cape Town
Melbourne Auckland

and associated companies in
Beirut Berlin Ibadan Nicosia

Oxford is a trade mark of Oxford University Press

First published 1984
Reprinted 1985, 1986 (twice)

British Library Cataloguing in Publication Data

Closed head injury.—(Oxford medical publications)
1. Brain—Wounds and injuries—Complications and
sequelae
I. Brooks, Neil
617'.48101   RD594
ISBN 0-19-261252-2

Library of Congress Cataloging in Publication Data

Main entry under title:
Closed head injury
Bibliography: p.
Includes index.
1. Brain—Wounds and injuries—Complications and
sequelae.   2. Cognition disorders.   3. Personality,
Disorders of.   4. Brain—Wounds and injuries—Social
aspects. I. Brooks, Neil, 1944—   .   (DNLM:
1. Head injuries—Psychology.   2. Head injuries—
Complications.   3. Cognition disorders—Etiology   . WE
706 C645)
RD663.C57   1983   617'.48101   83-13332
ISBN 0-19-261252-2

Printed in Great Britain by
Antony Rowe Ltd, Chippenham

Preface

This book arose directly out of a series of informal meetings held over a number of years in the mid-1970s both in Britain and in Holland. The meetings were attended by psychologists, neurosurgeons, and neurologists, and were designed as a medium for exchanging ideas about the study and management of psychological deficits after head injury. The meetings offered an opportunity to describe ongoing studies, to comment on trends in the literature, and to speculate about future developments. After one particularly fruitful meeting held in Oxford, the rather fanciful title of Trauma International was proposed for the informal group, and the label stuck.

Initially, the meetings were dominated by discussions of cognitive deficits—particularly deficits in memory, but as further meetings were held, the nature of the discussions changed, as we began to try to understand underlying mechanisms of cognitive disorder, and to assess the functional importance of cognitive disorder on a patient's everyday life. In addition, considerations of family, social, and vocational and behavioural outcome became more dominant, and later meetings began to consider topics such as family distress, personality change, and the management of behavioural change.

The topics dealt with in this book—ranging from cognitive and attentional deficits to the management of behaviour disorders—reflects neatly the discussions held by Trauma International, and not surprisingly, five of the contributors to the book, Brooks, Oddy, Van Zomeren, Deelman, Brouwer, were regular attenders at the meetings. A regular attender but a non-contributor to the book (pressure of work forced her to decline an invitation to contribute) was Dr Freda Newcombe of the MRC Neuropsychology Unit in Oxford. She initiated the meetings, and acted as a charming hostess and a stimulating research contributor.

It is hoped that the book will provide a data base and a conceptual framework for those intending to work clinically or in a research capacity with severely head-injured patients. The book aims to set out what is currently known about psychological outcome, and should be of use to physicians and surgeons, psychologists and psychiatrists, remedial therapists, and others involved in researching, treating, and managing the psychological consequences of severe head injury.

Many people deserve thanks for the direct or indirect efforts they have put into the book. First, Bryan Jennett for initially interesting me in the problems of head injury, and secondly, the contributors who have produced chapters which are not only scientifically erudite, but also interesting to read—a difficult combination. I must also thank all members of Trauma International (whether contributors to the book or not), for years of fruitful and stimulating discussion. Finally, I must thank the patients themselves and their relatives. Had they not given generously of their time and energy in taking part in our many research studies, the book would not have been written. The debt to them is a very real one, and I hope that a by-product of a book like this may be a marked and lasting improvement in the services for the long-term management of severely injured patients and their families.

Glasgow
July, 1983   D.N.B.

Contents

Contributors

Neil Brooks (editor): Senior Lecturer in Clinical Psychology, Department of Psychological Medicine, University of Glasgow.

Michael Bond: Professor of Psychological Medicine, Department of Psychological Medicine, University of Glasgow.

W. H. Brouwer: Experimental psychologist, Neuropsychology Unit, Academisch Ziekenhuis, Groningen, Holland.

B. G. Deelman: Experimental psychologist, Neuropsychology Unit, Academisch Ziekenhuis, Groningen, Holland.

Bryan Jennett: Professor of Neurosurgery, Institute of Neurological Sciences, University of Glasgow.

David Mendelow: Senior Lecturer in Neurosurgery, Institute of Neurological Sciences, University of Glasgow.

Michael Oddy: Senior Clinical Psychologist, St. Francis Hospital, Haywards Heath.

Graham Teasdale: Professor of Neurosurgery, Institute of Neurological Sciences, University of Glasgow.

A. H. Van Zomeren: Neuropsychologist, Neuropsychology Unit, Academisch Ziekenhuis, Groningen, Holland.

R. L. Wood: Clinical Psychologist, St. Andrew's Hospital, Northampton.

1 Introduction

Neil Brooks

Fifteen years ago, it would have been very unlikely that this book could have been written. At that time, head injury occupied very much an 'also ran' position in the clinical neurosciences, with little published information on psychological sequelae, and often a considerable therapeutic pessimism among the surgeons and physicians who dealt with acutely head-injured patients. Outcome after injury was considered in simplistic terms, and the long-term emotional, behavioural, and other psychological consequences were unknown, or ignored. This is no longer the case. The neurosurgical literature contains enormous amounts of valuable information about the early management of severe head injury, and there is an increasing body of knowledge about the long-term consequences—consequences which are almost by definition, psychological. These form the focus of this book.

Although the book is concerned with the psychological effects of head injury, the first two chapters are written by neurosurgeons—Professor Bryan Jennett, Professor Graham Teasdale, and Mr David Mendelow. All three are from Glasgow, and this is not simply a result of parochialism on the part of the Editor (also from Glasgow). The upsurge of interest in head injury in the 1970s was largely due to one man—Bryan Jennett, Dean of the Faculty of Medicine, The University of Glasgow, and Professor of Neurosurgery in Glasgow. He gathered around him a team of clinicians and scientists to begin a series of investigations of all aspects of head injury. The fact that one of the first research workers appointed was a psychologist demonstrates his commitment to understanding the long-term psychosocial sequelae—an aspect of outcome that may easily be forgotten in the hurly-burly of acute neurosurgical management.

The next two chapters in this book ('Pathophysiology of head injuries' and 'The measurement outcome') are not about psychological consequences, and at first sight it may be thought that these chapters sit somewhat uneasily with the rest of the book. This should not be the case, as the late psychological changes after head injury in patient and family do not occur in a vacuum. They are the end result of a complex series of processes that begin with physical damage to the brain, and an understanding of the mechanisms and dynamics of these early processes is crucial for understanding the range and severity of the psychological deficits that may follow later.

Psychological outcome is only one aspect of outcome, but as the time since injury increases, the study of outcome becomes dominated increasingly by psychological rather than physical factors. Except in a small number of cases—those remaining in persistent vegetative state, or those with persisting severe neurophysical damage (a relatively small proportion of the surviving conscious population)—the longer-term the perspective, the greater the psychological component. For this reason, Bryan Jennett's thought-provoking chapter on outcome serves as an additional crucial orientation point for the rest of the book.

The remaining chapters deal with various aspects of the psychological consequences of severe injury. To some extent, the organization of the book is arbitrary in that some topics have been relatively underplayed (for example the post-concussional syndrome), and some have had greater emphasis (for example cognitive factors), but the underlying structure has been a three-part one, viz. cognitive, social/family, and 'other' consequences. The general cognitive consequences are described by Brooks in Chapter 4, and the specifically attentional consequences in Chapter 5 by van Zomeren and his colleagues. The decision to separate the attentional from the other cognitive consequences was taken partly because the expertise of van Zomeren in this area made this a natural choice, but also because the attentional-deficit literature has taken rather a different course from the literature concerning other cognitive consequences. Researchers studying attentional deficits have often adopted an analytic, theory-driven approach, asking questions, and using measures derived from current psychological and neuropsychological theorizing. This has been much less obvious in the general cognitive literature, where questions have tended to be empirical and clinical. A further reason for devoting a separate chapter to attentional consequences is that these often loom very large, and in many patients it is possible that a disorder of attention may underlie many of the other cognitive disorders.

The broadly social consequences of injury are described in three chapters —those by Oddy on social and vocational outcome (Chapter 6), by Brooks on family outcome (Chapter 7), and Bond on psychiatric consequences (Chapter 8). The chapters of Oddy and Brooks are complementary, with Oddy considering vocational, interpersonal, and leisure aspects of life following head injury, and Brooks concentrating much more exclusively on the family and related aspects of outcome. Psychiatric aspects of closed head injury have until now been largely neglected. The excellent review by Lishman (1968) and the earlier accounts by Hillbom (1960) and Hillbom and Jarho (1966) mainly concern the consequences of focal missile wounds, so that Bond's chapter is particularly valuable, not only for understanding the phenomenology and dynamics of the emotional and other changes in the patient, but also for help in managing these long-term changes.

The management of late consequences of head injury is now being seen to be increasingly important. The Israeli group (Najenson, Mendelson, Shechter, David, Mintz, and Groswasser 1974) has written in detail describing their experiences using conventional interdisciplinary rehabilitation techniques, and others are now beginning to do the same (Tobis, Kasturi, Puri, and Sheldon 1982; Rosenthal, Griffith, Bond, and Miller 1983). The treatment of the specifically cognitive consequences is now being tackled with vigour in many centres, but management of the severe behavioural disturbance is not being described in any detail. However, a small number of centres are now trying to develop techniques in this area, and one approach in particular—the behavioural approach—is likely to be valuable in managing problems of the severely impaired patient. This approach is described in Chapter 10 by Wood.

Finally, one special topic is included—head injury in children, by Oddy (Chapter 9). This is another neglected area, although recent work from Rutter and co-workers (Rutter, Chadwick, Shaffer, and Brown 1980; Chadwick and Rutter 1981; and from Klonoff, Low, and Clark 1977) has added considerably to our knowledge here. Despite these studies, little is known in detail about the long-term psychological consequences of injury in children; clinical experience strongly suggests that the nature, natural history, and severity of the psychological changes in children are different from those in adults, and these topics are discussed in detail by Oddy.

REFERENCES

Chadwick, O. and Rutter, M. (1981). A prospective study of children with head injuries: IV Specific cognitive deficits. *J. clin. Neuropsychol.* **3**, 101–20.

Hillbom, E. (1960). After effects of brain injury. *Acta psychiat. neurol. Scand.* Suppl. 142.

Jarho, L. (1966). Post traumatic Korsakoff syndrome. In *Head injury* (ed. W. F. Caveness and A. E. Walker) Lippincott, Philadelphia, pp. 98–109.

Klonoff, H., Low, M. D., and Clark, C. (1977). Head injuries in children: A prospective five-year follow up. *J. Neurol. Neurosurg. Psychiat.* **40**, 1211–19.

Lishman, W. A. (1968). Brain damage in relation to psychiatric disability after head injury. *Br. J. Psychiat.* **116**, 373–410.

Najenson, T., Mendelson, L., Schechter, I., David, C., Mintz, N., and Groswasser, Z. (1974). Rehabilitation after severe head injury. *Scand. J. rehabil. Med.* **6**, 15–21.

Rosenthal, M., Griffiths, E. R., Bond, M. R., and Miller, J. D. (ed.) (1983). *Rehabilitation of the head injured adult.* F. A. Davis, Philadelphia.

Rutter, M., Chadwick, O., Shaffer, D., and Brown, G. (1980). A prospective study of children with head injuries. I: Design and methods. *Psychol. Med.* **10**, 633–45.

Tobis, J. S., Kasturi, B., Puri, D., and Sheldon, J. (1982). Rehabilitation of the severely brain injured patient. *Scand. J. rehabil. Med.* **14**, 83–8.

2 Pathophysiology of head injuries

Graham Teasdale and David Mendelow

Many mechanisms can cause brain damage after head injury. The type, severity, and location of damage determine the effects on the patient in both the early and late stages. Knowledge of intracranial events during life is still very limited and much of what is reliably known about traumatic brain damage is derived from recent detailed neuropathological studies performed after death. On the other hand, both clinical studies that make use of advances in investigations, such as CT scanning, and also experiments in animal models of head injury are helping to unravel the complexities of human head injury.

Neurosurgeons are particularly focused on the patterns and causation of brain damage in the early stages, because it is then that treatment has the greatest potential to make a difference to outcome. An understanding of the mechanisms of brain damage in the early stages is also a basis for comprehending some of the sequelae of head injury. Knowledge of these is even more limited but it is usually assumed (probably correctly) that the processes that are responsible for death in fatal cases are also responsible for disability in survivors.

Recent studies (Adams, Graham, Murray, and Scott 1982) have emphasized the importance of diffuse brain damage after head injury and there is now less interest in the neurological and the psychological syndromes produced by focal lesions. Although focal lesions may be particularly relevant with penetrating fractures and with gunshot wounds of the head we shall concentrate on the sequelae of 'impact' head injury. This is sustained when the head is accelerated after a blow or when the moving head undergoes deceleration, as occurs frequently in road traffic accidents.

CLASSIFICATION OF BRAIN DAMAGE

For many reasons it is useful to distinguish between primary and secondary brain damage. The former occurs at the time of injury, is the result of distinctive mechanical factors, and is seldom affected by treatment; the latter is a consequence of a complication and is potentially preventable or reversible with treatment.

PRIMARY BRAIN DAMAGE

This is also referred to as immediate or impact brain damage and produces two very different types of lesion: contusions and diffuse axonal injuries.

Contusions

When the brain is examined with the naked eye, the most obvious signs of primary brain damage are haemorrhagic contusions on the crests of the gyri of the cerebral cortex. The haemorrhage varies in the extent from a superficial layer of blood to one which involves the whole depth of the cortex and perhaps several adjacent gyri. Large contusions may coalesce and produce a sizeable cerebral clot. Wherever the impact on the head, contusions are found most frequently on the under-surfaces of the frontal lobes and around the pole of the temporal lobe. Usually present on both sides of the head, they may be more severe on one side. Contusions are very rarely seen in the occipital lobe, even with blows to the back of the head. Indeed, contusions are very uncommonly found under the site of the blow to the head, except when this has caused a depressed fracture of the skull—that is, one with in-driven bone fragments.

Adams, Scott, Parker, Graham, and Doyle (1980) devised a numerical index for assessing the severity of the distribution of contusions in fatal cases. Their study confirmed that whatever the site of impact, the maximal location for contusions was the frontal region.

Diffuse axonal injury in the white matter

Although this is now thought to be the most important mechanism of primary traumatic brain damage, it has remained largely undetected until recently. This was because it is very difficult to find in the early stages. The post-mortem observation of white-matter degeneration after head injury was made first by Strich (1956) working in Oxford. She observed hydrocephalus and loss of white matter in the brains of patients who died after having survived for some months in the vegetative state. Since then, careful microscopic surveys have revealed the frequency and characteristics of the lesions, which have been referred to as white-matter shearing injuries, or as diffuse axonal injuries.

Even when axonal tearing is extensive, there may be little trace of it on the brain surface or in brain sections. Careful examination will often show small areas of haemorrhage. These have a predilection for the corpus callosum and upper brainstem (Fig. 1). They may be bilateral but are often asymmetrical and may be accompanied by intraventricular bleeding. In the

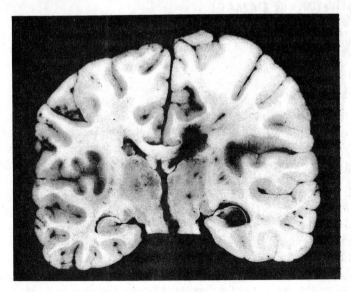

Fig. 2.1.

Diffuse damage to white matter (6-day survival after injury): there is a recent haemorrhagic lesion in the corpus callosum. (From Adams, J. H. (1975). *Handbook of clinical neurology* 23, North-Holland, Amsterdam.)

late stages these lesions are converted to brown scars and then are often associated with severe cerebral atrophy and hydrocephalus. It is when sections of the brain are treated with appropriate stains and are examined under the microscope that the striking features of axonal injury are seen. In the early stages, stains for nerve processes show the so-called 'retraction balls' (Fig. 2). Each of these indicates the site of a torn axon and is thought to represent extruded axoplasm. A few days after the injury there is a cellular reaction around the torn nerve fibres, forming a 'microglial' scar. After a few weeks, appropriate stains will show degeneration of the nerve processes distal to the site of the tear. These pick out the ascending and descending tracts of the brainstem and spinal cord, as well as associated fibres within the cerebral hemisphere. Axonal lesions are never seen in the brainstem alone; brainstem axonal lesions are always associated with lesions in the cerebral hemispheres.

Mechanisms responsible for primary brain damage

Clinical and experimental studies have each contributed to the development of concepts about the causation of primary brain damage. In Oxford, during the Second World War, Holbourne (1943) deduced that the effects of head injury on the brain were determined by the physical properties of the

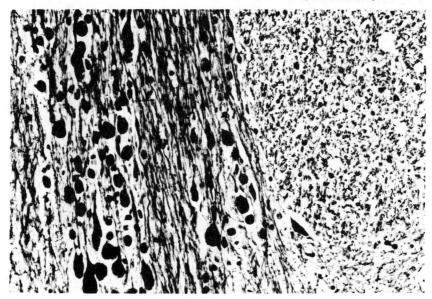

Fig. 2.2.

Diffuse damage to white matter (6-day survival after injury): there are numerous axonal retraction balls in basis pontis. Palmgren; ×250. (From Adams, J. H., Mitchell, D. E., Graham, D. I. and Doyle, D. (1977). *Brain*, **100**, 489–502. Reproduced with permission.)

brain and skull. Of particular importance in the production of contusions was the contrast between the skull, which is rigid and has an irregular internal contour, and the brain which lacks rigidity, but is incompressible. A head injury induces relative movement between the brain and the skull so that it is feasible to envisage the brain rotating and making contact with the inside of the skull. This results in forces which are maximal between the soft frontal and temporal lobes on the one hand, and the sharp wing of the sphenoid which separates the anterior and middle cranial fossae on the other. This is the reason that contusions are commonest in these sites.

Because contusions are so often remote from the site of impact they were previously thought to be produced by a contrecoup mechanism, with the force of the blow somehow transmitted to the opposite side of the brain. Evidence against this view was provided by Ommaya, Grubb, and Naumann (1971) who studied head injuries produced experimentally in monkeys. They found that contusions were maximal in the frontotemporal region, irrespective of whether the skull was struck in the frontal or occipital region. Adams *et al.*, in addition to confirming the frequency of contusions in the frontal and temporal regions, also found that when there was a skull fracture contusions were maximal on the same side of the brain, if the contrecoup explanation had been true they would have been anticipated to be greater on the opposite side (Adams, Scott, Parker, Graham, and Doyle, 1980).

Diffuse axonal injury is also explained by a shearing mechanism, in this case produced by movement between different components of the brain itself. Holbourne's analogy was to a deck of cards that had been changed from a rectangular pattern to a wedge. This deformity would result in disruption of any links across the interfaces between adjacent cards. Thus, movement of one part of the brain relative to another is responsible for damaging the nerve fibres in the white matter. The forces required to generate this shearing strain in the human result from rotational accelera-tion. Strictly linear movement of the head in any direction will not result in this type of acute injury. Holbourne also suggested that in rotational accel-eration, lesions would be more severe in the hemisphere than in the brainstem, a view supported by animal experiments (Ommaya and Gen-narelli 1974), by electrophysiological studies in patients (Greenberg *et al.* 1980), and by post-mortem studies in fatal cases (Adams, Graham, Murray, and Scott, 1982).

Clinical manifestations of primary brain damage

The best known and most consistent consequence of head injury is altered consciousness. Half a century ago Symonds (1928) suggested that the dura-tion of loss of consciousness might reflect the severity of brain damage sus-tained on injury. He also proposed that it was differences in the amount of brain damage, rather than the kind of lesion or its location, that determined whether a patient was unconscious for a few days or weeks rather than for minutes or seconds.

It now seems likely that different durations of unconsciousness reflect varying degrees of diffuse axonal injury. When coma is deep and persistent, axonal damage is severe and widespread. If a patient talks soon after a head injury then severe primary brain damage cannot have been sustained. On the other hand, it seems likely that even in so-called 'concussion' the basis for the brief traumatic unconsciousness is a degree of diffuse axonal injury in which most fibres escape permanent structural damage. This view is sup-ported by Oppenheimer's (1968) observation of microglial scars in patients who recovered from 'concussion lasting only a few minutes but who died from other extracranial complications'. It is also consistent with new psychological evidence of persisting but subtle damage after minor head in-jury and also with evidence of the cumulative effects of repeated mild con-cussion (Gronwall and Wrightson 1975). It is well known that lesions in the reticular activating system in the brainstem may induce loss of con-sciousness. This has led some to propose that the phenomenon of concus-sion is largely a brainstem event. There is recent evidence from experimental animals, in which the brain was damaged by a pulsed input of fluid with sufficient force to result in short periods of unconsciousness, that the endothelium and blood—brain barrier in blood vessels in the brainstem demonstrate early damage (Povlishock, Becker, Sullivan, and Miller 1978). On the other hand, there is evidence that in a closed head injury, associated with rotational acceleration, damage to the brainstem is preceded by damage in the hemispheres. Whether there is a degree of injury sufficient to disturb hemisphere function and produce unconsciousness without involving the brainstem has not been established.

The clinical significance of cortical contusions is much less than previously thought. Extremely large contusions or lesions in eloquent areas may produce clinical signs, especially when followed by swelling, oedema and local ischaemia. Scarring after contusions may later result in epilepsy. On the other hand, contusions cannot be invoked as the cause of loss of consciousness during injury. It is quite clear that even extensive contusions can be sustained without prolonged or even any loss of consciousness.

There are good reasons for discarding two terms that have been traditionally used to classify the severity of primary traumatic brain damage. 'Commotio cerebri' was held to represent a brief loss of consciousness without permanent brain damage, while 'contusio cerebri' was associated with a more prolonged disturbance of consciousness. One reason for the terms falling out of favour has been variable duration of the unconsciousness that was used to make the distinction. The main reason, however, has been the lack of validity of the underlying concepts. Brief unconsciousness can result in diffuse axonal injury and may leave a permanent mark on the brain, whereas even major contusions can be sustained without prolonged loss of consciousness.

SECONDARY BRAIN DAMAGE

When a patient who has been talking after injury subsequently loses consciousness, or when the responsiveness of a comatose patient deteriorates, it is likely that there is secondary brain damage. Some of the many factors that are responsible for secondary brain damage are listed below. They fall into two main types: intracranial and extracranial.

1. Intracranial factors: (i) intracranial haematomas; (ii) brain swelling; (iii) infection; (iv) subarachnoid haemorrhage; (v) hydrocephalus.

2. Extracranial factors: (i) respiratory failure and hypoxia; (ii) hypotension.

Whatever the primary factor, the ultimate mechanism responsible for the damage to the brain is usually either hypoxia/ischaemia or a shift with distortion and compression of the brain.

Causes of secondary brain damage

Intracranial factors

Intracranial haematoma
Bleeding inside the skull after a head injury leads to the development of a clot and, eventually, to compression of the brain. A clot may form between the skull and the meninges (extradural haematoma; Fig. 2.3) or may be deep to the dura (intradural haematoma; Fig. 2.4). An extradural haematoma is classically a complication of a skull fracture that has damaged the middle meningeal artery. It is typically associated with little or no primary brain damage whereas this is the rule with an intradural haematoma. Intradural haematomas are three times as common as extradural haematomas and may be subdural, intracerebral or often a mixture of the two. Results of evacuation of an extradural haematoma are usually good, but, because of their association with primary impact damage, treatment of an acute intradural haematoma is not universally successful. Whatever the kind of the haematoma if it is not removed in time its effects on the brain may trigger a series of pathological events which progress relentlessly, despite operation.

A chronic subdural haematoma presents weeks or months after the original head injury, which is often so trivial that it has been forgotten. It usually occurs without severe primary brain damage. The initial presentation is often suspicious of a stroke or a dementing process.

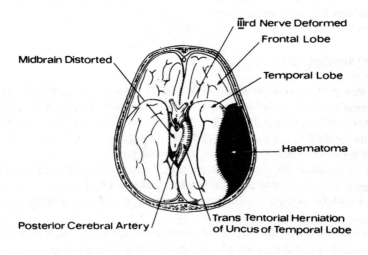

Fig. 2.3.

Extradural haematoma.

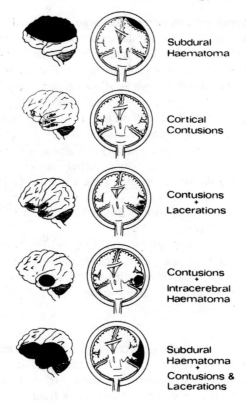

Subdural Haematoma

Cortical Contusions

Contusions
+
Lacerations

Contusions
+
Intracerebral Haematoma

Subdural Haematoma
+
Contusions & Lacerations

Fig. 2.4.

Intradural haematomas. (From Jennett, B. and Teasdale, G. (1981). *Management of head injuries*. F. A. Davis, Philadelphia. Reproduced with permission.)

Brain swelling

This term denotes an increase in the volume of the brain itself. It may affect the whole or more often only part of the brain and can be due either to an increase in cerebral volume (engorgement) or to an increase in the amount of intra- or extracellular fluid (oedema).

The cerebral blood volume is dependent upon the capacity of the arterial, capillary, and venous systems. As a general rule, hypoxia and hypercapnia tend to increase cerebral blood volume. Similarly, an increase in cerebral oedema may exert pressure on major cerebral veins producing obstruction and a concomitant increase in the blood volume. Although cerebral blood volume is a relatively small component of the intracranial contents it is the most easily manipulated by therapeutic measures and is therefore of great importance to clinicians.

Brain oedema can be divided into different types: vasogenic, cytotoxic, hydrostatic, and interstitial. In *vasogenic oedema* there is disruption of the blood–brain barrier with movement of large, osmotically active molecules from the plasma in the intravascular compartment to the fluid in the interstitial (extracellular) space. This increases osmotic pressure in the tissues and attracts fluid into the extracellular space. Because this mechanism is primarily due to damage in the walls of the cerebral vessels, it is known as vasogenic oedema. If vasogenic oedema and venous engorgement co-exist, a severe degree of brain swelling may occur. In *cytotoxic oedema* the accumulation of fluid occurs within the cell. This is usually a response to ischaemia and interference with their energy supply. *Hydrostatic oedema* is a result of an increase in intravascular pressure, either because of a disorder of cerebrovascular regulation or as a passive response to increased venous pressure. In *interstitial oedema* the fluid is mainly found around the ventricles and this is associated with hydrocephalus and an obstruction to the flow of cerebrospinal fluid.

Each type of oedema may follow a head injury. Depending on how much and what part of the brain is affected the result may be brain shift, raised intracranial pressure (ICP) or both. With almost all types of secondary brain damage, the ultimate effect is likely to be hypoxia/ischaemia with brain swelling due to cytotoxic oedema.

Infection

Infection rarely develops before several days after the head injury and may take one of two forms: brain abscess or meningitis. The predisposing factors which allow the offending organisms access to the brain are compound depressed fractures of the vault of the skull or fractures of the skull base and nasal sinuses. With the latter there may be leakage of cerebrospinal fluid. Brain abscess may produce increased ICP or brain shift or both. Meningitis, being a diffuse process, may produce increased ICP, or more commonly leads to communicating hydrocephalus.

Other intracranial mechanisms which produce secondary brain damage

These include subarachnoid haemorrhage and hydrocephalus. Subarachnoid haemorrhage occurs in a high proportion of head injuries. It may lead to (angiographic) vasospasm, with reduced cerebral blood flow and ischaemic brain damage (Macpherson and Graham 1978). The hydrocephalus which occurs early after a head injury is due to failure of CSF absorption in the arachnoid villi which become blocked with organized blood or white cells. Secondary elevation of the ICP may reduce cerebral perfusion pressure and so cause ischaemia.

Extracranial factors

An accident which causes a head injury often results in injuries to other parts of the body. These may damage the brain by causing either hypoxia or hypotension.

Respiratory failure and hypoxia

Injury to the chest may cause a pneumothorax, haemothorax, or multiple rib fractures (Fig. 2.5). Each of these can prevent adequate movement of air into and out of the lungs. Inadequate ventilation may also result from aspiration of vomit, especially if alcohol has been consumed, and may also

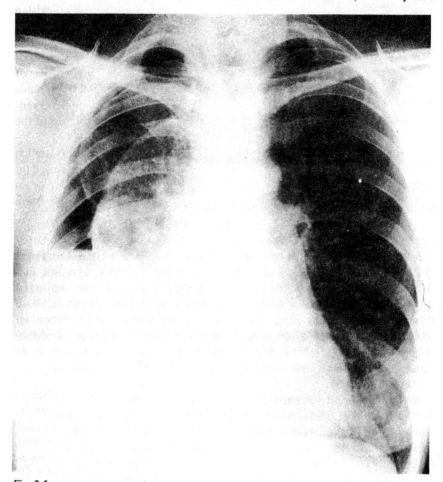

Fig. 2.5.

Chest X-ray showing haemopneumothorax.

be a consequence of asphyxiation during an epileptic seizure. Specific abnormalities of respiratory rhythm are frequently associated with severe head injury.

Inadequate ventilation leads to insufficient oxygen being available in the lungs for equilibration with the blood and therefore to a reduction in the content of oxygen in the arterial blood passing to the brain. Hypoxia can also be a result of such disorders as lung shunting and pulmonary oedema. These interfere with the exchange of oxygen between the lungs and the blood.

Hypotension
Blood loss from associated injuries can sometimes be substantial and lead to a fall in blood pressure and eventually to shock. Although normally the brain compensates for reductions in blood pressure, it may be unable to do so after a head injury. In the absence of blood loss, hypotension may be due to an associated spinal injury and may even by iatrogenic, especially if anaesthesia or drugs are given without due care and attention. A head injury by itself hardly ever results in a reduction in blood pressure.

Pathophysiology of secondary brain damage

Cerebral ischaemia/hypoxia
Secondary brain damage is usually ultimately due to a reduction in the energy supplied to the brain and there is general agreement that tissue hypoxia, in its widest sense, is the main factor in producing energy failure. It is known that the source of energy in the brain is almost exclusively from glycolysis and that the maintenance of neuronal function and viability depends upon an adequate and uninterrupted supply of the two main substrates: oxygen and glucose. A reduction in energy supply, if it is moderate or transient, produces only a temporary cessation of function, whereas if it is severe or prolonged, causes permanent damage. Graham, Adams, and Doyle (1978) showed that 91 per cent of a series of head-injured patients who died in a neurosurgical unit showed ischaemic brain damage at autopsy.

Both intracranial and extracranial abnormalities can cause hypoxic brain damage. Deficient respiratory function (systemic hypoxia) causes brain damage, even if the cerebral circulation is normal. On the other hand, brain damage occurs with a normal arterial oxygen content when there is a failure of cerebral circulation and ischaemia, either generalized or localized. This may result from systemic hypotension or from raised intracranial pressure, both of which lead to a fall in cerebral perfusion pressure.

Distribution of hypoxic damage at post-mortem
Two major patterns can be recognized:

1. Damage corresponding to the territory of one of the major intracranial arteries. This occurred in about half of the patients studied by Graham *et al.* (1978). In their series there was an infarct in the territory of the posterior cerebral artery in 30 per cent of patients (Fig. 2.6). This was usually a consequence of the artery being occluded during an episode of transtentorial her-

niation. In 27 per cent of patients there was infarction in the territory of either the anterior or middle cerebral artery, and in almost half of these patients there was bilateral damage.

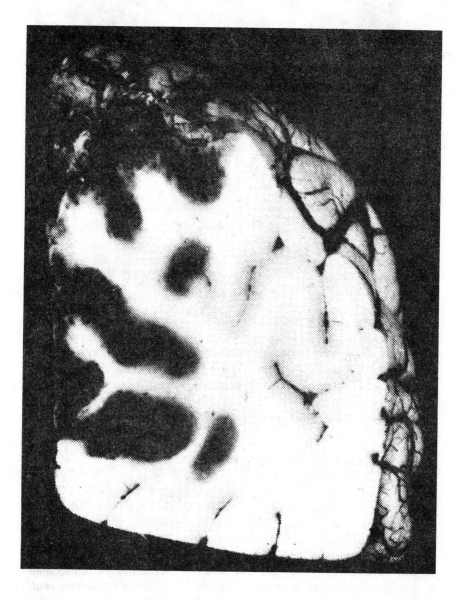

Fig. 2.6.
Posterior cerebral artery infarct. (From Jennett, B. and Teasdale, G. (1981). *Management of head injuries,* F. A. Davis, Philadelphia. Reproduced with permission.)

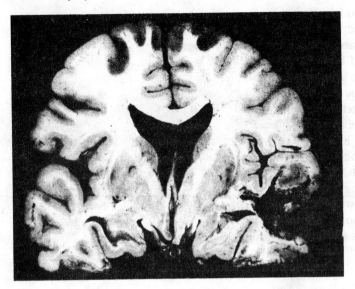

Fig. 2.7.

Bilateral haemorrhagic infarction in the cortex in the boundary zones between the anterior and middle cerebral arterial territories. There is also a 'burst' temporal lobe. (From Adams, J. H. (1975). *Handbook of clinical neurology* 23, North–Holland, Amsterdam.

2. The occurrence of ischaemic lesions in other distributions was even more common in their series. The most common sites were the basal ganglia and hippocampus, and these were involved in four out of five patients. About half the patients had lesions in the cerebral cortex that corresponded to the boundary zones between the adjacent major cerebral arteries (Fig. 2.7). The distribution of these ischaemic lesions suggests that the patients had suffered from profound reductions in overall cerebral blood flow some time before death.

Mechanisms involved in cerebral ischaemia/hypoxia

Reduction in cerebral blood flow (CBF) can follow a rise or a fall in mean blood pressure (MBP). Both of these lead to a drop in the cerebral perfusion pressure (CPP). Increases in ICP are a common consequence of intracranial complications; reductions in blood pressure represent extracranial complications. Moreover, MBP and ICP may both be abnormal after head injury. If a patient has a high ICP then his CPP will be lower for a given level of MBP than in the normal person. In the latter the ICP is usually about 10 mmHg; if MBP was 80 mmHg CPP would be 70 mmHg; a level that is unlikely to result in severe reduction in CBF. On the other hand, with an ICP of 50 mmHg and MBP of 80 mmHg, CPP would be only 30 mmHg and reductions in CBF would be expected.

Raised intracranial pressure

Raised ICP is common in severe head injury. When there is an intracranial haematoma the level can be extremely high. In many of the patients described by Graham *et al.* (1978) the cause of ischaemic damage was an increase in ICP in association with intracranial haematoma. Raised ICP may also be caused by brain swelling and by hydrocephalus.

Whether or not an intracranial lesion produces raised ICP depends upon its size and upon the capacity for compensatory reductions in the volume of other intracranial contents. Because the skull is rigid, an increase in the volume of any one of the components of the intracranial contents tends to increase intracranial pressure (Fig. 2.8). The effect becomes greater as the volume increases and the compensatory mechanisms fail. This relationship is shown in Fig. 2.9. A patient with a high ICP is therefore very sensitive to any further increases in volume; The CPP becomes critically balanced and in this situation any alteration in haemodynamics can be disastrous.

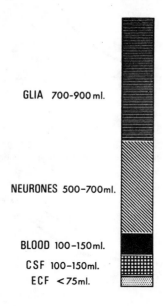

GLIA 700-900 ml.

NEURONES 500-700 ml.

BLOOD 100-150 ml.

CSF 100-150 ml.

ECF <75 ml.

Fig. 2.8.

Approximate volumes of normal intracranial contents. (From Jennett, B. (1977). *Introduction to neurosurgery,* 3rd ed. Heinemann, London. Reproduced with permission.)

To relate CPP to CBF we must first consider some of the normal physiological aspects of CBF in man. Normally the brain receives 15 per cent of cardiac output (50 ml blood (100 g brain)$^{-1}$ min^{-1}). In undamaged brain CBF remains constant despite a fairly wide range of CPP. This phenomenon is known as autoregulation and has been described in man and animals (Harper 1966), and is illustrated in Fig. 2.10. In severe head injuries the phenomenon of autoregulation is often lost (Overgaard and Tweed 1974; Fieschi, Battistini, Beduschi, Boselli, and Rossanda 1974), so that CBF becomes passively pressure dependent, as illustrated in Fig. 2.10. Thus any fall in CPP (even if still in excess of 50 mmHg) may result in a reduction in CBF to a critically low level. It has been difficult to document the relationship between CPP and CBF in human head injury because changes are

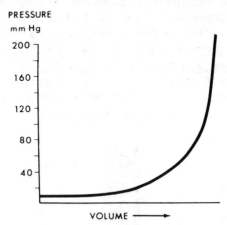

Fig. 2.9.

Intracranial pressure responses to unit volume change. (From Jennett, B. (1977). *Introduction to Neurosurgery*, 3rd edn, Heinemann, London. Reproduced with permission.)

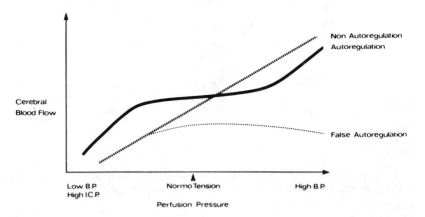

Fig. 2.10.

Effect of cerebral perfusion pressure on cerebral blood flow. In damaged brain non-autoregulation or false autoregulation may account for low flow states. BP = Blood pressure; ICP = intracranial pressure. (From Jennett, B. and Teasdale, G. (1981). *Management of head injuries*. F. A. Davis, Philadelphia. Reproduced with permission.)

often transient and occur within a short time of the injury. Studies of CBF in man following head injury are also complex and require specialized equipment and personnel with the result that it is frequently not possible to 'capture' the moment of ischaemia. Instead, the majority of studies have been done on head injuries after resuscitation and under steady-state conditions, so that the information yield has been small. Our knowledge of the fleeting moments of ischaemia in head injury is therefore dependent upon experimental studies which have clearly shown that a progressive rise in ICP produces a fall in CBF (Fig. 2.11). It is likely that more important information will now be discovered in a recent model of head injury in the primate which has, for the first time, produced diffuse axonal injury in addition to secondary brain damage (Gennarelli, Thibault, Adams, Graham, Thompson, and Marcincin 1982).

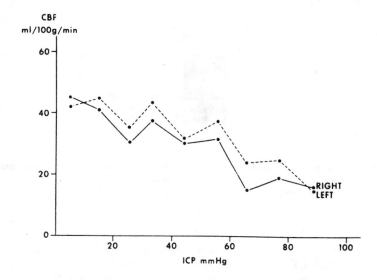

Fig. 2.11.

Effect of rising intracranial pressure (ICP) on cerebral blood flow (CBF). (From Johnston, I. H. and Rowan, J. O. (1974). *J. Neurol. Neurosurg. Psychiat.* **37**, 585–92. Reproduced with permission.)

Progressive reductions of CBF produce an orderly sequence of changes which have been related to certain critical flow thresholds. A flow below 20 ml blood (100 g brain)$^{-1}$ min^{-1} results in coma. Below 16 ml blood (100 g brain)$^{-1}$ min^{-1} cerebral electrical activity is lost. If this level of flow persists for any length of time, water begins to accumulate in the brain. Between 12 and 16 ml (100 g brain)$^{-1}$ min^{-1} there is a reversible increase in the level of potassium in the extracellular space and below 8–10 ml blood (100 g brain)$^{-1}$ min^{-1} a profound increase occurs, indicating a failure of the mechanisms responsible for maintaining the membrane potential. If this degree of ischaemia persists for more than 30 minutes, irreversible damage to neurones occurs. Changes are associated with the accumulation of metabolites such as lactic acid and potassium and with loss of energy from cellular stores. These changes are depicted diagrammatically in Fig. 2.12.

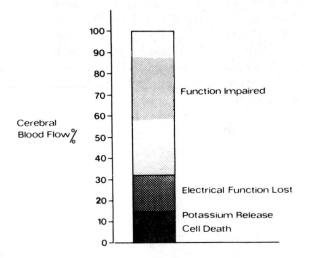

Fig. 2.12.

Effect of reduced cerebral blood flow on cerebral function and cellular homeostasis. (From Jennett, B. and Teasdale, G. (1981). *Management of head injuries*. F. A. Davis, Philadelphia. Reproduced with permission.)

Brain shifts

The growth of a localized intracranial lesion, such as a haematoma, as well as causing raised ICP, can produce brain shift. With a supratentorial mass a shift occurs from one side to another (sub-falcine herniation) or from the supratentorial compartment into the posterior fossa, through the hiatus in the dural fold which forms the tentorium cerebelli. This phenomenon is known as a transtentorial hernia (Fig. 2.13). Displacement from the posterior fossa into the spinal canal occurs through the foramen magnum and is often called tonsillar herniation. Tentorial and tonsillar hernias compress several important structures.

Tentorial herniation—Compression of the oculomotor nerve is characterized by ptosis, dilatation of the pupil, and loss of eye movements. Distortion of the brainstem and the blood supply lead to dysfunction of the midbrain and characteristically to decerebrate rigidity. This is a posture in which there is extension of the limbs as a result of the removal of the inhibitory influences of higher centres above the brainstem. When there has

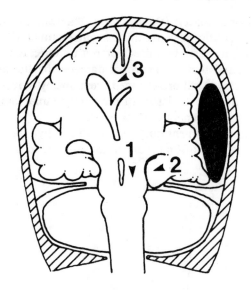

Fig. 2.13.

Shifts with a unilateral supratentorial hematoma: **1.** Downward displacement of brain stem; **2.** Herniation of uncus of temporal lobe into tentorial hiatus; **3.** Herniation of cingulate gyrus below falx cerebri. Note also shift of the ventricles, compression of the ventricle on the same side as the clot, and dilatation on the opposite side. (From Jennett B. and Teasdale G., *Management of head injuries*. F. A. Davis, Philadelphia. Reproduced with permission.)

been raised ICP and tentorial herniation, local necrosis of the parahippo-campal gyrus is found at autopsy. This phenomenon may correlate with the frequency of memory disability in survivors of severe head injury.

Tonsillar herniation—When a space-occupying effect encroaches on the posterior fossa, the medulla and cerebellar tonsils are extruded through the foramen magnum. Compression of the medulla leads to vasomotor and respiratory disturbances which eventually cause respiratory arrest and death.

Systemic hypoxia
Just as a reduction in CBF leads to an orderly sequence of events, so the consequences of hypoxia have been worked out. Mild hypoxia initially pro-duces a loss of dark-adapted vision. Moderate degrees produce amnesia, nausea, and blurring of vision, and finally coma. Surprisingly, however, man is able to tolerate fairly severe degrees of hypoxia (as low as 25 mmHg) without ill effects provided that disorders of the cardiovascular system are not present. Normally, progressive hypoxia is associated with a compen-satory increase in CBF so that the oxygen delivery to brain is maintained and the cerebral metabolic rate for oxygen ($CMRO_2$) remains constant. Once CBF has reached its maximal potential there is then a switch to anaerobic metabolism. Hypoxia also leads to an alteration in the synthesis

of various neurotransmitters (Davis, Giron, Stanton, and Maury 1978), but the biological significance of this is uncertain and the release of neurotransmitters by nerve impulses may not be affected by hypoxia. It has also been postulated that the neuronal damage that occurs with hypoxia may occur as a delayed but pre-destined event during the phase of reoxygenation. The fully developed picture of the damage may therefore by dependent on an oxidative mechanism (Siesjo 1981).

Because the main compensatory mechanism in hypoxia is an increase in CBF, it is essential that this mechanism can operate to prevent cell damage

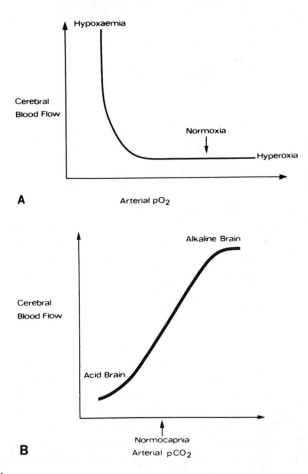

Fig. 2.14.

Chemical influence on cerebal blood flow: (*a*) arterial oxygen level (*b*) arterial carbon dioxide level. (From Jennett, B. and Teasdale, G. (1981). *Management of head injuries*. F. A. Davis, Philadelphia. Reproduced with permission.)

(the normal response to hypoxia is illustrated in Fig. 2.14). However, if there is an associated fall in CPP (because of hypovolaemic shock or increased ICP) then a mild degree of hypoxia may lead to profound neuronal damage because the normal compensatory increase in CBF illustrated in Fig. 2.14 cannot take place. It is a long-established principle that it is vital to maintain a head-injured patient's blood pressure and PaO_2 within normal limits at all times. Unfortunately, in practice, this is not always achieved.

Summary of early events which produce secondary brain damage

The complex factors in the foregoing account of the pathophysiology of acute head injury are summarized in Fig. 2.15. In practice, the quantity and distribution of the brain damage depends upon the interplay of these various factors. Thus a minor head injury with associated chest injuries producing hypoxia and perhaps limb fractures producing hypotension may prove fatal, while a severe head injury with contusions in a well-resuscitated patient may be associated with a favourable outcome. Once a cycle of ischaemia with brain oedema is established the process may progress

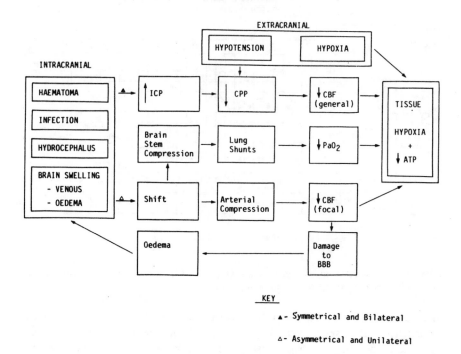

Fig. 2.15

Dynamic pathology following head injury. CBF = cerebral blood flow; CPP = cerebral perfusion pressure; ICP = intracerebral pressure.

relentlessly. It is therefore extremely difficult to correlate sequelae of head injury with specific structural brain damage, as the combination of the various factors so modify the original lesion that the final outcome may be totally different, given identical starting points in different patients.

MEASUREMENT OF BRAIN DAMAGE IN LIFE

Conscious level

The importance of conscious level as an indicator of brain damage is reflected in the many systems that have been proposed for its assessment. This task is now widely performed by the scale that was devised in Glasgow which has become known as the Glasgow Coma Scale (Fig. 2.16). This scale depends upon separate assessments of eye, verbal and motor responsiveness to build up an overall picture of the severity of dysfunction of the brain. Each response can be scored and the numbers summed to produce a useful summary of the severity of injury (Teasdale and Jennett 1974). The depth

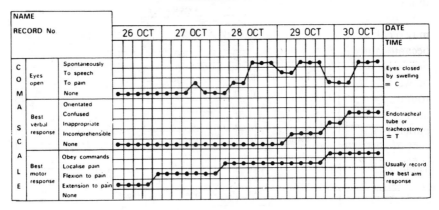

INSTITUTE OF NEUROLOGICAL SCIENCES, GLASGOW
OBSERVATION CHART

Fig. 2.16.

Coma chart. (From Jennett, B. and Teasdale, G. (1981). *Management of head injuries*, F. A. Davis, Philadelphia. Reproduced with permission.)

and duration of coma can be judged by the scale and they are closely related to prognosis after severe head injury (Teasdale and Jennett 1976). It is even possible to define coma rigorously, using the absence of eye opening, the absence of comprehensible verbal response and an absence of a response to command (Teasdale and Jennett 1976). Among 1000 head-injury patients studied in a collaborative venture between several centres, in half the patients there was a secondary intracranial lesion, usually a haematoma. A third of the remaining patients had talked and therefore did not have severe primary brain damage but this was responsible for coma in the remainder. When coma persists for several hours this is a reliable indicator of severe brain damage and in the series of 1000 patients the mortality was almost 50 per cent (Jennett, Teasdale, Braakman, Minderhoud, Heiden, and Kurze 1979).

Various other clinical features can be useful in assessing focal damage in specific sites. These include motor responsiveness, pupil reactions and eye movements. The last two are particularly useful in assessing brainstem damage.

Post-traumatic amnesia

Russell proposed that the time elapsed until the recovery of full consciousness, and the return of on-going memory, correlated with the extent of brain damage that had occurred. The interval between the injury and return to full consciousness is referred to as post-traumatic amnesia (PTA). This can only be assessed in retrospect but is nevertheless a very useful index.

Sometimes the end of amnesia can be determined precisely: the patient may recall a particular event, or his relatives will recognize the stage that 'he became himself'. However, it is not necessary to measure the duration precisely; it is sufficient to judge whether it lasts for minutes, hours, days, or weeks. The scale proposed by Russell, with some expansion, has been found to be useful (Table 2.1). PTA is often several times longer than the interval from injury to when the patient speaks. In the series of 1000 patients referred to above, all had a PTA of more than 2 days and 94 per cent of survivors had PTA of more than 1 week.

Table 2.1 *Causes of hypoxia in head injuries*

---

1. Ventilatory failure
   Perhipheral: Chest injury, —pneumothorax, —haemothorax, —flail chest, —lung contusion
         Airway obstruction
         Aspiration
         Infection
   Central: Apnoea
         Abnormalities of rate and rhythm

2. Failure of oxygenation
   Lung shunts (venous admixture)
   Pulmonary oedema
   Fat emboli

MEASUREMENT OF BRAIN DAMAGE BY INVESTIGATION

Radiology

Radiological tests are more useful in diagnosing the nature rather than assessing the severity of brain damage. Skull X-ray often shows a fracture in severely injured patients, especially those who are liable to secondary intracranial complications. It may therefore provide evidence that a patient had indeed a head injury of some severity and that the impact has been in a particular site. However, the relationship of fracture either to the type or location of damage is inconsistant and both severe primary damage and secondary damage can result with no skull fracture.

CT scanning

Although the advent of CT scanning has provided an opportunity to revolutionize the management of intracranial haematomas, it has been of less value in demonstrating lesions in the parenchyma of the brain. It will show if and where the brain is swollen but not from what cause. It shows only larger contusions and only very occasionally does it pick out the small haemorrhages which accompany diffuse axonal injury. It is most useful and accurate in the diagnosis of intracranial haematomas (Fig. 2.17). Recently devised techniques of imaging the brain by nuclear magnetic resonance signals have a greater potential.

Biochemical markers

The injured brain leaks its chemicals into the CSF and blood. The chemicals that have been studied include brain-specific enzymes such as creatine kinase (Hedman and Rabow 1978), lactic dehydrogenase (Lindblom 1971), and also brain-specific proteins with levels measured using immunological techniques (Thomas, Palfreyman, and Ratcliffe 1978). Whatever the marker and the study the level tends to rise sooner when there is primary brain damage than in patients with secondary brain damage. The level reached relates to the severity of the injury as judged by the depth of consciousness and high levels correlate with poor outcomes. The attractiveness of these markers to clinicians is that all that is needed is to draw blood samples which can then be stored for later analysis. The disadvantage is that they do not show dynamic changes and are therefore of limited value in monitoring a patient's progress.

Electrophysiological techniques

The spontaneous EEG proved of little use in assessing the type, location, or severity of damage. Recent interest has been in computerized analysis of the

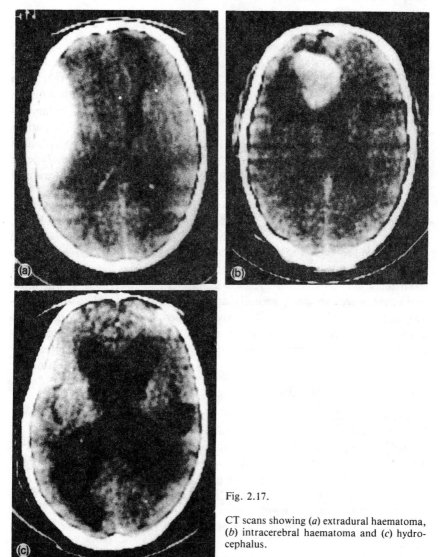

Fig. 2.17.

CT scans showing (*a*) extradural haematoma, (*b*) intracerebral haematoma and (*c*) hydrocephalus.

EEG and of conduction in various specific sensory systems (Greenberg *et al.* 1977). With increased severity of injury there is disorganization of the wave pattern of the evoked response and eventually no response can be elicited. Measurement of the rate of conduction in the central white matter (central conduction time, CCT) can also be performed and slow rates of conduction are found in patients with deeper conscious levels and with poorer prognosis (Lindsay, Pasaoglu, Kennedy, Mills, and Teasdale 1982). The advantage of this approach is that it provides a numerical index which can be repeated extremely frequently.

Other measurements

The measurement of ICP, cerebral blood volume, CBF and brain water content have been referred to in the discussion above. Their use is restricted largely to centres with facilities for detailed clinical measurement and, while useful in evaluating the pathophysiological events in head injury, they are not of general application.

RECOVERY AFTER HEAD INJURY

It is a unique but fortunate feature of head injury that after the initial insult, most patients progressively recover. There is general agreement that recovery is less effective with increasing age and that it can be impeded at any age by the development of secondary complications. On the other hand, there is still little known about the mechanisms of recovery. Several mechanisms are likely to be responsible for this return of function after the injury. Those responsible for rapid improvement may be quite different from those responsible for the slow improvement over months and even years that is seen in many severely head-injured patients. What is particularly controversial is how much recovery depends on return of function to damaged, but structurally intact, neurones, and how much is due to structural changes in the nervous system.

Early recovery of function

This is most likely to be due to the abatement of some disorder of neuronal function. It has been suggested that concussion is accompanied by an abrupt discharge within the nervous system. This may be followed by loss of neurotransmitters which then have to be replenished. Another possibility is that shearing forces within the white matter may produce degrees of axonal damage, short of loss of continuity. This could result in loss of membrane potential which is subsequently restored by the continued operation of the sodium–potassium pump. Shearing may also interfere with axoplasmic flow.

It is therefore easier to understand rapid recovery of function once some potential cause of secondary brain damage has been dealt with. For example, after reversal of a temporary period of cerebral hypoxia, restoration of energy supply can rapidly lead to the return of normal metabolism, restitution of membrane potential and recovery of synaptic transmission. Rapid recovery may follow the removal of a haematoma, or the restoration of normal blood flow or oxygenation. On the other hand, recovery that depends upon the waning of brain oedema or resolution of a disorder of CSF circulation may take days rather than hours.

Late recovery

Whereas rapid initial recovery probably reflects the return of function to structurally intact cells, and the reactivation of established pathways, late recovery may involve much more profound adaptive changes in the nervous system. Essentially two theories have emerged.

The first view holds that recovery of function reflects the use of other neuronal pathways than those originally damaged. Such pathways may be merely alternatives of previously redundant connections and the process is seen basically as a learning phenomenon. Soh *et al.* (1977) utilized CBF measurements to illustrate the use of alternative circuits. They showed that dysphasic patients when attempting to speak, did not show the usual focal increase in blood flow in the speech areas of the brain but instead showed an increase in flow in the adjacent sub-frontal and parietal regions of the cortex. This was the first objective evidence that other cortical regions could compensate for adjacent areas of dysfunction. It is not surprising that children are most rapid in relearning whereas elderly people recover more slowly and less completely. The ability of children to transfer functions within the brain is sometimes referred to as 'plasticity' but this can also imply the occurrence of structural changes in the nervous system, the alternative mechanism of late recovery.

Growth of neuronal tissue

Evidence that neuronal growth is responsible for recovery of function is scant, but two distinct phenomena may be involved. In the first, after dissolution of continuity of the axon, the distal portion is replaced by regeneration from the proximal stump. Peripheral nerves have considerable potential for this, but it has been thought that it occurs little, if at all, within the central nervous system. This may be because most studies have involved surgical lesions of the brain or spinal cord, which are followed by the development of a glial barrier at the site of division. By contrast, diffuse axonal injuries might result in axonal damage within intact glial sheaths, so that the opportunity for regeneration may be substantial. Striking regeneration of nerve fibres can occur in the hypothalamo-neurohypophyseal tract of some animals (Daniel and Pritchard 1975; Adams, Daniel, and Pritchard 1971). Moreover, following heavy-particle irradiation, nerve fibres grow into areas of necrosis and become myelinated (Rose, Malis, Krugner, and Baker 1960; Maxwell and Krugner 1964; Estable-Puig, de Estable, Tobias, and Haymaker 1965).

Animal experiments have shown another response within the central nervous system when, because of damage to its source of innervation, a neurone is deprived of its synaptic contacts. It may subsequently gain synaptic contacts as a result of the sprouting of adjacent intact axons. How far this process goes to re-establish normal function has not yet been established (Matthews, Cotman, and Lynch 1976; Raisman 1969). At present it is fair to conclude that there is little evidence that structural neuronal regeneration contributes significantly to recovery following head injury in man.

THE BASIS OF DISABILITY AFTER HEAD INJURY

Specific late complications

Epilepsy

Epilepsy is a symptom of cortical damage with persistent cortical scarring. In his major monograph, Jennett (1975) has shown that several factors predispose to the development of late epilepsy—an early seizure, post-traumatic amnesia lasting more than 24 hours, dural tearing with compound depressed fractures, focal neurological signs, and intracranial haematomas (Fig. 2.18).

There is controversy as to whether the epileptic seizure in itself can produce brain damage. Clearly a patient may become hypoxic during a fit and hypoxic damage may therefore occur, but Meldrum and Horton (1973) have indicated that focal damage may be produced in the absence of hypoxia; however, this is controversial.

Chronic subdural haematoma

This so often appears to be unrelated to any injury. This may be because the injury has been so trivial as to have been ignored. However, the majority of cases are post-traumatic and blood fills the subdural space, which is often enlarged because of advancing age with brain atrophy and sometimes chronic alcoholism. The patient then becomes confused and may present with dementia. Classically the level of consciousness fluctuates and this has been ascribed to changes in the volume of fluid in the subdural space—the fluid haematoma comes to lie within a thickened membrane which is thought to display changing permeability to water and colloid substances. These osmotic changes produce shifts of water which increase or decrease the size of subdural fluid collection. In children the fluid becomes yellow and clear and the condition is then called a subdural hygroma which is quite different from the adult form which frequently contains black liquid fluid of increased viscosity.

Hydrocephalus

The late development of ventricular dilatation is most commonly due to a loss of brain substance—the ventricles enlarge passively as the brain volume

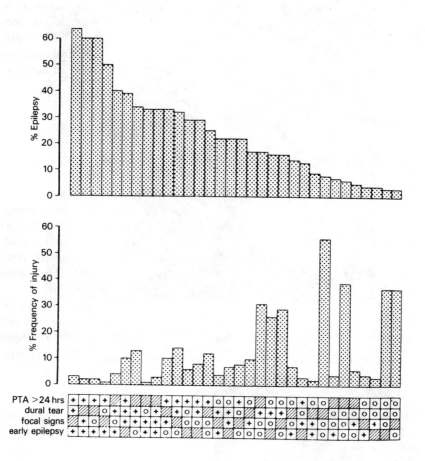

Fig. 2.18.

Epilepsy after head injury. Predisposing factors for (*b*) also apply to (*a*). (From Jennett, B. (1975). *Epilepsy after non-missile head injuries*, 2nd ed. Heinemann, London. Reproduced with permission.)

decreases with scarring. This may be due to a diffuse loss of white matter in which case the process is symmetrical (Fig. 2.19) or it may occur in relation to an area of focal damage (for example with intracerebral haematoma or contusion) with subsequent focal degeneration and porencephaly. In the latter situation one part of the ventricular system may undergo localized dilatation (Fig. 2.20). This form of ventricular enlargement occurs *ex vacuo* and is a marker of brain damage, rather than a factor which continues to produce neuronal dysfunction.

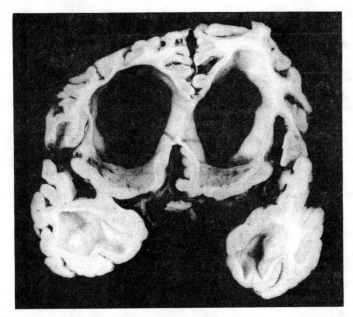

Fig. 2.19.

Diffuse neocortical necrosis after several months survival in vegetative state following cardiac arrest shortly after sustaining a head injury. (From Jennett, B. and Teasdale, G. (1981). *Management of head injuries*. F. A. Davis, Philadelphia. Reproduced with permission.)

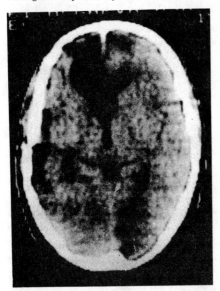

Fig. 2.20.

CT scan showing post-traumatic porencephaly.

Hydrocephalus also occurs from obstruction to CSF flow caused by blood in the subarachnoid space and in the arachnoid villi. Here the obstruction causes an increase in ICP which may retard recovery. A special type of hydrocephalus has been recognized where the ICP appears to be normal at least on random lumbar puncture. This syndrome is characterized by the clinical triad of dementia, urinary incompetence, and gait apraxia and has been termed 'normal pressure hydrocephalus'. So-called normal pressure hydrocephalus will respond to cerebrospinal fluid shunting procedures and needs to be distinguished from those patients with *ex vacuo* hydrocephalus.

DISABILITIES DUE TO PERSISTING BRAIN DAMAGE

Neurophysical

Deficits such as a hemiparesis or a cranial nerve palsy usually reflect a focal area of irreversible brain damage. This may have been caused at the time of the impact. Thus, blindness or disorders of eye movement may follow a fracture of the orbit that has involved the optic nerve or the innervation of the ocular muscles. Large contusions or lacerations may produce a cerebral hemisphere deficit. On the other hand, they are probably more often due to secondary complications. Dysphasia, hemiparesis, or movement disorders may be due to the local effects of an intracranial haematoma, especially if intracerebral. They may also follow ischaemia in the cortex or basal ganglia as a consequence of raised intracranial pressure, particularly incurred when there is associated brain shift. A special example of this is the occurrence of hemianopia as the result of an infarct in the posterior cerebral artery. This is usually a consequence of pressure on the artery during herniation at the tentorium (see Fig. 2.6). Incoordination or dysarthria are likely to be consequences of deep lesions, perhaps in the basal ganglia or even in the structures in the posterior fossa.

Mental sequelae

Mental changes after a head injury are the chief determinants of disability and relate to the severity of diffuse damage sustained in the early stage, either from primary axonal injury or from secondary ischaemia. Which of the two has been more important may be impossible to decide in retrospect, except that the patient who talks is unlikely to have severe primary damage. The severity of diffuse damage is related to the depth and duration of coma, to the duration of any post-traumatic amnesia and both of these relate to the degree of recovery after a head injury. Structural corroboration of the relationship between the extent of brain damage and the degree of disability is provided by studies of ventricular size in survivors. Van Dongan and

Braakman (1980) have shown that cortical atrophy, hydrocephalus *ex vacuo* and atrophy in posterior fossa structures correlate with the occurrence of severe degrees of disability.

Although diffuse damage is a major factor, some mental factors may reflect damage which has been particularly severe in one area. Thus, patients who have left-hemisphere lesions, even if they do not show an obvious deficit in ordinary speech, tend to perform poorly on some cognitive tests. On the other hand, right-hemisphere lesions are more liable to be followed by visuospatial difficulties and perceptual problems. Both of these may considerably interfere with recovery. The frequency of memory disorders may be a reflection of how often there is damage to both temporal lobes. Likewise, the prominence of frontal lobe contusions may account for the frequency of personality disorders after a head injury, and in particular the so-called 'frontal lobe syndrome'.

REFERENCES

Adams, J. H., Graham, D. I., Murray, L. S., and Scott, G. (1982). Diffuse axonal injury due to non-missile injury in humans: an analysis of 45 cases. *Ann. Neurol.* **12**, 557–63.

——, Scott, G., Parker, L. S., Graham, D. I., and Doyle, D. (1980). The contusion index: a quantitative approach to cerebral contusions in head injury. *Neuropathol. appl. Neurobiol.* **6**, 319–24.

——, Daniel, P. M., and Pritchard, M. M. L. (1971). Changes in the hypothalamus associated with regeneration of the hypothalamo-neurohypophyseal tract after pituitary stalk section in the ferret. *J. Comp. Neurol.* **142**, 109–24.

Daniel, P. M. and Pritchard, M. M. L. (1975). Studies of the hypothalamus and the pituitary gland: with special reference to the effects of transection of the pituitary stalk. *Acta Endocrinol.* **80**, 201–16.

Davis, J. N., Giron, L. T., Stanton, E., and Maury, W. (1978). The effect of hypoxia on brain neurotransmitter systems. *Adv. Neurol.* **26**, 219–23.

Estable-Puig, J. F., de Estable, R. F., Tobias, C., and Haymaker, W. (1965). Degeneration and regeneration of myelinated fibres in the cerebral and cerebellar cortex following damage from ionizing particle radiation. *Acta Neuropathol.* **4**, 175–90.

Fieschi, C., Battistini, N., Beduschi, A., Boselli, L., and Rossanda, M. (1974). Regional cerebral blood flow and intraventricular pressure in acute head injuries. *J. Neurol. Neurosurg. Psychiat.* **37**, 1378–88.

Gennarelli, T. A., Thibault, L. E., Adams, J. H., Graham, D. I., Thompson, C. J., and Marcincin, R. P. (1982). Diffuse axonal injury and traumatic coma in the primate. *Ann. Neurol.* **12**, 564–74.

Graham, D. I., Adams, J. H., and Doyle, D. (1978). Ischaemic brain damage in fatal non-missile head injuries. *J. Neurol. Sci.* **39**, 213–34.

Greenberg, R. P., Becker, D. P., Miller, J. D., and Mayer, D. J. (1977). Evaluation of brain function in severe head trauma with multimodality evoked potentials. Part II. Localisation of brain dysfunction and correlation with post traumatic neurological condition. *J. Neurosurg.* **47**, 163–77.

Gronwall, D. and Wrightson, P. (1975). Cumulative effects of concussion. *Lancet* **ii**, 995–7.

Harper, A. M. (1966). Autoregulation of cerebral blood flow: influence of the arterial blood pressure on the blood flow through the cerebral cortex. *J. Neurol. Neurosurg. Psychiat.* **29**, 398–403.

Hedman, G. and Rabow, L. (1978). *CKbb-isoenzymstegrint som tecekn pa tij ampurenkyn – skaela.* Svensks Lakersall skapets Riksstamma, Stockholm.

Holbourne, A. H. S. (1943). Mechanics of head injuries. *Lancet* **ii**, 438–41.

Jennett, B. (1975). *Epilepsy after non-missile head injuries*, 2nd edn., Heinemann, London.

——, Teasdale, G., Braakman, R., Minderhoud, J., Heiden, J., and Kurze, T. (1979). Prognosis in series of patients with severe head injury. *Neurosurgery* **4**, 283–8.

Lindblom, A. (1971). The pattern of serum LDH isoenzymes and S-GOT after traumatic brain injury. *Scand. J. rehabil. Med.* **4**, 61–72.

Lindsay, K. W., Pasaoglu, A., Kennedy, I., Mills, G., and Teasdale, G. (1982). Somatosensory and auditory brainstem conduction time after head injury. *Br. J. Surg.* **69**, 294.

Macpherson, P. and Graham, D. I. (1978). Correlations between angiographic findings and the ischaemia of head injury. *J. Neurol. Neurosurg. Psychiat.* **41**, 122–7.

Matthews, D. A., Cotman, C., and Lynch, G. (1976). An electron microscopic study of lesion-induced synaptogenesis in the dentate gyrus of the adult rat. 1. Magnitude and time course of degeneration. *Brain Res.* **115**, 1–21.

Maxwell, D. S. and Krugner, L. (1964). Electron microscopy of radiation induced laminar lesions in the cerebral cortex of the rat. In *Response of the nervous system to ionizing radiation* (ed. T. J. Hale, and R. S. Snider), Little Brown, Boston, pp. 54–83.

Meldrum, B. S. and Horton, R. W. (1973). Physiology of status epilepticus in primates. *Arch. Neurol.*, **28**, 1–9.

Ommaya, A. K., Grubb, R. L., and Naumann, R. A. (1971). Coup and contrecoup injury: observations on the mechanics of visible brain injuries in the rhesus monkey. *J. Neurosurg.* **35**, 503–16.

——, and Gennarelli, T. I. (1974). Cerebral concussion and traumatic unconsciousness: correlations of experimental and clinical observations on blunt head injuries. *Brain*, **97**, 633–54.

Oppenheimer, D. R. (1968). Microscopic lesions in the brain following head injury. *J. Neurol. Neurosurg. Psychiat.* **31**, 299–306.

Overgaard, J. and Tweed, W. A. (1974). Cerebral circulation after head injury. Part 1: Cerebral blood flow and its autoregulation after closed head injury with emphasis on clinical correlations. *J. Neurosurg.* **41**, 531–41.

Povlishock, J. T., Becker, D. P., Sullivan, H. G., and Miller, J. D. (1978). Vascular permeability alterations to horseradish peroxidase in experimental brain injury. *Brain Res.* **153**, 223–39.

Raisman, G. (1969). Neural plasticity in the septal nuclei of the adult rat. *Brain Res.* **14**, 25–48.

Rose, J. E., Malis, L. I., Krugner, L., and Baker, C. P. (1960). Effects of heavy, ionizing, monoenergetic particles on the cerebral cortex. II. Histological appearances of laminar lesions and growth of nerve fibres after laminar destructions. *J. Comp. Neurol.* **115**, 243–96.

Siesjo, B. K. (1981). Cell damage in the brain: a speculative synthesis. *J. Cerebral Blood Flow Metab.* **1**, 155–85.

Soh, K., Larsen, B., Skinhøj, E., and Lassen, N. A. (1977). rCBF in aphasia. *Acta*

Neurol. Scand. **56**, 270–1.

Strich, S. J. (1956). Diffuse degeneration of the cerebral white matter in severe dementia following head injury. *J. Neurol. Neurosurg. Psychiat.* **19**, 163–85.

Symonds, C. P. (1928). The differential diagnosis and treatment of cerebral states consequent upon head injuries. *Br. Med. J.* **iv**, 829–32.

Teasdale, G. and Jennett, B. (1974). Assessment of coma and impaired consciousness. *Lancet* **ii**, 81–4.

——, ——, (1976). Assessment and prognosis of coma after head injury. *Acta Neurochir.* **34**, 45–55.

Thomas, D. G. T., Palfreyman, J. W., and Ratcliffe, J. G. (1978). Serum basic protein assay in diagnosis and prognosis of patients with head injury. *Lancet* **i**, 113–15.

Van Dongen, K. J. and Braakman, R. (1980). Late computed tomography in survivors of severe head injury. *Neurosurgery* **7**, 14–22.

3 The measurement of outcome

Bryan Jennett

Measuring outcome after severe brain damage attracts much less attention from doctors than does assessment of the degree of dysfunction soon after injury. Yet the temporary crises of the first few days fade into insignificance beside the life-long disability which many survivors after severe injury are destined to suffer. There are several reasons why it is necessary to categorize satisfactorily the different kinds and varying degrees of disability that result. Until this is done it is not possible to assess systematically the result of treatment, either in the acute state or during rehabilitation, so as to be able to compare the efficacy of alternative methods. Nor can recovery of different degrees be related to features soon after injury in order to identify predictive factors and to formulate statistical rules for prognosis. Making appropriate arrangements for the continued care of patients with prolonged or permanent disability also requires that the nature of their handicap be defined in unambiguous and simple terms.

Until recently the terms commonly used to describe outcome after head injury were vague—good, fair, poor, practical, worthwhile, and acceptable. What one assessor regarded as a good result another might consider poor; a consensus could not perhaps be expected about terms which involved value judgements about the quality of life. Further confusion was added by the various intervals after injury when outcome was assessed—this might be on discharge from the acute neurosurgical service (ranging from a week or so to many months, according to local policies); or, for a series of patients, it might be an *average* period after injury, or a *minimum* period—figures of limited value unless accompanied by the range and standard deviation of the observations.

THE GLASGOW OUTCOME SCALE

What is really needed is a limited number of clearly defined categories of outcome to which patients are allocated at a series of specified times after injury. The Glasgow Outcome Scale (Jennett and Bond 1975) was devised to meet this need, not only after head injury but following other kinds of acute brain damage. Used at six months or one year after injury it has proved practical in a number of studies involving centres in different countries, and it has now been adopted for many prospective investigations of head injury and of non-traumatic coma. This scale summarizes the overall social out-come, without considering the separate components of the disability. There are four outcome categories for surviving patients.

Vegetative state

This state implies absence of function in the cerebral cortex due either to disconnection (because of diffuse white-matter shearing lesions) or to destruction (because of hypoxic damage). It should be restricted to patients who show no evidence of psychologically meaningful responsiveness, as Jennett and Plum (1972) emphasized when they described this state. Patients who obey even simple commands, or who utter even a single word, are assigned to the next category (severe disability). Vegetative patients breathe spontaneously, have periods of spontaneous eye opening when they may follow moving objects with their eyes, show reflex responses in their limbs (to postural or painful stimuli), and they may swallow food placed in their mouths. Inexperienced observers, particularly the patient's family, are apt to interpret the visual tracking and grasp reflex as evidence of the recovery of voluntary activity. This non-sentient state must be distinguished from other conditions of wakeful reduced responsiveness—such as the locked-in syndrome, akinetic mutism and total global aphasia.

Severe disability

This indicates that a patient is conscious but needs the assistance of another person for some activities of daily living every day. This may range from continuous total dependency (for feeding and washing) to the need for assistance with only one activity—such as dressing, getting out of bed, moving about the house, or going outside to shop. More often dependency is due to a combination of physical and mental disability—because when physical disability is severe after head injury there is almost always considerable mental deficit. And some patients who have little or no physical deficit are so mentally handicapped that they are unable to organize their day-to-day lives effectively and must be classified as severely disabled. The worst affected of these requires the care and protection which only a mental hospital can provide, while others cope at home with the support of attentive relatives, but could not be left overnight because they would be unable to plan their meals or to deal with callers, or any domestic crisis which might arise. The severely disabled can be described as 'conscious but dependent'.

Moderate disability

These patients may be summarized as 'independent but disabled'. Such a patient is able to look after himself at home, to get out and about and to use public transport. However, some previous activities, either at work or in social life, are now no longer possible by reason of either mental or physical deficit, often both. Some patients in this category are able to return to certain kinds of work, even to their own job, if this happens not to be affected by their major deficit.

Good recovery

This indicates the capacity to resume normal occupational and social activities, although there may be minor physical or mental deficits. However, for various reasons, the patient may not have resumed all his previous activities, and in particular may not be working.

The originators of this scale have since proposed that each of the three highest categories (describing conscious survivors) might be subdivided into a better and worse level—in order to provide a more sensitive measure (Jennett, Snoek, Bond, and Brooks 1981). On the other hand it is possible to collapse the scale to a smaller number of categories, as may be required when making statistical predictions in the first few days after injury. Other scales which have been published tend either to be over-simple, allowing only two categories of survivor; or to be weighted with several subdivisions of dependency. More than half the categories from five recent scales refer to these severely disabled patients who make up less than a fifth of survivors six months after severe head injury.

TIME SCALE OF RECOVERY

Recovery is a dynamic process, but for how long substantial improvement may continue is a matter of controversy. Isolated reports of dramatic recovery years after injury seldom include well-documented details—but they lead some clinicians to hold out the prospect of further significant recovery for longer than is realistic, and to put off for too long the assessment of outcome. Maintaining unrealistic expectations tends to delay the acceptance by the patient and his family of the certainty that some degree of disability is likely to be permanent, which in turn postpones the taking of practical steps to adjust to this and to plan an appropriate future.

Of a large series of patients who one year after injury were moderately disabled or made a good recovery, two-thirds had already attained this category of recovery within 3 months, and over 90 per cent within 6 months of injury. Considerable improvement *within* one of these large categories of outcome frequently occurs during the latter part of the first year, and even thereafter; but in only a few does this overall functional recovery justify reclassification on this scale. What is regarded as improvement after 6 or 12 months frequently proves not to be associated with any significant diminution of measurable deficit. Instead it reflects a better social adjustment because the disabilities have been accepted and appropriate adaptations made.

NATURE OF DEFICITS CONTRIBUTING TO SOCIAL OUTCOME

These were studied in a consecutive series of 150 patients who had regained consciousness after a severe head injury (more than six hours' coma, more than two days PTA). Almost all patients had some deficit, but this was often mild. Three-quarters had neurophysical deficits (including epilepsy), and two-thirds had personality change. Measurable cognitive deficits occurred in about 60 per cent of cases. Most patients with marked cognitive or physical deficits also had definite evidence of personality change; but in a third of patients with change in personality this was the only significant deficit.

The commonest *neurological (physical) deficit* was hemiparesis or dysphasia, or both. This was found in 60 per cent of patients six months after severe injury, but it was often not a major handicap. In patients classified as severely disabled, however, there was frequently very marked paralysis and dysphasia. One or more cranial nerve palsies were recorded in a third of this series; most frequent was visual loss in one or both eyes, disordered ocular movement causing diplopia; sensorineural deafness; and anosmia.

Traumatic epilepsy is a serious complication because of its social implications—particularly when it occurs in someone who has otherwise made a good or moderate recovery. It is particularly common after intracranial haematoma, more than a third of survivors being affected. Fits frequently take the form of temporal lobe attacks, the true nature of which may go unrecognized for some time and which also contribute to behaviour disorders. Once one late fit (after the first week) has occurred then the liability to have further attacks remains, and this constitutes a social disability even if actual seizures are infrequent. In modern society the inability to drive a car can be a serious handicap, even more so to someone already disabled in some degree. About half the patients destined to develop late epilepsy have their first attack within a year of injury; but this complication is not infrequently delayed for four years or more. The likelihood that epilepsy will occur in an individual patient can be calculated soon after injury, because it depends on the degree and nature of the brain damage suffered and on early complications (Jennett 1975; Jennett and Teasdale 1981). It varies from over 60 per cent for some injuries to less than 3 per cent for others.

It has long since been recognized that *mental disorders* (including personality change) contribute more significantly to overall handicap after head injury than do neurological deficits—although it is the combination that makes disability after head injury so devastating in many cases. Our series of severely injured patients has quantified this impression (Jennett and Teasdale 1981; Jennett, *et al.* 1981). Mental deficits that were more significant than, or at least equally important as, any neurological impairment were recorded in more than 70 per cent of patients in each of the three categories of conscious survivor. Most of the rest of this book is about the nature and consequence of these disorders of mental function—in its widest sense.

Although a detailed neurological examination and formal psychometric testing are required to construct a comprehensive profile of a patient's disability the overall outcome can be assessed more simply. Indeed we have found that attempting to measure disability by aggregating all the deficits found by exhaustive examinations is apt to exaggerate the degree of disability experienced by the patient in everyday life. On the other hand, the extent of the social handicap attributable to disorders of personality and memory can readily be underestimated if care is not taken to include an interview with close relatives or associates of the patient. Given this, however, it is usually possible to place a patient on the Glasgow Scale on the basis of a simple interview with the patient and a family member, because this scale summarizes the social disability without requiring analysis of its component parts.

More detailed measurements may be needed in order to assess the response to specific rehabilitation methods, or to decide how best to advise the patient and his family to cope with his deficits. This may require a decision about the extent to which the disability is due to neurosensory impairment or is due to deficits in memory, learning or motivation.

FALLACIES IN JUDGING OUTCOME

The word 'judging' is used here advisedly—because, however objective the measurement of outcome is, a comparison must eventually be made between the patient's final state of health and what he was like before. That comparison may be seen very differently, according to the viewpoint of the observer. Doctors and other members of the therapeutic team tend to compare the present state of recovery with the earlier post-traumatic condition of the patient, when he was in life-threatening coma; in their view the patient may now seem to be well recovered 'considering how bad he was'. This explains why patients with substantial disability are frequently referred to as having made a 'remarkable recovery'.

The patient himself remains oblivious of how bad he was in the early stages after injury, thanks to the protective effect of PTA; his comparison is therefore with his pre-traumatic state, and the contrast may be stark. The patient's family is in a more complex position—knowing something of the patient's previous state, but being aware also of how bad he was soon after injury. In the first few weeks or months after injury the relatives may share the optimistic view of the therapeutic team, based on the amount of recovery since the patient was in coma, rather than comparing him with his state before injury. Later the family will have to face up to the latter comparison, and a new fallacy may then appear; the family may overstate the positive attributes of the patient prior to injury. In fact, many victims of head injury prove to have been socially deviant to some extent before this injury (e.g. liable to drunkenness, to violence, to committing driving offences or crime); unless reliable data are available about the pre-morbid state it may be assumed that such behaviour after the head injury is the result of brain damage.

Much is heard nowadays about the quality of life, but little about how it should be assessed. Inevitably, assessment must depend heavily on subjective impressions and on value judgements. However, there has been increasing acceptance in recent years that it is reasonable to question whether survival with certain degrees of disability is in fact acceptable. For example, most now agree that to survive in a vegetative state is no better than death, and from some viewpoints, worse (Jennett 1976). That some patients can come to terms with overwhelming physical disability has been demonstrated many times, but there is a fallacy in extrapolating this to survival after severe brain damage—when the reserves of emotional drive, the stability of personality and the intellectual resources that are all so essential to coping with disability are themselves affected. The age of the patient is also important in affecting the way that the patient himself regards his state of existence; here the fallacy is to extrapolate from geriatric models of disability rating, which place much emphasis on activities of daily living (ADL). It may indeed be a matter of satisfaction for an 80-year-old to have limited mobility within his room; but a youth of 21, with 40 years' disability stretching ahead of him, will likely view it differently. Some of the factors that might be considered in assessing quality of life are:

1. Activities of daily living (ADL).
2. Mobility/life organization.
3. Social relationships.
4. Work (level).
5. Present satisfaction.
6. Future prospects.

REFERENCES

Jennett, B. (1975). *Epilepsy after non-missile head injuries*, 2nd edn. Heinemann, London.
—— (1976). Resource allocation for the severly brain damaged. *Arch. Neurol.* **33**, 595–7.

—— and Bond, M. (1975). Assessment of outcome after severe brain damage. *Lancet* i, 480–4.

—— and Plum, F. (1972). Persistent vegetative state after brain damage. *Lancet* i, 734–7.

——, Snoek, J., Bond, M. R., and Brooks, N. (1981). Disability after severe head injury: observations on the use of the Glasgow Outcome Scale. *J. Neurol. Neurosurg. Psychiat.* **44**, 285–93.

—— and Teasdale, G. (1981). *Management of head injuries.* F. A. Davis, Philadelphia.

4 Cognitive deficits after head injury

Neil Brooks

INTRODUCTION

The fact that head injury can lead to serious cognitive deficits is well known. Clinical accounts of memory deficits were published by Russell in the 1930s (see Russell 1971, for collected papers), and in the late 1930s and early 1940s two research studies of cognitive effects of head injury were carried out (Conkey 1938; Ruesch 1944). A trickle of reports appeared thereafter (Reynell 1944; Tooth 1947) but it was not until the early 1970s that interest increased again in this field.

The Conkey and Ruesch studies are worth close examination: their reports were poor by present-day research standards, with inadequate description of the patients studied, but their papers raised many of the problems and questions which dominated subsequent research. For example, both Conkey and Ruesch attempted to chart *recovery* during the first year after injury, and both used a wide battery of cognitive tests for this purpose. Conkey was aware of the importance of distinguishing genuine cognitive recovery from simple increased familiarity with the psychological tests on which patients had been re-examined—still very much a current concern—and she and Ruesch were both interested in the extent to which different cognitive functions are differentially affected by trauma. In addition, Conkey was anxious to discover whether different functions recovered at different *rates*; and Ruesch tried to predict levels of cognitive functioning using neurological indices obtained early after injury —again both very much current concerns.

These topics will be used to structure the present chapter, which will consider firstly the extent to which different cognitive functions are differentially affected by trauma. Having identified the main deficits, these will then be considered in detail: within each area of deficit, its severity, its rate and level of recovery, and its relationship to severity of brain injury will be discussed. Finally, the chapter will consider the relationship between deficits on cognitive tests and those in everyday life and will discuss briefly current attempts at remediation of such deficits.

ARE ALL COGNITIVE FUNCTIONS EQUALLY AFFECTED?

Although a number of different approaches have been reported in the literature, there are some common elements: for example, some researchers have employed a broad test battery to try to build up a general profile of head-injury deficits, whereas others have focused on specific aspects of function such as learning, intelligence, language, or perception. This section will, therefore, deal firstly with the broad battery approach, and will then consider more specific aspects of cognitive deficit.

General test batteries

Often batteries used have been those designed for the examination of a wide range of brain-damaged patients, rather than the specific examination of the head-injured patient. The batteries frequently involved the assumption that ability to recall and use information acquired *before* injury will be less vulnerable than ability to acquire new information *after* injury, and this was a key characteristic of Conkey's study, in which she employed the Babcock series of tests (Babcock 1930) enabling her to examine a range of simple and complex functions, e.g. 'simple mental activities; more complex and symbolic activities dependent mainly on old knowledge; new learning and appreciation and perception of an abstract sort'. Conkey compared her 24 mildly head-injured patients with two non-injured control groups during the first year after injury. Throughout the study, head-injured patients performed more poorly on tests of learning, perception and memory than on other tests, and Conkey noted that although performance on simpler cognitive tests was often accurate, it was slow. Her final conclusion was that permanent cognitive deterioration was only likely to be found on tests 'involving more complex functions . . . or a greater degree of memory'.

Conkey's study should be treated as a source of hypotheses rather than as a series of firm conclusions. Her table of results summarizes performance on a wide variety of different tasks which have been combined together rather obscurely. However, her conclusions, particularly those concerning speed of performance and the vulnerability of a number of different cognitive functions were amply supported by Ruesch (Ruesch and Moore 1943; Ruesch 1944). Like Conkey, Ruesch studied rather mild injuries, and there are other similarities between the studies. Ruesch studied recovery, although over a shorter time (Ruesch and Moore 1943), and like Conkey he initially tested patients as early as possible. His tests, being designed with early assessment in mind, involving simple measures such as the serial subtraction of 7's (from $100 - 7$), the recall of strings of digits (digit span), and the detection of similarities and absurdities in pictures, etc. His results suggest that 'serial 7's' was one of the most sensitive measures, showing disturbances even when patients were able to perform adequately on many other tests. Ruesch, like Conkey, commented on performance speed, noting that accuracy of performance on serial 7's showing an earlier trend of improvement than did speed. He concluded that those patients with 'uncomplicated' injuries showed a rapid return to normal on most tests, except serial 7's, on which complete restitution required a period of some weeks.

The following year (1944) Ruesch published a more detailed account of a wider battery of tests, showing that 'during the first few weeks after mild injury, the most severely damaged functions were 'judgement, mental speed, and the ability to keep up a sustained effort'. Ruesch noted that most of his patients improved significantly on his tests over the period of a few months, and he felt that in these mildly injured patients, the defects were 'slight and reversible'. In more severe cases this need not necessarily be the case, although 'only a very small percentage' of his 48 cases failed to show improvement over the three months after injury.

The Conkey and Ruesch studies are important in that they raise many of the issues that have come to dominate more recent cognitive outcome studies, and many of the later studies have served largely as replications of their work.

Other workers also used broad test batteries: Reynell (1944) used measures of general intelligence as well as 'arithmetical reasoning', and digit span, on 522 cases of varying severity seen at unspecified times after injury. These were patients referred specifically for psychiatric examination and psychological testing, and Reynell found that the patients who performed worst (particularly on 'performance' tests, reasoning, retention and 'relational thought') were most likely to show more prolonged occupational disability. Reynell's patients had all been military personnel, as were the 100 cases reported by Tooth (1947), although unlike Reynell's cases they comprised a consecutive series of head-injury admissions. Many patients (42) had been injured at least 1 year before psychological examination, although twenty-six had been injured less than 3 months before. On many tests Tooth found little evidence of severe deficit: head-injured patients performed at the same level as normals on digit span, and on a sorting task. Despite this, Tooth was careful to document the wide variation in performance of individual head-injured patients, and he felt that his test battery did 'not give sufficient quantitative discriminations between head injured and normals to be of much practical importance in the assessment of the individual case'.

Apart from an ill-described study by Aita, Armitage, Reitan, and Rabinovitz (1947), little psychological research on severe closed head injury appeared for some years, and the work that did appear began to change in character. Many of the studies published from the early 1970s onwards were concerned with specific aspects of cognitive function, e.g. memory, etc., and the broad-battery approach was less common. Where batteries were used it was often because the specific battery had already been widely used in general clinical neuropsychological practice, e.g. the Hallstead—Reitan battery (Hallstead 1974, Reitan 1958) used by Kløve and Cleeland (1972) and Dye, Milby, and Saxon (1979); or had been designed to examine specific aspects of post-head-injury cognitive function (Smith 1974, Roberts

1979, Brooks and Aughton 1979 *a*, *b*, and Brooks, Aughton, Bond, Jones, and Rizvi 1980).

The results of the different 'battery' studies show similarities. Many authors have commented upon the poor head-injury performance on tasks involving memory, and the report of a general slowing of performance is common. The scores of head-injured patients on more perceptual or 'performance' aspects of intelligence are often found to be worse than on 'verbal' aspects, and in general the ability to recall and use information acquired before the accident is less affected than the ability to acquire new information after the accident.

Much of the rest of the chapter is devoted to a discussion of deficits on specific cognitive function, beginning with deficits in learning and memory, followed by disorders of intellect, language and perception. Disorders of slowing and attention which are common and often severe, will be discussed in detail in Chapter 5.

Learning and memory

This area has been investigated intensively, and reviews exist both of clinical (Russell 1971; Gronwall and Wrightson 1980) and experimental (Schacter and Crovitz 1977) studies of memory deficit. One of the most obvious early consequences of closed head injury is not simply loss of consciousness but also a loss of memory for current events, and loss of an ability to recall information about events prior to the injury. The latter type of difficulty is known as Retrograde Amnesia (RA), and the former (defined as the interval between the injury and regaining continuous day-to-day memory) is known as post traumatic amnesia (PTA). These two aspects of amnesia were described in detail by Russell in a series of papers collected together in *The traumatic amnesias*, published in 1971. Russell and Smith (1961), using the definition given above, found a wide distribution of PTA. Combining the data for four separate groups comprising 1324 patients showed that 9 per cent of patients had no PTA; 20 per cent had PTA less than an hour; 29 per cent of 1–24 hours; 23 per cent of 1–7 days; and 19 per cent of greater than 7 days. This distribution is completely unlike that for RA which is typically much shorter and more skewed in distribution.

One major reason for an interest in PTA is that it has often been used as a predictor of later outcome. Russell showed that patients with long PTAs were more likely to take longer to return to full duties in military life, and having returned there the likelihood of fully adequate performance was inversely related to PTA length. Many other studies have shown a relationship between PTA and increased later disability, so much so that PTA duration has become one of the most common single measures of severity used in psychological studies of closed head injury. However, as Gronwall and Wrightson (1980) point out, researchers often fail to give their criteria for

PTA assessment, or use different criteria in different studies. Furthermore, the reliability of a retrospective assessment of PTA may be low.

Despite this, the use of PTA as an index of severity of injury is common, although there are very few studies of cognitive performance during PTA itself, and those that exist have major problems (Fodor 1972; Dunn and Brooks 1974). For example, in Fodor's study, it is difficult to be sure exactly what procedures she used: she refers to the recall and recognition of 'related' and 'unrelated' items of information, but what she means by this is unclear, and her conclusion that in PTA the primary deficit is in retrieval of information cannot be accepted without further replication. The pilot study reported by the present author (Dunn and Brooks 1974) also has problems, as only five head-injured patients and five controls were tested, and in a test paradigm open to the influence of guessing. Comparison of spontaneous and cued recall of random and 'clustered' lists of words showed that the head-injured patients were able to recall more information when a cue was given, and this may suggest that difficulties in retrieval, in addition to initial learning difficulties, may be a major problem during PTA. The conclusion of Dunn and Brooks that memory performance in PTA is quantitatively rather than qualitatively different from normal is worth investigating on larger number of cases, but currently it is dangerous to generalize from results gained on only five patients.

Most studies of learning and memory after head injury have concentrated on memory deficits *after* the end of PTA, and this research was foreshadowed by Russell (1932) who reported clinically on the 'late' memory performance of 72 patients, showing that four showed a 'severe' deficit; 22 a 'slight' deficit, and 42 had no deficit in memory. Subsequently, Russell and Smith (1961) found that 23 per cent of 1324 patients developed a memory and/or calculation deficit, although in neither study were criteria for the presence of a deficit clearly specified.

Memory deficits have been studied in Glasgow using a variety of tests to compare severely head-injured patients with non-head-injured controls. Typically, head-injured patients performed significantly worse than non-head-injured controls on a variety of tests involving recall, recognition, and relearning of both verbal and non-verbal material—a very widespread deficit indeed (Brooks 1972; Brooks 1974a, b, 1975, 1976). The results using the Wechsler Memory Scale (Wechsler 1945) on 82 severely injured cases are illustrative (Brooks 1976): most of the patients in this study were seen within two years of injury, and had particular difficulties on tests involving timed or paced performance. They showed a normal or near-normal performance on digit span, but were impaired when the recall of the digits was in reversed order, and had particular difficulties in immediate and delayed recall of simple stories (Logical Memory), and in learning new pairs of words (Associate Learning). Subsequent reports by Brooks and Aughton (1979a, b); and Brooks, Aughton, Bond, Jones, and Rizvi (1980) replicated these findings, and similar results were obtained by Groher (1977).

Thomsen (1977) studied verbal learning within 3 years of injury in 41 severely head-injured patients, referred initially for speech therapy, of whom 19 were still aphasic. The patients were required to learn a complex sentence and a list of ten unrelated words, and to recall the substance of a story. When compared with non-injured controls, both aphasic and non-aphasic head-injured patients were highly significantly worse on all measures, and on most measures the aphasics had greater difficulty than non-aphasics.

The Wechsler Memory Scale data had shown that head-injured patients were least severely affected on the immediate recall of simple information (e.g. digit span), but had serious difficulties on any task involving the learning and recall of more substantial amounts of information for longer periods of time. An earlier detailed investigation of this had been described by Brooks (1975) using a technique relying on immediate and delayed free recall of lists of words—a technique that enables the separation of short- and long-term memory components. If in normals the probability of recall of a given word is plotted (Y-axis) against the position of that word in the list, it is found that with immediate recall, words at the beginning (Primacy) and the end (Recency) are recalled consistently better than those in the middle. It is assumed that this is because those at the beginning have been transferred into a more permanent long-term memory (LTM), and those at the end in a relatively transient short-term memory (STM). If recall is delayed for 20 or 30 seconds and the subject not allowed to rehearse the information, the curve changes: items at the beginning (in LTM) are likely to be recalled, but other items are likely to be lost. This technique was used with 30 severely injured patients, who recalled the same number of words from the end of the list as non-injured controls (STM) and slightly (non-significant) fewer from the beginning of the list at immediate recall (LTM). At delayed recall, they recalled significantly fewer, and this was taken as evidence for poor LTM but normal STM.

A similar technique was used by Parker and Serrats (1976) in 108 head-injured patients with severities ranging from coma durations of 'a few minutes to several weeks'. This was a selected group of patients, as only those who were felt by the authors to have abnormalities of memory were included in the study: they were tested on immediate recall of lists of 12 words. The patient group were then divided into sub-groups according to the pattern of recall. Unfortunately the number of patients in each sub-group is not given, nor is the precise method of subdivision. However, the authors identified varying sub-groups: one showed a general deterioration of both LTM and STM; one showed poor LTM and normal STM, and one showed the unusual pattern of normal LTM and abnormal STM.

An attempt at measuring more prolonged learning and memory processes was made by Brooks (1974*a*, *b*) in 34 head-injured patients seen from 1 to 32 months after injury. The patients were tested on a task known as the Continuous Recognition Test derived from a method developed by Kimura (1963). In this test the patient is presented with 160 cards each containing a simple design. The 160 designs reappear a total of eight times and each recurring design does so once in every 20 cards. The patient must recognize each design as 'new' or 'old'. This enabled a measure of the number of correct recognitions (corrected for guessing); the number of false-positive errors (incorrectly identifying a 'new' shape as a recurrence); and the number of false-negative errors (failing to identify a recurring item). Initial analysis of the results showed that head-injured patients had a slower rate of learning than controls. However, an analysis of error type showed that head-injured patients made a greater number of false negatives. These data were reanalysed using methods derived from Signal Detection Theory (an approach criticized by Richardson (1979)), which enabled a separation of memory 'efficiency' from decision criteria (i.e. how cautious a patient is in making his response). This showed that head-injured patients were indeed severely affected in purely learning and memory capacity but that they also had a more cautious approach to the task than the controls.

Levin and his colleagues have reported results on an interesting test of memory (Levin, Grossman, Rose, and Teasdale 1979), in 27 severely head-injured patients seen at least six months after injury. The test used was the Buschke Selective Reminding Technique (Buschke and Fuld 1974) which attempts to separate memory storage and memory retrieval, in a task involving learning lists of 12 words. The results suggested that memory storage was defective in nine patients, although there were naturally wide individual variations. Retrieval from memory storage was defective in ten patients, suggesting that about a third of the patients showed disorders of memory storage or retrieval or both. This might be thought to be a relatively small number of patients still showing deficits, but the patients studied by Levin were not a random sample of head-injured patients, being restricted to those with ages ranging from 16 to 50 years, and excluding patients with 'a negative pre-injury history for alcoholism, drug abuse, and neuropsychiatric disorders'.

The studies reviewed so far have concentrated on patients seen usually within 2–3 years after injury, and often within a few months. This may be thought of as 'late' outcome, yet it is unusual to see analyses of recovery beyond this period. However, a study of late cognitive outcome (10–20 years) in 77 severely injured right-handed men (Smith 1976, Roberts 1979) showed persisting disorders (usually mild) of learning and memory even at this late stage.

The prediction of memory disturbance

Not all patients show severe memory disturbance and in large series of patients memory performance may range from normal to very severely impaired. Many researchers have addressed themselves specifically to the problem of predicting the severity of deficit, using variables such as post-traumatic amnesia and coma duration as estimates of diffuse brain damage; and skull fracture, haematoma, or the presence of residual neurological signs as evidence of focal damage.

Coma and PTA

The influence of coma. This was estimated indirectly in the Ruesch studies already extensively referred to. Ruesch compared cognitive performance of patients with short coma tested soon after injury, with the performance of patients with longer disturbances of conscious level tested later. The two groups did not differ significantly cognitively although patients with shorter coma tended to perform better. Tooth (1947) investigated PTA, and found on digit span that patients with PTAs less than 1 hour, 1–24 hours, and more than 24 hours showed a graduation of scores, with shortest PTA cases obtaining the highest, and longest PTA cases the lowest scores—a conclusion reached also by Russell and Smith (1961).

The Glasgow studies have consistently used PTA as an index of severity, and an association has frequently been found between severity of memory disturbance and increasing PTA. In the 1974 study of continuous recognition memory, Brooks found that PTA duration showed a significant negative correlation with memory performance, although this was not the case in the analysis of long- and short-term memory (Brooks 1975). However, these two studies both involved rather small numbers of cases (34 and 30 respectively) and a subsequent (1976) analysis of performance on the Wechsler Memory Scale involved 82 patients, and showed a very clear association between PTA and memory.

Further analysis showed that patients with a PTA longer than seven days were usually significantly worse than non-head-injured controls, but those with a PTA of seven days or less differed only slightly from controls on the recall of short stories and the learning of pairs of words. On the digit span test used by Tooth (1947), there was no significant influence of PTA, but a slight influence was found on digits recalled in a reverse order where the shorter PTA cases again gained the highest scores.

A partial replication of these results on a further 89 severely injured cases was reported by Brooks and Aughton (1979*a*, *b*). In this study PTA sub-divisions of 1 week or less, 8–27 days and over 27 days were used, and on all the three memory tests used (word learning, stories recall, and design recall) the difference between the three PTA sub-groups was significant, with a consistent reduction in memory score with increasing PTA. This was particularly marked in the recall of the complex design, the Rey figure (Rey 1941) where the scores for the three PTA sub-groups were 19.1, 13.0, and 10.4. Of these 89 cases, 62 had been assessed during the early period on the Glasgow Coma Scale (Teasdale and Jennett 1974), and the influence of coma duration on later cognitive performance could be examined by sub-dividing the total group of patients into 22 with coma of 1 day or less, 26 with coma of 2–3 days, and 13 with coma of 4 days or more, and comparing cognitive performance across the three sub-groups. Here there were no statistically significant differences, although the patients with a coma of 1 day or less tended to show the best memory scores. The effect, however, was slight.

In the study reported by Levin *et al.* (1979), the Glasgow Coma Scale was again used, although coma estimates were made retrospectively in some of the 27 patients. Patients with prolonged coma were much more likely to show a poor 'general' outcome assessed on the Glasgow Outcome Scale (Jennett and Bond 1975). When patients in three outcome grades were com-pared on learning and memory using the Buschke technique already des-cribed, there was a consistent relationship between increasing disability on the Outcome Scale (itself associated with coma) and increasing disturbance in both memory storage and retrieval. Despite this statistical relationship it is obvious from Levin's data that there must be considerable overlap be-tween patients' scores in the three outcome groups, and the presence of pro-longed coma is by no means a certain predictor of cognitive outcome.

Smith's (1974) very long term follow-up incorporated estimates of PTA, and she found no statistically significant relationship between PTA assessed at time of hospitalization, and memory performance 10–20 years later. However, inspection of her data suggests that patients with a shorter PTA (21 days or less) performed somewhat better than those with longer PTAs (mean story recall for shorter PTA = 6.0; for longer PTA = 4.8).

The Parker and Serrats (1976) analysis of long- and short-term memory examined performance in relation to 'post-traumatic disorientation' (PTD), rather than PTA. Their definition of PTD was unclear and, as Von Wowern (1966), Sisler and Penner (1975), and Gronwall and Wrightson (1980) showed, the relationship between PTD and PTA may not be close. Thirty cases had a PTD less than 24 hours, 38 had a PTD of 24 hours to 14 days; 20 had 15–28 days; and 12 had PTD longer than 28 days. This meant that there must have been very small numbers for analysis when the patients were also subdivided into three different memory recall patterns. Despite this, Parker and Serrats suggest that the memory recall pattern suggestive of both long- and short-term memory deficit was found mainly in patients with short-term PTDs (less than two weeks) tested early in recovery, who thereafter returned to normal. Longer PTD patients were much more likely to show a pattern suggesting a specific deficit in either short- or long-term memory, and the deficits were usually found to be severe. The authors estimated that 92 per cent of patients with a PTD of 24 hours or less had reached a normal memory by 2 years whereas only 50 per cent of those with PTD longer than 28 days had reached normal. Furthermore, all the cases of severe memory dysfunction at two years after injury were found to have suffered long

PTDs, and these cases were likely to show other signs of brain damage. This was not, however, the case in the 8 per cent of short PTD patients who had failed to recover normal memory by 2 years, but who showed no other abnormalities. Parker and Serrats hint that this may reflect a 'compensation neurosis', although equally it may merely indicate that memory deficits are common, persistent, and difficult to predict even in apparently mildly injured cases.

Lezak (1979) used coma rather than PTA in her study of 24 cases but, as is frequently the case, she did not give precise criteria of coma assessment. When patients with comas longer than two weeks were compared with those with shorter coma on a range of memory tests, there was only one significant difference three years after injury on her six measures. However, the likelihood of memory dysfunction at three years was consistently higher in the longer coma group, and at three years 54 per cent of the shorter coma patients were showing a normal digit span performance whereas only 20 per cent of longer coma cases were. Similarly on two of her measures of auditory verbal learning, the corresponding percentages were 46 and 9; and 85 and 27, suggesting that comas of longer than two weeks may have prognostic significance.

Focal damage. The possible importance of skull fracture has often been studied in relation to cognitive outcome with very varied results. Ruesch (1944) felt that fracture was of no significance in predicting outcome within a few months after mild injury, whereas Tooth (1947) found that a fracture alone had only a slight negative influence on memory outcome, although cases with skull fracture were more likely to have prolonged PTA. Similarly in the Kløve and Cleeland study (1972) fracture was found to be of no significance in predicting cognitive outcome within two years after injury, a finding reported also by Brooks (1976), and Brooks *et al.* (1980). However, in the 1975 study of long- and short-term memory Brooks found that the 16 patients with a skull fracture were worse than the 14 patients without, on many of the measures of memory performance used, although the differences only reached significance on one measure. In Smith's long follow-up (1974) the site of skull impact was used to attempt to predict the pattern of cognitive deficit (assuming a contrecoup model of brain damage in which left-sided impact leads to right hemisphere damage and *vice versa*). Smith found that patients with right-sided impact performed significantly worse than left-sided impact cases on both verbal and visuospatial measures of memory, although inspection of their raw data casts some doubt on the generality of this result. The report had suggested that the difference between left- and right-sided impact effects was distributed across all fracture sites within a hemisphere, whereas inspection of the raw data suggests that the effect was most noticeable for posterior impact cases but less so for frontal and lateral impact. In view of Smith's results, Brooks *et al.* (1980)

carried out a more detailed examination of the potential significance of skull fracture. No difference was found between patients with any fracture and those without: the 32 cases with left-sided fracture were then compared with the 23 right-sided fracture cases excluding bilateral cases, and no differences in cognitive performance were found between the two groups. Patients with linear fracture only were then compared with those with depressed fracture only and again no significant differences were found.

Other studies have reported neurological evidence of focal (usually hemispheric) brain damage, and a number of authors have compared the cognitive performance of patients showing persisting neurological signs with those without. Tooth (1947) showed that patients with persisting signs were also likely to have had longer PTAs. When those patients showing persisting neurological abnormalities were examined they were likely to show poor memory performance, but as many had also had longer PTAs a separation of the two effects of focal and diffuse damage is difficult.

The Glasgow psychological studies have examined the significance of continuing neurological signs by separating out those patients still showing moderate to severe signs from those showing mild or absent signs and comparing the two groups. On the Wechsler Memory Scale (Brooks 1976), patients with continuing signs did not score significantly worse than other patients, whereas in the analysis of Levin *et al.* (1979) only patients showing signs of brainstem damage performed poorly on memory, although this may indicate greater severity of diffuse rather than focal brain damage (Ommaya and Gennarelli 1974). Kløve and Cleeland (1972) showed that the presence of continuing signs was significantly associated with poorer performance on a tactile memory task, and on a number of other cognitive tests there was a non-significant trend for neurologically impaired patients to show poorer performance than unimpaired patients within two years of injury.

The studies of Smith (1974), Dye *et al.* (1975), and Levin *et al.* (1979) concerned the influence of very early neurological signs on later outcome. Smith showed that patients with abnormal motor patterns early after injury (e.g. decerebrate response) were likely to show subsequently more severe verbal learning deficits, but this was only evident in right-sided rather than in left-sided impact cases. However, inspection of Smith's raw data for the recall of stories suggests that the differences between the patients who did and those who did not show decerebrate response is very slight. Dye's study compared 11 patients with early 'severe' neurological status with 37 patients showing 'mild' early status. 'Severe' status was defined in terms of abnormal motor patterns. On the tactile memory test referred to earlier, both 'mild' and 'severe' early status patients were worse than non-injured controls three years after injury, but the two head-injury sub-groups also differed significantly, with the early 'severe' cases showing a poorer subsequent performance. Levin *et al.* (1979) found that early hemiparesis, oculovestibular deficit, and bilateral non-reactive pupils were associated with increasingly poor memory storage and retrieval months or years after injury. The differences between the severity sub-groups were statistically significant for the presence of hemiparesis and oculovestibular deficits. Indeed for the latter sign, the differences betwen patients who had and those who had not shown the sign were very great indeed. The seven cases with early oculovestibular deficit showed severely deteriorated cognitive performance and no overlap with the score distribution of the patients who had not shown the sign.

In neurosurgical series, many cases have sustained an intracranial haematoma for which they underwent operation. The six patients of Kløve and Cleeland (1972) who had had subdural haematomas evacuated were compared with six who had not undergone operation. The haematoma cases had slightly lower scores on many of the tests used, but this was not found in the study of eighty-nine patients by Brooks *et al.* (1980), of whom 52 were operated on for removal of an intracranial haematoma. These were compared with 24 cases not operated, and the haematoma cases were no worse cognitively. Indeed on the recall of simple stories, the operated cases performed significantly better, and this appeared to be due to their less severe diffuse brain damage (reflected by their shorter PTAs). The haematoma site proved insignificant when the 22 left-sided patients were compared with the 26 right-sided cases.

Other predictors. Some authors have investigated the influence of the patient's age on cognitive outcome, and Russell (1971) in his early work found a relationship between increasing age and increasing duration of PTA. On visual recognition memory Brooks (1974, 1975), no difference in performance was found between patients aged above and below 30. In Brooks' later analysis of Wechsler Memory Scale performance (1976) there was some evidence that patients aged 30 or above might have a slightly poorer performance on word learning, but the effect was neither large nor consistent. A subsequent analysis of age effects (Brooks *et al.* 1980) found that the recall of stories and the learning of word pairs was no poorer in older patients, although the recall of the complex Rey figure was significantly worse in patients aged 30 or above. Lezak (1979) failed to find any significant difference in learning between the patients above and below 25 years of age.

Rate of recovery of memory

Few studies have attempted to determine the rate and eventual level of recovery by testing the same patients on a number of occasions. Those that have used this method have often encountered methodological problems in attempting to separate practice effects (the effects of increased familiarity with test material, due to repeated testing), from genuine recovery (Shatz 1981). A further problem mentioned by Conkey (1938) and Brooks and

Aughton (1979*b*), is that of patient drop-out, as many patients fail to present for follow-up examination.

The earliest reported test–retest studies were those of Conkey and Ruesch already extensively referred to. Conkey attempted to examine her patients five times during the year after injury, but the difficulty in follow-up can be deduced from the fact that she tested 25 patients on the first occasion, but only four on all occasions. Conkey was well aware of the necessity to distinguish practice from recovery, and she included a retested control group of non-injured hospital patients (to control for the effects of hospitalization *per se*), together with a non-hospitalized normal control group. This latter group proved to be important, as some of her tests were difficult even for non-injured patients.

Using her wide battery of tests Conkey concluded that behaviours involving memory lagged behind other behaviours in both rate and level of recovery. On inspection of her recovery curves it is evident that on all measures the patients were severely deteriorated at first assessment (while still in hospital, and possibly still in PTA), and the greatest change seemed to be between first and second assessments (within 30–40 days of injury). This is the interval where one would expect the greatest degree of practice, but Conkey's results show little change for the retested control group here, so the great improvement in head-injury performance appears to be due to genuine recovery. Conkey went on to show that although the head-injured patients as a group had reached the level of controls by the fourth testing, this was not until 8 months after injury, suggesting a prolonged recovery even in mildy injured patients.

Parker and Serrats (1976) extended the recovery period by testing 108 severely injured patients seven times over the first 24 months after injury, using the recall of lists of words. Both the rate and level of recovery seemed to be related to severity of injury judged by duration of post-traumatic disorientation. The Groher (1977) analysis of long- and short-term memory concerned earlier recovery in patients retested five times at intervals of 120 days following initial testing within a week of injury. A significant improvement was found from test to retest, but the greatest change occurred between the first and second examination—possibly including the period of PTA.

More recently, Lezak (1979) tested patients four times during the first three years after injury, noting for each time of testing, the percentage of patients falling within normal limits on each test. She found consistent improvements on digit span, with 47 per cent of head-injured patients showing normal performance at third testing, and 83 per cent at fourth testing: on the more difficult verbal learning tasks there was little change over time, and on a measure of auditory verbal learning, 6 per cent of patients were normal at first testing and 29 per cent at last. As Lezak points out, only 30 per cent of patients achieved a normal score on her two learning measures.

Lezak was also interested in the influence of coma and site of damage on recovery, and she compared patients with comas of less than two weeks with those showing longer comas, finding that the longer coma patients performed more poorly on the verbal learning tests; however, by the final test the two groups differed significantly on only one measure of verbal learning, although at all time periods the shorter coma cases were more likely to show a normal performance. There appeared to be considerable variability in performance of the longer coma group: none of them showed a normal performance on any test at first assessment, 9 per cent were normal at second assessment, 27 per cent at third, and none at fourth, on one of the measures of auditory verbal learning.

Lezak estimated laterality of damage using varying criteria, and this had little influence on recovery. Patients estimated to have right-hemisphere damage did better at each time interval, but the differences between right- and left-sided patients were slight. Estimates of laterality of damage are likely to be unreliable in severe closed-head injury which has resulted in diffuse damage in addition to any focal effects.

Recovery of memory was also examined by Brooks and Aughton (1979*b*), and Brooks, Deelman, Van Zomeren, Van Dongen, Van Harskamp, and Aughton (1983) using a range of tests including the recall of stories from the Wechsler Memory Scale, the learning of three pairs of words, and the recall of the complex Rey figure. In the Brooks and Aughton study, 24 patients were tested three times during the period 3–12 months after injury, and a further 12 were seen four times at 1, 3, 6, and 12 months after injury. A control group of 30 non-head-injured patients was used, of whom ten were retested after a 6-week period. At first assessment, the head-injured patients were compared with the controls at *their* first assessment, and at subsequent assessments the comparison was made with the controls at their *second* test. The head-injured patients tested four times were still significantly worse than controls at 12 months on word learning. On recall of stories and the Rey figure, the change in head-injury performance from test to retest was small in the patients tested three times. This was also the case in patients tested four times, except for the word learning test on which performance remained very poor up to the third test at 6 months, and then showed a marked improvement (although not to a normal level) by 12 months.

It is difficult to draw together the different studies of recovery of memory, as they have varied widely in terms of number and type of patients studied, adequacy of description of the patients, length of follow-up, type of test, and adequacy of statistical and experimental methods. However, studies using very simple measures of short-term or immediate memory, e.g. digit span, have found marked recovery within three years or less of injury, often up to a normal level. The studies that have incorporated measures of verbal learning have found slow recovery and marked deficits up to at least a year after injury and after many retestings. This is not the case with many other functions (to be examined later) which often approach normal by 1 year.

A few studies have attempted to estimate the effects of severity of injury on rate or level of recovery, but interpretation is often made more difficult because of unclear description of patient population, or the formation of conclusions from a small number of cases.

A comparison *across* different reports comparing those studying mild and those studying severe patients does suggest that as might be expected severity of injury influences the level of cognitive performance reached within the first year, but its influence on *rate* of recovery is difficult to estimate.

Intelligence

Many researchers have estimated the effects of head injury on intellectual performance and of all the measures used, the most popular have been the Wechsler series of tests—either the earlier Wechsler–Bellevue (WB) or the later Wechsler Adult Intelligence Scale (WAIS) (Wechsler 1958). Both tests are similar involving a series of verbal and performance sub-tests. The two series of sub-tests give separate verbal and performance IQs, and the performance sub-tests are done under time pressure whereas (with the exception of one measure) this is not the case with the verbal tests.

Although Conkey did not use explicit measures of IQ, many of her tests were of the kind that would be incorporated in a general test of intelligence. Her results showed that the more intellectually demanding the test, that is, the more it rested on 'more complex mental activity', the more likely it was to show impairment early after injury, and the slower the rate, and the lower the final level of recovery. Many of Ruesch's (1944) test items were taken from the WB, and he found that the perception of pictorial absurdities and visual span for objects (both 'performance' type items) were especially vulnerable to injury. However, Block Design—another 'performance' item—was relatively unimpaired as was the perception of verbal similarities and verbal comprehension. Ruesch concluded that whereas 'judgement' and 'keeping up a sustained effort' were vulnerable to injury, those functions least affected were 'related to old and well-established mental habits (verbal similarities, pictorial abstractions, comprehension)'.

Many other workers used Wechsler's tests (Reynell 1944; Aita *et al.* 1947; Tooth 1947, Mandleberg 1975, *a*, *b*, Mandleberg and Brooks 1975, Vigouroux, Baurand, Nacquet, Chament, Choux, Benayoun, Bureau, Charpy, Clamen-guey and Guey 1971; Dye *et al.* 1979; and Levin *et al.* 1979), and the results have shown substantial agreement, with scores on 'verbal' sub-test showing recovery to a normal or near normal level, but scores on the 'performance' sub-test showing a marked and often prolonged deficit.

The earlier Glasgow studies reported by Mandleberg (1975 *a*, *b*, Mandleberg and Brooks 1975) used the Wechsler series of tests, but later work (Brooks and Aughton 1979 *a*, *b*; Brooks *et al*. 1980), used the Progressive Matrices (Raven 1960), and associated Mill Hill Vocabulary Scale (Raven 1962). The Matrices consists of a series of designs with a part missing, and the patient has to supply the missing part from among six or eight alternatives. The tests become increasingly difficult: the early items involve a simple perceptual task but the later items are conceptual in nature in which the patient has to identify an appropriate principle rather than a perceptual pattern. The Mill Hill Scale gives an estimate of a patient's vocabulary level. A comparison of 89 severely head-injured patients with non-head-injured controls showed that head-injured patients were significantly worse on both tasks: on the Matrices Scale they scored 9 IQ points below controls and on the Mill Hill Scale 5 IQ points below. The absolute magnitude of the difference was, therefore, greater on the Matrices Scale.

The results for intelligence testing have shown considerable consistency but despite this it is not easy to say precisely *why* head-injured patients find performance items more difficult. Hints come from Ruesch (1944) who talked about 'difficulty in keeping up a sustained effort' and from Conkey (1938) who together with Ruesch talked about the difficulties in tasks involving a speed component. Similarly Aita *et al*. (1947) speculated about the role of decreased learning and lack of sensori-motor control, and Mandleberg and Brooks (1975) suggested that the differential sensitivity may result from the more complex nature of the performance items. They suggested that verbal items can often be answered by a readily elicited simple response, whereas success on the performance tasks may demand the integration of a number of complex functions which would include learning, perception, dexterity, speed, etc., and a disorder of any one of these functions may impair the final performance.

The prediction of intellectual disturbance

PTA and coma

Reynell (1944) and Aita *et al*. (1947) using rather vague criteria of severity of injury concluded that severity affected mainly the 'performance' items of the Wechsler Scale. Mandleberg (1975*a*) investigated the influence of PTA by comparing score patterns of patients in and out of PTA. During PTA, all intellectual functions were impaired, although performance items were quite disproportionately impaired with mean scores nearly three standard deviations below the mean of normals on two sub-tests. To gain scores of this level many individual patients must have been totally untestable, and these results are, therefore, difficult to interpret. During PTA, verbal and performance IQs were 74.6 and 50.6, whereas a group of patients out of

PTA gained IQs of 98.0 and 80.1. The difference between the two IQ scores in the two groups of patients is of the same order of magnitude.

The Glasgow studies using the Progressive Matrices and Mill Hill Scale (Brooks and Aughton 1979*a*, Brooks *et al.* 1980) found similar results, with the Mill Hill Scale showing less effect of increasing PTA than the matrices. On the Mill Hill Scale only cases with a PTA of more than two weeks scored below controls. On the Matrices there was a consistent reduction in Progressive Matrices IQ with increasing PTA. Coma duration, however, had no influence on intellectual outcome within two years of injury.

Focal damage

Aita *et al.* (1947) looked at the influence of skull damage rather than brain damage, by comparing IQ results of twleve patients who had had a posterior skull impact with twenty patients with anterior impact, concluding that posterior impact was more serious in its intellectual effects, although no test scores are given. Smith (1974) analyzed the effects of site of impact on very late cognitive performance, showing that neither the side nor site of impact predicted late intellectual performance. Her Table of Results (Table 5, Smith 1947) does, however, suggest that compared with other impact groups, the right posterior impact patients were more severely impaired on the Progressive Matrices. Tooth (1947) found that patients with a fracture were more likely than those without to show poor intellectual scores, but the effects were small and were contaminated by longer PTAs in fracture cases. In his study patients still showing abnormal neurological signs had particular difficulties on arithmetic problems, and in the perception of verbal similarities as well as on simple memory: they were also worse on concept formation and on a block construction task but this may also reflect increasing PTA (i.e. diffuse damage) as the patients showing neurological signs were also those who had longer PTA.

Kløve and Cleeland (1972) compared 20 patients with, and 20 without skull fracture matched on other possible contaminating variables, and found no significant difference between the two groups on IQ scores. The patients found to be still showing abnormal signs had lower verbal and performance IQs than those without, but the difference between the two groups was signficant only for the performance IQ ($p = 0.05$). In addition these patients were worse on mental arithmetic. This study differs from that of Tooth in that the patients with and those without signs had been carefully matched on other possibly important variables (e.g. duration of unconsciousness).

The Mandleberg study (1975*b*) showed that the presence of a skull fracture had a slight relationship with intellectual performance but the study was based on a small group of cases ($n = 16$), and the PTA duration of patients with a fracture is unknown. Additionally Mandleberg found that patients with persisting motor dysfunction performed more poorly on performance tests, but simple motor slowness and awkwardness may have accounted for that. Both Dye *et al.* (1979) and Leven *et al.* (1979) investigated the effect of early neurological signs (which at that stage may reflect increasing diffuse damage) on susbequent cognitive outcome, finding that cases with more severe early signs had poorer cognitive outcome, particularly on the 'performance' items of the Wechsler Scale.

Rate of recovery of intellectual function

Conkey (1938) and Ruesch (1944) both found that the more complex and intellectually demanding the test, the slower its rate of recovery, at least within the short time scale of their analyses. More recent studies support this, with Vigouroux *et al.* (1971), Brown (1975), and Mandleberg and Brooks (1975) finding that 'performance' functions recover at a slower rate than 'verbal' functions. Mandleberg subsequently investigated PTA as a predictor of rate of intellectual recovery, finding a signficant influence of PTA on performance, but not on verbal sub-tests of the Wechsler Scale.

Further work from Glasgow (Brooks and Aughton 1979*b*) using the Raven's tests on 24 severely injured patients showed normal vocabulary IQ even at the first testing 3 months after injury, but low (non-significant) performance on the Progressive Matrices—up until 6 months after injury.

The evidence concerning rate of recovery of intellectual functions shows a slower recovery rate for 'performance' type functions, perhaps merely because the initial deficit on these tasks is greater. This range of functions may reach normal by around 12 months after injury when large groups of cases are examined, but many individual patients will still not be fully recovered by then. The severity of injury does not seem to have any specific effect on rate of recovery, with more severely injured patients recovering at essentially the same rate as less severely injured patients, but to a lower level.

Language

Many psychological studies of closed head injury have incorporated some measures of language functioning, if only in terms of vocabulary level, or verbal comprehension as part of a general intelligence test. The Conkey and Ruesch studies had used simple language tasks (e.g. saying the days of the week, months of the year, etc.), and Conkey found that her patients had difficulties early after injury, which disappeared by the fourth assessment (34 weeks after injury). Indeed, these were the first measures to recover to a normal level. Even when performance was poor on these tests, it was usually because of slowness rather than inaccuracy or inability. The more complex language tests (e.g. giving opposites, comprehending directions, etc.) were much more severely affected and recovered much more slowly.

Few workers have examined language functions specifically in head-injured patients using the sort of test procedures that are found in the assessment of dysphasia. Heilman, Safran and Geshwind (1971) found formal dysphasic symptomatology in only 2 per cent of 750 cases of all severities. Thomsen (1975) selected 12 severely injured aphasic patients for examination, initially some weeks after injury, and again some 29 months later. She carried out a detailed assessment of aphasic symptomatology, and found marked defects even at the later follow-up, at which time many patients still showed amnestic and perseverative errors.

Levin, Grossman, and Kelly (1976), Levin Grossman, Sarwar, and Meyers (1981); and Najenson, Sazbon, Fiselzon, Becher, and Schechter (1978) also studied aphasic symptomatology (see Levin, 1981, for recent review). Levin, testing patients early after injury found that 40 per cent had disorders of object naming. The ability to repeat was not impaired, but there was a slight impairment in verbal fluency, and 34 per cent of his patients showed impaired oral comprehension. In terms of a conventional aphasic classification, the most frequent defects were 'expressive aphasia', and specific anomic defects.

The Najenson study involved intensive serial examination of 15 very severely injured patients. The extreme severity of injury makes interpretation of results difficult as at least three patients appear to have remained in Persistent Vegetative State throughout, therefore showing no language output, and 'minimal or no evidence of any comprehension'. Nine other patients did show considerable recovery in language, and by 6 months after injury their performance seemed to be approaching normal on all the language functions assessed, except oral expression.

Groher (1977) tested 14 severely injured patients 4 months after injury, and found a 'reduction in expressive and receptive language capabilities', although all patients could converse well with staff and relatives, and none were unable to make their needs known. However, writing had not by any means returned to normal, showing 'errors of spelling, incomplete sentence construction, and poor syntax'.

Recent work in Glasgow (Brooks and Aughton 1979*a* and Brooks *et al.* 1980) used two simple measures of language function, the Token Test (De Renzi and Vignolo 1962), and Word Fluency (Borkowski, Benton and Spreen 1967). Most head-injured patients had little difficulty with the Token Test, but found word fluency extremely difficult at least within the first 6 months after injury producing many fewer words than non-injured controls. By 12 months, performance in the head-injury group was reaching normal, although the head-injured patients still produced fewer (non-significant) words than controls.

The prediction of language disturbance

Coma and PTA

The long-term study of Smith (1974) examined both speed and accuracy of object naming as a function of PTA. The 77 patients were subdivided (10–20 years after injury) into four PTA sub-groups and within each sub-group a separate subdivision was made into left- or right-sided impact. The wisdom of the laterality subdivision may be doubted, not only because of the well-recognized diffuse nature of blunt head injury, but also because the further subdivisions resulted in unacceptably small numbers of cases, e.g. four left impact short PTA cases, and two left impact long PTA cases. PTA had no effect on accuracy or latency of object naming, although the small group sizes makes unequivocal interpretation difficult. Levin *et al.* (1976) used coma rather than PTA duration, and found significant correlations between coma duration and severity of language defect. The strongest association was between coma and reading comprehension, but there were further significant correlations between coma and visual naming, word association (a test of word fluency), and aural language comprehension. Only two tests—sentence repetition and Token test—were not significantly correlated with coma. It is difficult to know how far one can generalize from Levin's results, as many of the patients were tested early after injury while still in hospital and, in some cases at least, while still confused. It is quite possible that coma may therefore not correlate so markedly with language functioning later after injury, and this was indeed found to be the case in the study of 62 cases reported by Brooks *et al.* (1980) and the 14 cases of Groher (1977).

Focal damage

Smith (1974) and Roberts (1979) found that very late after injury, patients with right-sided impact performed significantly worse on a speed of object naming than those with a left-sided impact, and this difference was more noticeable for parietal than frontal or temporal impact cases.

Neither Kløve and Cleeland (1972), Levin *et al.* (1976) or Brooks *et al* (1980) found an association between the presence of skull fracture and performance on any of a wide variety of language measures. In the Kløve and Cleeland study patients with persisting neurological signs within two years of trauma were consistently (but not significantly) worse than those without on various test involving reading, and on a general aphasia screening test, and Levin *et al.* (1976) concluded that early neurological signs indicating brainstem injury were associated with defective language functioning. This may, however, merely indicate that the brainstem patients had more severe diffuse damage.

The effects of intracranial haematoma on subsequent language function have only occasionally been assessed, but Kløve and Cleeland (1972) did compare six patients with evacuated subdural haematoma with six well-matched patients without haematoma, finding that the haematoma cases were worse on an aphasia screening test, and on reading and spelling, although the differences between the two patient groups were not significant. This was not so in the study of Brooks *et al.* (1980) in which patients with operated haematomas were compared with those without, on the Token Test and word fluency. Operated patients were significantly better on fluency, but this was considered to be due to their less severe diffuse damage. One reason for the discrepancy between the Kløve and Brooks study may be that Kløve and Cleeland attempted to equalize severity of diffuse damage in their two groups of patients.

Age as a possible predictor has also been reported, with Smith (1974), and Brooks *et al.* (1980) showing that age at injury or at assessment had no significant effect on accuracy of object naming, or obeying verbal comments.

Rate of recovery of language

Thomsen (1975) commented that the prognosis of post traumatic aphasia is 'rather good', but she concluded that none of her 12 patients had a completely normal language function even 3 years after injury. Groher (1977) carefully observed language recovery in 14 patients. He found improvement during the 4-month test interval on all measures, although in each case this was obviously greatest between the first and second testing—that is, early after injury. Verbal skills showed a significant improvement up to the fourth assessment, but gestural and graphic skills only improved significantly up to the second assessment. The recovery here was, therefore, rapid (within some three months of injury), but to a low level, for as Thomsen (1975) found, the scores were still indicative of a reduction in expressive and receptive language capabilities even after the four-month period.

The study of Najenson *et al.* (1978) also involved a small number of cases (15) of whom six remained very severely disabled. The nine patients who made some recovery showed two main patterns. The first involved a regular recovery up to two years, with visual and auditory comprehension preceding oral expression, reading, and writing. Signs of recovery in these patients were observed from three weeks to five months after injury, and complete recovery was observed by four to nine months. However, what Najenson referred to as 'the motor aspect of speech' recovers much more slowly and much less completely. The second pattern involved incomplete recovery, with patients showing persisting deficits even two years after injury. Najenson concluded his analysis by pointing out not only that severely injured cases may make a 'considerable degree of recovery', but also that this may not begin to appear until 5–7 months after injury. This was certainly not the case in the Groher study, although Groher does quote group means (which mask individual patterns), whereas Najenson reports individual cases analysed as individuals.

In the Brooks and Aughton account (1979*b*) injured patients were still scoring below controls on comprehension and fluency, at 12 months.

However, the difference was not significant, and head-injured patients were only significantly worse than controls at three months.

Perceptual functions

To a large extent, this aspect of cognitive function has already been dealt with in the discussion of intellectual changes following head injury. Many of the 'performance' intelligence tests (e.g. Raven's Matrices, Block Design, etc.) are perceptual in nature, and such measures have often found to be vulnerable to the effects of head injury.

Some authors have reported performance on perceptual tests of the kind that have not usually been included in general measures of intelligence, and these will be discussed very briefly. Both Klóve and Cleeland (1972), and Dye *et al.* (1979), used the Halstead/Reitan Battery which incorporates a number of measures of perceptual functions such as Speech Perception, Rhythm Discrimination, Fingertip Writing, Sensory Inattention, Roughness Discrimination, etc. These studies were concerned more with within-head injury effects (e.g. the effects of severity of injury, etc.), rather than comparison between head-injury and control patients, and in the Klóve study patients with intracerebral haematoma, or with persisting neurological signs, were worse (although non-significantly) than those without, on all the perceptual tests. Dye *et al.* compared 'mild' and 'severe' head-injury patients and found no differences on Speech Perception or Rhythm Discrimination, although when the two head-injured groups were compared with a non-injured control group, head-injured patients were (not significantly) worse.

An interesting study of auditory perceptual function was reported by the Najenson group (Bergman, Hirsch, and Najenson 1977) showing subtle defects of auditory perception and attention in a series of individual head-injured patients. Further work in this area was reported by Cant, Gronwall, and Burgess (1975).

Smith (1974), and Roberts (1979) used the Ellithorn Maze Test (Ellithorn, Kerr, and Jones 1963) which requires the patient to trace with a pencil a path through a series of dots placed at the intersection of crossing diagonal lines. Right-sided impact cases performed significantly worse than left on this test, with right posterior cases showing the worst score. The longer the PTA the worse the performance on the test—particularly so for right-sided impact cases.

THE DAY-TO-DAY CONSEQUENCES OF COGNITIVE DEFICITS

Many of the studies of cognitive deficit after head injury have made the implicit assumption that deficits identified by psychological tests have a major impact on the patient in his everyday life. It is difficult to gather evidence about this, as the assessment of real-life consequences of (for example) memory disturbance relies on behavioural observation (very difficult to achieve for memory functions) or questionnaire techniques (of doubtful validity in a severely head-injured patient lacking in insight), or some kind of analogue of real-life memory (e.g. the study by Wilkins and Baddeley 1978).

Currently the tendency is to assume that cognitive test performance may map fairly closely on to real-life cognitive performance but this need not necessarily be the case, as Wilkins and Baddeley (1978) demonstrated in a sample of normal volunteer subjects. The subjects were required to press a button on a small box every four hours. Inside the box was a small digital watch which was photographed every time the button was pressed, thereby giving a neat and effective record of accuracy of performance. The subjects also underwent a free recall memory test involving learning lists of words. Wilkins and Baddeley found that the subjects who performed worst on free recall performed best on the button pressing. Obviously one cannot infer thereby that the laboratory tests never map on to real-life performance: the motivation of volunteers pressing a button may well not be the same as that of taking a test, but the results remain worrying.

The questionnaire approach has been used in Glasgow (Brooks 1979), and in Cambridge (Sunderland, Harris, and Baddeley 1982, 1983). The Glasgow study involved severely head-injured patients tested at three, six, and 12 months after injury on conventional clinical memory tests (story recall and Rey figure) as well as on a simple 12-item memory questionnaire devised by Alan Sunderland of the Applied Psychology Unit in Cambridge. The questionnaire concerning the patient was filled in by a close relative, and the results showed that at three and six months after injury the main everyday life memory problems involved continually repeating questions, forgetting names of friends, and misplacing objects in the house. At three months after injury highly significant correlations were found between two clinical psychological tests, and a number of the questionnaire items. Despite the high statistical significance, none of the Pearson Product correlations was greater than -0.4, which leaves much variance 'unexplained', and shows that at least as far as the questionnaire is concerned, memory test performance need not usefully predict functional memory in an *individual* patient. Against this finding must be placed results from the same study (Brooks and Aughton 1979a; McKinlay, Brooks, Bond, Martinage, and Marshall 1981) in which relatives were asked to report symptoms and difficulties in the patient following head injury. When the different symptoms reported by the relative were ranked, memory disturbances consistently came out high with 73 per cent of relatives reporting memory disturbances in the patient at three months, 59 per cent at six months, and 69 per cent at 12 months. Relatives, therefore, do recognize a day-to-day impairment in memory in the patient, and in that sense a poor memory test performance of head-injured patients does reflect an underlying reality. However, relatives were also asked to rate the overall severity of memory disturbance in the patient from 'absent—mild' to 'severe', and when these were subdivided into three severity sub-groups, and the patients in these sub-groups compared on cognitive test performance using analysis of variance, there were no significant differences. The 'severe' sub-group did, however, perform at the lowest level, and the 'absent—mild' at the highest.

REMEDIATION OF COGNITIVE DEFICITS

Until very recently, there have been few concerted efforts at treating the cognitive deficits which follow head injury (see Brooks 1979, 1981, and Diller and Gordon 1981, for recent accounts). Indeed, cognitive rehabilitation in general is in an early phase of development, and has often been concerned more with deficits found after focal rather than diffuse traumatic damage. Much work has been carried out in Russia by Luria and his colleagues (Luria, Naydin, Tsetkova, and Vinarskaya 1969), and the Luria programme serves as one fundamental model for development in this area. Luria proposes a precise neuropsychological analysis of the individual patient's difficulties in order to understand exactly how the cognitive system has broken down. This is necessary in Luria's view, because deficits that at first sight seem identical may in fact be the result of quite different underlying disorders, and a rehabilitation scheme that involves submitting all patients to one particular regimen will, therefore, be bound to be inefficient or ineffective for some patients, depending on their particular problems.

In head injury, the most prominent defect is one of learning and remembering, although problems in attention and slowness may also be severe. The rehabilitation schemes proposed for dealing with memory deficits have been of two general types, involving on the one hand a cognitive approach and the use of mnemonic systems, and on the other a broadly behaviour therapy approach. These are well described in Diller and Gordon's excellent recent review (1981).

Cognitive approach

Yates (1966) in his book *The art of memory* discusses the memory training techniques in use by the Greek orators. Often the technique involved visual imagery: objects or (if possible) concepts to be remembered were 'distributed' around prominent locations in a building, and the orator would then 'walk' in his mind around the locations, plucking out each idea or object as he came to it. The technique is intuitively appealing for rehabilitation and reports have appeared describing the use of imagery in helping brain-damaged patients. For example, Patten (1972) described four patients with focal lesions resulting in verbal memory deficits, who were taught to form visual images in conjunction with a 'peg list' to help recall lists of items. The peg list comprised the numbers 1–10, each of which was paired with a specific and easily visualized object: 1, BUN; 2, SHOE; 3 . . . 10, HEN.

Given a list of words to be learned, the patient forms a vivid image of the first word in the list, and then interacts this image in some bizarre or striking way with the image of a bun. For example, if the first word to be remembered was 'cheese', the patient might picture a bun with an enormous piece of cheese in the middle, and so on for the rest of the list. Obviously the technique is easiest for concrete nouns, but with practice it may be extended further. The four patients described by Patten proved able to learn the list and to use it to improve their memory. Without the system the patients still had poor memories, so the system acts as an external aid or prothesis. Patten noted that three other patients had not benefited, and these were patients who were unaware of their deficits, and were so seriously damaged as to be unable to learn the original peg list.

Patten's study was a clinical one involving the description of cases rather than the experimental manipulation of variables. More detailed experimental work has come from Glasgow, Zeiss, Barreira, and Lewinsohn (1977); Lewinsohn, Danaher, and Kikel (1977); Gianutsos and Gianutsos (1979); and Crovitz (1979). The Lewinsohn study involved 19 vascular brain-damaged patients who were taught the use of visual images to facilitate verbal recall. Their verbal memory performance was improved at 30 minutes recall, but not at 1 week. Gianutsos used elaborative rehearsal, in which patients invent a story to link the words to be remembered: her four patients all benefited, although by relatively small amounts in three cases.

The use of imagery and the elaborative coding methods offers a possible tool for alleviating some of the head-injury memory defects, but its effectiveness needs to be studied in much greater detail before it can be considered a reliable and predictable method for memory rehabilitation (Wilson 1982).

Behavioural approaches

An alternative approach is a broadly behavioural one which was used by Lomranz (1974) in a series of individual head-injury case studies, and by Fowler, Hart, and Sheehan (1972) in the treatment of a single severely head-injured patient. Fowler used a treatment which involved memory aids—a printed schedule of the patient's daily activities together with a portable hour timer which the patient had to set and reset for 5 minutes before each appointment. The timer and schedule together provided the patient with cues and information about the time, location, and sequence of daily activities, and in the event of the patient successfully arriving at a given activity, he was given warm praise and encouragement by the hospital staff. If he failed to arrive on time (within 10 minutes) he was firmly ignored. The scheme contains the two essential elements of behavioural treatment—a precise specification of the necessary behaviour (arriving at a given sequence of appointments within given time limits), and instant feedback (by means of praise and social reinforcement) for successful behaviour. Before the scheme started the patient consistently missed every one of his 24 possible daily appointments. By the second week of treatment he missed only two out of a possible 23. Within a very short time the timer was 'faded out' as was the schedule. Later it was found that the patient had in fact obtained an appointment book of his own (identical with that used by the senior author of the study), and had transcribed his daily schedule into it, and was successfully meeting all his appointments.

It is a mistake to consider cognitive rehabilitation schemes as involving *either* cognitive *or* behavioural approaches (Ben Yishay and Diller 1983). Schemes that use elements of both approaches may well be more successful than those which use just one, but until the detailed research is carried out it is difficult to prescribe individual treatments with confidence. In the next few years it is very likely that a spate of research reports will appear giving much greater guidance to rehabilitation specialists about assisting patients with cognitive deficits.

CONCLUSIONS

Severe head injury leads to marked and persistent defects in various areas of cognitive functioning, but most particularly in learning and memory and in 'speed'. Many patients have continuing cognitive difficulties for months or years after injury, and although the precise research is not yet available, it does seem that defects identified on cognitive testing may also have a deleterious effect on the patient's everyday life. The more severe the injury, the greater the cognitive defect, but there are still wide individual variations, and whereas a patient with a PTA of more than 4 weeks is almost certain to have a persisting severe learning and memory defect, there is no guarantee that a patient with a PTA of a matter of days will *not* have cognitive defects. Each case has to be evaluated on its own merits.

Having come to these conclusions, it must be said that the precise reasons why patients have persisting cognitive deficits remain remarkably under-researched. Much of the work on the cognitive effects of head injury has been clinical and empirical, and often divorced entirely from psychological or neuropsychological theorizing. There are a few exceptions: for example, the use of a primary and secondary memory model (Brooks 1975; Parker and Serrats 1976; Wilson, Brooks, and Phillips 1982), the use of attention models by Van Zomeren in Chapter 5, and Levin's examination of possible hemispheric disconnection (Levin, Grossman, Sarwar, and Meyers 1981). Other than these studies, however, the cognitive research has been largely atheoretical. This has led almost inevitably to replication and re-replication of similar findings (consider the number of reports of memory impairment), and to a curiously 'unfocused' feel to the literature in this area.

That cognitive deficits are severe, often persistent, and related broadly to severity of brain damage has been reported time after time, but exactly *why* the deficits are found, and precisely *what* underlying sensory and cognitive processes are affected is not clear. There is a great need for analytically based programmes of research using test procedure derived from current models of normal cognitive processing, in addition to the more conventional clinical tests. This sort of approach is now becoming the norm elsewhere in neuropsychology, and its adoption will help not only in understanding the nature of the deficits, but in planning their effective rehabilitation.

REFERENCES

Aita, J. A., Armitage, S.G., Reitan, R. M., and Rabinovitz, A. (1947). The use of certain psychological tests in the evaluation of brain injury. *J. Gen. Psychol.* **37**, 25–44.

Babcock, H. (1930). An experiment in the measurement of mental deterioration. *Arch. Psychol.* **117**, 105.

Ben Yishay, Y., and Diller, L. (1983). Cognitive deficits. *Rehabilitation of the head injured adult* (ed. M. Rosenthal *et al*). pp. 167–84. F. A. Davis, Philadelphia.

Bergman, M., Hirsch, S., and Najenson, T. (1977). Tests of auditory perception in the assessment and management of patients with cerebral cranial injury. *Scand. J. rehabil. Med.* **9**, 173–7.

Borkowski, J. G., Benton, A. L., and Spreen, O. (1967). Word fluency and brain damage. *Neuropsychologia* **5**, 135–40.

Brooks, D. N. (1972). Memory and head injury. *J. nerv. ment. Dis.* **155**, 350–5.

——, (1974*a*). Recognition memory and head injury. *J. Neurol. Neurosurg. Psychiat.* **37**, 794–801.

——, (1974*b*). Recognition memory after head injury: A signal detection analysis. *Cortex* **10**, 224–30.

——, (1975). Long- and short-term memory in head-injured patients. *Cortex* **11**, 329–40.

——, (1976). Wechsler Memory Scale performance and its relationship to brain damage after severe closed head injury. *J. Neurol. Neurosurg. Psychiat.*, **39**, 593.

——, (1979). Psychological deficits after severe blunt head injury: Their significance and rehabilitation. In *Research in psychology and medicine*, (ed. A. B. Oborne, C. D.Gruneberg, and E. F. Eiser) Vol. II, pp. 469–76, Academic Press, London.

——, (1983). Disorders of memory. *Rehabilitation of the head-injured adult* (ed. M. Rosenthal *et al.*, pp. 185–96, F. A. Davis, Philadelphia.

—— and Aughton, M. E. (1979*a*). Psychological consequences of blunt head injury. *Int. rehabil. Med.* **1**, 160–5.

——, ——, Bond, M. R., Jones, P,, and Rizvi, S. (1980). Cognitive sequelae in relationship to early indices of severity of brain damage after severe blunt head injury. *J. Neurol. Neurosurg. Psychiat.* **43**, 529–34.

——, Deelman, B. G., Van Zomeren, A. H., Van Dongen, H. R., Van Harskamp, F., and Aughton, M. E. (1983). Methodological problems in measuring the process of cognitive recovery after severe head injury. *J. Clin. Neuropsychol.* (In press.)

Brown, J. C. (1975). Late recovery from head injury: Case report and review. *Psychol. Med.* **5**, 239–48.

Buschke, H. and Fuld, P. A. (1974). Evaluating storage, retention and retrieval in disordered memory and learning. *Neurology* **24**, 1019–25.

Cant, B. R., Gronwall, D. M. A., and Burgess, R. (1975). Recovery process of the slow auditory response following head injury. *Revue De Laryngologie* **96**, 199–206.

Conkey, R. C. (1938). Psychological changes associated with head injuries. *Arch. Psychol.* **232**, 1–62.

Crovitz, H. F. (1979). Memory retraining in brain damaged patients: The airplane list. *Cortex,* **15**, 131–4.

De Renzi, E. and Vignolo, L. A. (1962). The token test: a sensitive test to detect receptive disturbances in aphasia. *Brain* **85**, 665–78.

Diller, L. and Gordon, W. A. (1981). Intervention for cognitive deficits in brain-injured adults. *J. Consult. Clin. Psychol.* **49**, 822–34.

Dunn, J. and Brooks, D. N. (1974). Memory and post traumatic amnesia. *J. Int. Res. Commun.* **2**, 1497.

Dye, O. A., Milby, J. B., and Saxon, S. A. (1979). Effects of early neurological problems following head trauma on subsequent neuropsychological performance. *Acta Neurol. Scand.* **59**, 10–14.

Elithorn, A., Kerr, M., and Jones, D. (1963). A binary perceptual maze. *Am. J. Psychol.* **76**, 506–8.

Fodor, I. E. (1972). Impairment of memory functions after acute head injury. *J. Neurol. Neurosurg. Psychiat.* **35**, 818–24.

Fowler, R. S., Hart, J., and Sheehan, M. (1972). A prosthetic memory: an application of the prosthetic environment concept. *Rehab. Counselling Bull.,* December, 80–5.

Gianutsos, R. and Gianutsos, J. (1979). Rehabilitating the verbal recall of brain injured patients by mnemonic training: an experimental demonstration using single-case methodology. *J. Clin. Neuropsychol.* **1**, 117–35.

Glasgow, R. E., Zeiss, R. A., Barrera, M., and Lewinsohn, P. M. (1977). Case studies on remediating memory deficits in brain damaged individuals. *J. Clin. Psychol.* **33**, 1049–54.

Groher, M. (1977). Language and memory disorders following closed head trauma. *J. Speech Hearing Res.* **20**, 212–23.

Gronwall, D. and Wrightson, P. (1980). Duration of post-traumatic amnesia after mild head injury. *J. Clin. Neuropsychol.* **2**, 51–60.

Halstead, W. C. (1947). *Brain and intelligence: a quantitative study of the frontal lobes.* University of Chicago Press.

Heilman, K. M. Safran, A., and Geshwind, N. (1971). Closed head trauma and aphasia. *J. Neurol. Neurosurg. Psychiat.* **34**, 265–9.

Jennett, B. and Bond, M. R. (1975). Assessment of outcome after severe brain damage: A practical scale. *Lancet* **i**, 480–7.

Kimura, D. (1963). Right temporal lobe damage. *Arch. Neurol.,* **8**, 264–71.

Kløve, H. and Cleeland, C. S. (1972). The relationship of neuropsychological impairment to other indices of severity of head injury. *Scand. J. rehabil. Med.* **4**, 55–60.

Levin, H. S. (1981). Aphasia in closed head injury. In *Acquired Aphasia* (ed. A. B. Sarno) pp. 427–64. Academic Press, London.

——, Grossman, R. G., and Kelly, P. (1976). Aphasic disorder in patients with closed head injury. *J. Neurol. Neurosurg. Psychiat.* **39**, 1062–70.

——, ——, Rose, J. E., and Teasdale, G. (1979). Long term neuropsychological outcome of closed head injury. *J. Neurosurg.* **50**, 412–22.

——, Grossman, R. G., Sarwar, M., and Meyers, C. A. (1981). Linguistic recovery after closed head injury. *Brain Lang.* **12**, 360–74.

Lewinsohn, P. M., Danaher, B. G., and Kikel, S. (1977). Visual imagery as a mnemonic aid for brain injured persons. *J. Consult. Clin. Psychol.* **45**, 717–23.

Lezak, M. (1979). Recovery of memory and learning functions following traumatic brain injury. *Cortex* **15**, 63–72.

Lomranz, J. (1976). *Rehabilitation of brain injured Veterans; progress report.* Neuropsychological Unit for Rehabilitation and Research, Department of Psychology, Tel-Aviv University.

Luria, A. R., Naydin, V. L., Tsetkova, L. S., and Vinarskaya, E. N. (1969). Restoration of higher cortical function following local brain damage. In *Handbook of clinical neurology* (ed. A. B. Vinken and C. D. Brayn) Vol. 3, pp. 368–433. North–Holland, Amsterdam.

McKinlay, W. W., Brooks, D. N., Bond, M. R., Martinage, D., and Marshall, M. M. (1981). The short-term outcome of severe blunt head injury as reported by relatives of the injured person. *J. Neurol. Neurosurg. Psychiat.* **44**, 527–33.

Mandleberg, I. A. (1975*a*). Cognitive recovery after severe head injury, 2. Wechsler Adult Intelligence Scale during post-traumatic amnesia. *J. Neurol. Neurosurg. Psychiat.* **38**, 1127–32.

——,. (1975*b*). Cognitive recovery after severe head injury, 3. WAIS Verbal and Performance IQ's as a function of post-traumatic amnesia duration and time from injury. *J. Neurol. Neurosurg. Psychiat.* **39**, 1001–7.

—— and Brooks, D. N. (1975). Cognitive recovery after severe head injury, 1. Serial testing on the Wechsler Adult Intelligence Scale. *J. Neurol. Neurosurg. Psychiat.* **38**, 1121–6.

Najenson, T., Sazbon, L., Fiselzon, J., Becker, E., and Schechter, I. (1978). Recovery of cognitive functions after prolonged traumatic coma. *Scand. J. Rehabil. Med.* **10**, 15–21.

Ommaya, A. K. and Gennarelli, T. A. (1974). Cerebral concussions and traumatic unconsciousness: correlations of experimental and clinical observations on blunt head injuries. *Brain* **97**, 633–54.

Parker, S. A. and Serrats, A. F. (1976). Memory recovery after traumatic coma. *Acta Neurochir.* **34**, 71–7.

Patten, B. M. (1972). The ancient art of memory: usefulness in treatment. *Arch. Neurol.* **26**, 25–31.

Raven, J. C. (1960). *Guide to the standard progressive matrices.* H. K. Lewis, London.

——, (1962). *Extended Guide to the Mill Hill Vocabulary Scales,* H. K. Lewis, London.

Reitan, R. M. (1958). The validity of the Trail Making Test as an indicator of organic brain damage. *Percept. Motor Skills* **8**, 271.

Rey, A. (1941). L'examen psychologique dans les cas d'encephelopathie traumatique. *Archives de Psychologie* **28**, 286–340.

Reynell, W. R. (1944). A Psychometric method of determining intellectual loss following head injury. *J. Mental Sci.* **90**, 710–19.

Richardson, J. T. (1979). Signal detection theory and the effects of severe head injury upon recognition memory. *Cortex* **15**, 145–8.

Roberts, A. H. (1979). *Severe accidental head injury.* McMillan, London.

Ruesch, J. (1944). Intellectual impairment in head injuries. *Am. J. Psychiat.* **100**, 480–96.

——, Moore, B. E. (1943). Measurement of intellectual functions in the acute stage of head injury. *Arch. Neurol. Psychiat.* **50**, 165–70.

Russell, W. R. (1932). Cerebral involvement in head injury. *Brain* **35**, 549–603.

——, (1971). *The traumatic amnesias.* Oxford University Press, London.

—— and Smith, A. (1961). Post-traumatic amnesia in closed head injury. *Arch. Neurol.* **5**, 16–29.

Schacter, D. L. and Crovitz, H. F. (1977). Memory function after closed head injury: a review of the quantitative research. *Cortex*, **13**, 150–76.

Shatz, M. W. (1981). WAIS practice effects in clinical neuropsychology. *J. Clin. Neuropsychol.* **3**, 171–9.

Sisler, G. and Penner, H. (1975). Amnesia following severe head injury. *Can. Psychiat. Assoc. J.* **20**, 333–6.

Smith, E. (1974). Influence of site of impact upon cognitive performance persisting long after severe closed head injury. *J. Neurol. Neurosurg. Psychiat.* **37**, 719–26.

Sunderland, A., Harris, J. E., and Baddeley, A. D. (1982). Everyday memory and test performance following severe closed head injury. Paper presented at *5th Annual Conference of International Neuropsychological Society*, June 15–18th, Deauville, France.

——, ——, —— (1983). Do laboratory tests predict everyday memory? A neuropsychological study. *J. Verb. Learn. Verb. Behaviour.* (In press.)

Teasdale, G. and Jennett, B. (1974). Assessment of coma and impaired consciousness. A practical scale. *Lancet* **ii**, 81–4.

Thomsen, I. V. (1975). Evaluation and outcome of aphasia in patients with severe closed head trauma. *J. Neurol. Neurosurg. Psychiat.* **38**, 713–18.

——, (1977). Verbal learning in aphasic and non-aphasic patients with severe head injuries. *Scand. J. Rehabil. Med.* **9**, 73–7.

Tooth, G. (1947). On the use of mental tests for the measurement of disability after head injury. *J. Neurol. Neurosurg. Psychiat.*, **10**, 1–11.

Vigouroux, R. P., Baurand, C., Nacquet, R., Chament, J. H., Choux, M., Benayoun, R., Bureau, M., Charpy, J. P., Clamen-Guey, J., and Guey, J. (1971). A series of patients with cranio-cerebral injuries, studied neurologically, psychometrically, electroencephalographically, and socially. In *Head injuries: proceedings of an international symposium held in Edinburgh and Madrid*, Churchill Livingstone, Edinburgh, pp. 335–410.

Von Wowern, F. (1966). Post-traumatic amnesia and confusion as an index of severity in head injury. *Acta Neurol. Scand.* **42**, 373–8.

Wechsler, D. (1945). A standardised memory scale for clinical use. *J. Psychol.* **19**, 87–95.

——, (1958). *The measurement and appraisal of adult intelligence.* Williams & Wilkins, Baltimore.

Wilkins, A. J. and Baddeley A. D. (1978). Remembering to recall in everyday life: an approach to absentmindedness. In *Practical aspects of memory* (ed. A. B. Gruneberg, *et. al.*) pp. 27–34. Academic Press, London.

Wilson, B. (1982). Success and failure in memory training following a cerebral vascular accident. *Cortex* **18**, 581–94.

Wilson, J. T. L., Brooks, D. N., and Phillips, W. A. (1982). Using a microcomputer to study perception, memory and attention after head injury. Paper presented at *5th Annual Conference of International Neuropsychological Society*, June 15–18th, Deauville, France.

Yates, F. A. (1966). *The art of memory.* University of Chicago Press.

5 Attentional deficits: the riddles of selectivity, speed, and alertness

A. H. van Zomeren, W. H. Brouwer, and B. G. Deelman

INTRODUCTION

References to deficits of attention in head-injured patients are numerous, even in older literature. Meyer (1904) in discussing the clinical varieties of traumatic insanity, extensively quoted his German colleague Köppen: 'These patients are unable to concentrate their attention, even in occupations which serve for mere entertainment, such as reading or playing cards. They like best to brood unoccupied. . . .'

It will be clear that Köppen was referring to the behaviour of very severely injured patients, in whom the deficit borders upon apathy. Nevertheless, similar observations have been described for people with all grades of severity of injury. When interviewing patients one may hear that they are easily distracted, and that concentrating on a task is unusually tiring. Likewise, some of them report difficulties in doing two tasks simultaneously, which suggests that they cannot divide their attention adequately.

These clinical impressions were apparently confirmed when psychologists introduced their specific methods of investigation in the field of head injury. The first psychological report on the sequelae of such injuries was published by Conkey in 1938. She administered a battery of 30 different tests, and according to her five of them tested the ability to concentrate or to focus attention. However, this selection of five tests seems to have been rather arbitrary, and not based on an explicit theory or even definition of attention. Nevertheless, her conclusions were that a principal result of head injury seemed to be a loss of power to sustain attention. In later studies too (Ruesch 1944 *a*, *b*; Dencker and Löfving 1958) statements about attentional deficits are found that in retrospect seem not fully justified, or even post-hoc interpretations. Moreover, attentional deficits are sometimes assumed to explain poor performance on tasks that were meant to test other psychological functions. So-called 'lapses of attention' in particular have been serving as scapegoats in some studies. Thus, although psychologists repeated the statements of early clinical observers, their views were mainly based on poor performance of patients on a variety of psychological tests.

This is hardly surprising, considering the lack of attentional theories at the time of their investigations. Still, their results may have significance in the framework of theories that have since been developed. In this chapter, we will attempt to review both older and recent literature in terms of these theories. Unless stated otherwise, all patient studies described below are concerned with attentional deficits in subjects who were no longer in a state of PTA. This PTA is characterized by an obvious lack of continuous memory, and the duration of PTA is often considered the best index of severity in the case of closed head injury (Schacter and Crovitz 1977, and see Chapter 4).

'Everyone knows what attention is', William James said in 1890. In a sense he was right, as attention was a favourite topic for introspection by his contemporaries. James continued as follows: 'Focalization, concentration of consciousness are of its essence. It implies withdrawal from some things in order to deal better with others.' However, the rise of Gestalt psychology and Behaviourism for some time banished the very word attention from psychology, as both schools tried to do without the concept, and attention as a concept was non-existent for the science of psychology from 1920 up till the 'fifties. Following the Second World War there was a revival of interest, which stemmed from practical questions. In the armed services a troublesome decrease of vigilance had been observed in people doing monotonous watch-keeping tasks (sonar, radar) while in industry the development of complicated man—machine systems had likewise revealed the limitations of attention. The research on attention was highly stimulated by the publication of Broadbent's book *Perception and communication* (1958) which introduced the 'human information processing' approach. The next decade saw an outburst of books, chapters, and articles devoted to the subject, but this did not bring theoretical consensus or even a generally agreed upon definition of attention. In 1969 Moray stated that the terminology related to the subject was 'at best confusing and at worst a mess'. Or, to paraphrase James, it seemed that everyone thought that he alone knew what attention was. Another decade later, it may be concluded that the terminological confusion was the result of the growing apart of three different approaches to attention, each approach bringing its own definitions and concepts. The approaches can be characterized by the concepts of selectivity, speed of information processing, and alertness. The structure of the present chapter is determined by this triad, while in addition a paragraph is dedicated to the so-called 'coping hypothesis'. A short overview of the issues in all four fields will be given in the next paragraphs, each paragraph considering both theories of normal functioning and data on pathological functioning derived from experimental studies with head-injured subjects.

SELECTIVE ATTENTION

Theories

Selectivity is the oldest meaning in which the word attention is used, as can be seen in the James' quotation above. All day long a continuous stream of stimulation reaches our senses, but the bulk of this stimulation is apparently ignored. At the same time a vast amount of information is present in the memory system, but again the actual behaviour of an organism is determined by a fraction of this information only. Thus, selective mechanisms must play an important role. A well-known illustration of our selectivity is found in the so-called cocktail party phenomenon: in a crowded room with a hum of voices, we can easily focus on the voice of our conversation partner while ignoring the others. In the laboratory selective attention has been studied extensively with the 'speech shadowing task': a subject is presented simultaneously with two different auditory messages, and he is instructed to repeat (shadow) one of them word by word. Subjects have little problem in performing such tasks, at least when the messages can be discriminated on the basis of obvious physical cues. For example, shadowing can be perfect when the relevant message is fed by earphones into the right ear, while the irrelevant message is fed into the left ear. Likewise, subjects can shadow easily when one message is spoken in a female voice and the other one in a male voice (Broadbent 1971).

This selectivity is of course very efficient, but at the same time it introduces a bottleneck in the information processing of an organism: beyond a certain point in time between stimulation and responding, only the selected stimulus can be processed and responded to. Theories of attention have always been concerned with the question where this bottleneck should be located in the information processing system.

Implied in most theories of selective attention is the notion that levels of abstraction can be specified in the analysis of sensory stimulation. At first, obvious physical characteristics are extracted, like the colour of a stimulus or its position in space. Thereupon patterns or Gestalts are formed, and subsequently interpretation occurs. Finally, a motor programme may be selected and executed. Until recently all theories had a strong structural component, in the sense that they located the selective mechanisms at a fixed level of abstraction. After Broadbent (1958) all theories in essence accepted an early stage in which stimulation from different sources was processed in parallel through separate channels, but they differed in respect to the level at which this parallel processing was supposed to stop. Broadbent's filter theory assumed that selection occurred immediately after abstracting raw physical features from the various channels, the filter excluding all other information (Fig. 5.1).

This view was shown to be untenable, as can be illustrated with daily events: even when a reader is completely involved in a fascinating book, he

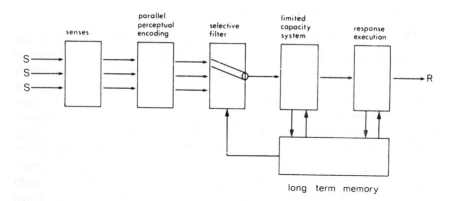

Fig. 5.1.

Broadbent's filter model in a slightly modified version.

will raise his head when his name is spoken. This indicates that auditory stimulation was processed up to the semantic or meaning level along with the visual information from the book. In the laboratory too it has been noted that intrusions occur, i.e. parts of the irrelevant message may slip in when they fit well into the context of the relevant message (Gray and Wedderburn 1960). Such evidence led Deutsch and Deutsch (1963) to the theory that the bottleneck occurs *after* the extraction of meaning, in the stage of response selection.

However, the weakness of this latter theory was that it could not explain why selection based on obvious physical cues was much easier than selection based on meaning. Therefore, the most recent generation of structural models featured two selective mechanisms: one at the stage of the filter, and one at the stage of the response selection (Treisman 1964; Broadbent 1971). In these theories it was held that the filter did not operate in an all-or-none fashion. Rather, it was assumed that the filter attenuated the information from different channels to degrees controlled by the subject. Stimulation that had to be ignored was supposed to be given a much shallower processing, and it would only control behaviour if the outcome of its processing was highly pertinent in the situation—for example, when it presented a signal of imminent danger. The latter selection mechanism was called 'pigeon-holing' and had to do with the setting of 'pertinence thresholds' for the outcome of earlier processing. If the threshold was very low for a particular outcome stemming from irrelevant stimulation (e.g. fitting quite well in the context of the attended message), this irrelevant stimulation would as yet control behaviour.

Norman (1969) formulates his critique against such a two-stage theory of selective attention as follows (page 33):

The problem with this is simply that it is difficult to see how Treisman can both have a savings in the number of signals that must be analyzed (an attenuated signal, after all, acts like it is hardly there at all) and an analysis of all signals when it is convenient (the attenuated signal is still there, after all).

Fundamentally, this critique also applies to the theory presented by Broadbent, as qualitative differences between 'limited capacity' processing of selected information and 'shallow' processing of attenuated information are not specified. Recent approaches to selective attention focus on the specification of such a qualitative difference by postulating automatic (pre-attentive) versus consciously controlled (attentive, limited capacity) modes of information processing.

When looking at the human information processor, one is struck by his astonishing capacity to perform two separate complex activities simultaneously. For example, we can sing a song while driving our car, and we can even go on singing while shifting gears—at least during the chorus. The point is that even complex motor patterns do not seem 'to ask our attention', provided that they are well trained. This ease in performing an overlearned skill contrasts sharply with the laborious process of the initial learning, when the task demanded our full attention. The distinction between processes that do and do not ask our attention led Neisser (1967) to postulate a dichotomy of pre-attentive and attentive processes. Learning or practise played an important role in his theory, and he demonstrated that detection in a visual search task may become automatic by practise. Although the distinction between attentive and non-attentive processes has been elaborated in several models (La Berge 1973, Shiffrin 1975) the present chapter is best served by the two-process theory of Shiffrin and Schneider (1977). Their theory emphasizes attentional limitations, and thus it might provide a link with pathological limitations that are encountered in the study of psychological deficits after head injury. The theory contrasts with the 'structural' theories described above by the important feature that selectivity is not structurally connected to any fixed level of abstraction, or stage of processing (see Fig. 5.2).

Shiffrin and Schneider distinguish two forms of information processing, that is, *automatic* versus *controlled*. All information entering the system is processed automatically up till the highest level possible without conscious control. This processing is based on activation of a learned sequence of long-term memory elements; it is initiated by appropriate inputs, and then proceeds automatically. It is even possible that a complete stimulus-response chain occurs automatically, in particular in familiar situations. In other words, automatic processing happens without subject control, without stressing the capacity limitations of the system and without demanding

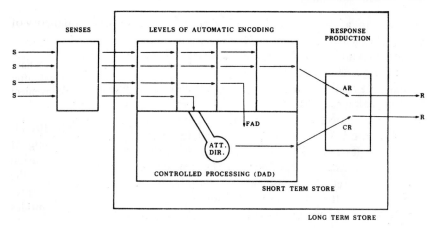

Fig. 5.2.

The two-process model of information processing as described by Shiffrin and Schneider (1977). ATT DIR = Attention director; AR = Automatic response, is this case compatible with CR = controlled response; FAD = Focused attention deficit, a result of automatic processing intruding in the domain of controlled processing. DAD = Divided attention deficit, when rate of controlled processing is too low. Note that short-term store is an activated part of long-term store.

attention. The importance of learning can be illustrated with the example of reading: when a text is presented to a skilled reader this text will be processed automatically up till a level of global meaning. On the other hand, when a Chinese text is presented automatic processing will stop at a level where the subject sees some figures that are meaningless, at least to him. The results of automatic processing can 'come to our attention' in two ways. A learned response tendency may interfere with the task at hand, or the results of automatic processing may be read out by conscious processes under control of the subject. Controlled processing is a temporary activation of a sequence of elements that can be set up quickly and easily, but requires attention. It is capacity limited, and usually serial in nature. It typically occurs in new situations where the subject cannot rely on prior experience.

Within this two-process model a dichotomy is specified of qualitatively different limitations of selective attention. The first class is termed Focused Attention Deficits (FADs). These result from automatic response tendencies which conflict with responses required in the task at hand. The second class is termed Divided Attention Deficits (DADs). These result from speed limitations of consciously controlled processing. Because of their intimate connection with processing speed, DADs will be discussed in the paragraph on 'Speed of processing'.

In normal subjects FADs tend to occur when an unfamiliar response must be given to a stimulus which has a conflicting response tendency very strongly attached to it. This conflicting stimulus-response bond is the result of earlier training in a comparable context, to a degree at which automatization of processing occurred.

In most situations, healthy subjects are able to suppress the execution of the conflicting response, the only evidence for the occurrence of distraction being the low speed of executing the new, less-familiar task. A classic example of such a FAD is found in the interference effect of the Stroop Color Word Test (Stroop 1935). This test consists of three sub-tests. In the first, the subject is asked to read aloud 100 simple colour names, like red, blue, blue, yellow, red etc., as quickly as possible. In the second sub-test, he is asked to name the colours of 100 coloured blocks printed on a card in the same array as the words in the first sub-test. Finally, 100 colour names are presented, likewise printed on a card. However, each word is now printed in coloured ink, and the actual colour of the letters does not fit the word meaning. Thus, the subject may see the word 'red' printed in blue. He is then asked to name the colours of the words as quickly as possible, while ignoring the word meaning. This turns out to be very difficult, as the word meanings are constantly entering the domain of conscious processing. Therefore, every subject, unless illiterate or in need of reading glasses, will need much more time for colour naming on the third card, and the magnitude of the difference is an index for the interference effect. This Stroop test clearly illustrates the mechanism of a FAD: although the subject knows quite well which input is relevant, he cannot avoid the irrelevant input—due to automatic response tendencies found in every skilled reader. FAD's are not just laboratory phenomena, but occur frequently in daily life. The man who has bought a new car of a make that he never drove before will find out that in the first days behind the steering wheel he will start automatic actions that lead him nowhere—as the trafficator lever is now situated on the other side of the steering column. Or, to give another example of interruption by results of automatic processing: suppose we are in a restaurant, enjoying a good meal and a merry conversation. Without eavesdropping we may suddenly notice that behind our back, at the next table, a foreign language is spoken. This proves that these auditory stimuli coming from human sources had been processed automatically, hence without any effort on our part, up till the phonetic level. Thus it came to our attention that peculiar phonemes were to be heard, which were then classified by conscious processing as stemming from a particular foreign language.

Before reviewing evidence on focused attention in head-injured patients, we will summarize briefly the evolution that took place in the theorizing about selectivity. At first, selective attention was assumed to be a perceptual phenomenon occurring in an early stage of information processing. As it became clear that irrelevant information may also give intrusions on higher levels of abstraction (for example, by its meaning) subsequent theories located the structural bottleneck in the response selection stage. At the same time, investigators began to emphasize the distinction between pre-attentive and attentive processes. This distinction became the essential feature in the two-process model of Shiffrin and Schneider that elaborated two forms of information processing: automatic and controlled. The first form does not demand conscious effort, and is the result of practise or learning. The products of automatic processing may interfere with conscious processing in *any* stage, implying that the two-process model does not locate a bottleneck in a particular stage of processing like the preceding structural models did.

Pathology of focused attention

In terms of the Shiffrin and Schneider theory, deficits of focused attention occur only when automatized response tendencies are attached to irrelevant stimulation. However, the older theories gave a somewhat broader definition of focused attention (Broadbent 1971). Most of them postulated that even irrelevant information to which no response tendencies were attached had to be *actively* attenuated by the 'filter'. According to Shiffrin and Schneider, however, this information would just *passively* decay in short-term-memory, and henceforth would not require any selective mechanism to stop it. As we want to do justice to older head-injury research aimed at focused attention as well, we must discuss two experiments that do not fit into the theoretical framework adopted in this chapter: in two studies an attempt has been made to assess the integrity of filtering.

As stated in the Introduction early psychological investigators (Conkey 1938; Ruesch 1944, *a*, *b*) had some doubts about their subjects' ability to concentrate on a given task. However, remarks about selectivity in these papers seemed to be based mainly on careful observation of patients during tests. Dencker and Löfving (1958) were the first investigators who used specific tests aiming at attentional deficits. They tested 28 monozygotic twins, in whom one had sustained a closed head injury, while his brother or sister served as a control subject. Two-thirds of the patients had shown a PTA duration of 1 hour or less, making them cases of 'mild concussion' in terms of the Russell classification of severity (1934). They were tested at an average interval of 10 years after injury, which forces us to assume that many of the mild injury cases had recovered more or less completely. Dencker and Löfving presented two texts to their subjects, by reading them aloud — the first story was about a French acrobat, the second about a Dutch sportsman. While the story about the acrobat was read, a record was played of about a dozen persons talking simultaneously. In this way Dencker and Löfving wanted to test sensitivity to distraction with the hypothesis that this would be increased in the head-injured group. Immediately after presentation of the text, seven questions were asked about its content. It turned out that the irrelevant stimulation had no effect at all on the performance of either group, as judged by the number of correctly answered questions. Both the head-injured patients and their siblings knew the fortunes of the French acrobat as well as those of the Dutch sportsman. Therefore the conclusion was that this experimental group showed no deficit in focusing based on an obvious physical dimension. It must be stressed however, that there were no well-trained interfering response tendencies attached to the irrelevant stimulation.

Gronwall and Sampson (1974) tested focused attention in the 'Broadbent sense' in five concussed patients with a duration of PTA of less than 1 hour. Within 24 hours after admission to the hospital these subjects were tested with dichotic stimulation: by headphones two messages were presented simultaneously, and subjects were instructed to 'shadow' the message in their left ear while ignoring the other one. In Part I of the experiment, two word lists were presented; in Part II the relevant message was a text on dieting and the irrelevant message a text on drug-taking. As there were no intrusions at all from the irrelevant messages the authors concluded that their patients showed no deficit in selectivity.

These two studies made use of very obvious cues to decide on relevance: experimenter versus record, left ear versus right ear. In other words, selection in these experiments was possible on the basis of physical dimensions and did not demand much of the selective strategy the subjects used. Moray (1969), for example, has pointed out that ear of presentation is a very potent cue to selective attention. Also, there were no conflicting response tendencies attached to the distracting stimulation. In terms of Shiffrin and Schneider's theory these results only indicate that the patients' strategy for reading out activated memories was about as efficient as the one of the control group. Next, a series of experiments will be described that were also concerned with focused attention. They differ from the experiments reviewed so far by introducing in the tests well-trained response tendencies attached to irrelevant stimulation, and thus they should be good techniques to assess abnormal FADs after head injury. Dencker and Löfving (1958) included in their investigation a test of mirror-drawing; this test requires the suppression of the habitual visuo-motor responses in order to deal with the new situation of visual feedback in mirror image. This is clearly an example of interference from overtrained responses, that is, of a FAD in terms of Shiffrin and Schneider. The task is usually experienced as difficult by normal subjects, but the head-injured group in the Swedish study took significantly more time to complete the task than a control group. Still, this cannot be explained conclusively as a sign of pathological response interference in the patients: no comparison was made of drawing speed in both groups without the hindrance of mirror feedback, and thus it could be stated that the experimental group is only performing slower, but without qualitative differences from the control group.

In two British studies the Stroop Color Word Test has been presented to head-injury patients. The reader will remember that this test consists of three sub-tests: reading colour names, naming the colours of blocks, and naming the colours of words that are themselves colour names. Chadwick (1976) compared head-injured children with orthopaedic controls, testing them one and four months after injury. He found a difference between groups, the head-injured children being slower on all three sub-tests. However, there was no specific effect of response interference in the last sub-test. Thomas (1977) reported similar results when studying a group of adult patients with mild concussions.

In our own laboratory we studied response interference by means of visual choice reaction times (RT). Twenty patients with injuries ranging from mild to very severe in the Russell scale were tested between three and 12 months after injury. Their RT was registrated in a four-choice task with a very high stimulus–response compatibility: the stimuli were themselves push-buttons that had to be pushed as quickly as possible when they were lighted. Total RT was split up into a decision time (DT), being the interval from stimulus onset until the beginning of the subject's movement towards the light, and a movement time (MT), being the interval required for switching off the light after leaving the resting point. Next, this four-choice task was repeated, but this time an irrelevant stimulus appeared simultaneously with each relevant one. That is, on the panel were additional lights in close proximity to the stimulus lights, and these were physically completely identical with the latter ones. As a result, the presentation of these twin lights evoked conflicting response tendencies in the subjects. When comparing the performance of the patients with a group of control subjects matched on age and sex, in an analysis of variance two main effects were found on DT. The patients had significantly longer DTs ($F = 49.55$, df 1, $p < 0.001$) than the controls, and both groups had significantly longer DTs on the distraction task than on the original four-choice task. ($F = 2475.67$, df 1,38, $p < 0.001$). Moreover, there was a significant interaction between groups and tasks: the irrelevant stimuli had a much stronger distracting effect on the head-injured group than on the control group ($F = 184.69$, df 1, $p < 0.001$). That distraction was effective by inducing response interference, was confirmed in an experiment on normal subjects. Twelve medical students performed the basic four-choice task, and the same task under distraction, on two successive days: once with a warning signal, and once without. Presenting a warning signal implies reduction of time uncertainty, and this variable is known (Sternberg 1969) to influence the stage of response selection in information processing. Applying Sternberg's 'additive factor method' we found an interaction between time uncertainty and distraction, and this indicated that the distraction by irrelevant stimuli indeed affected the stage of response selection. Concerning MT in the head-injured group: the analysis of variance revealed that the patients moved significantly slower than the controls, overall MT being 242 ms for the head-injury group and 185 ms for the control group ($F = 11.50$, df 1, $p < 0.01$). Distraction did not prolong MT, which suggests that both patients and controls 'looked before they leapt' and then moved at a speed comparable with their speed in the basic task.

The outcome of this experiment was statistically very clear: distraction had a disproportionate effect on the patients. The theoretical explanation is nevertheless difficult. The distraction effect cannot be explained as a FAD, as subjects had never been trained to react to the irrelevant stimuli. On the other hand, because of their close proximity and resemblance one could state that they evoked the response tendencies that were shaped during training on the relevant lights, by stimulus generalization. In our view, the distraction effect is best explained as a DAD, that is, as a slowing down of consciously controlled processing. Both patients and control subjects experience response conflict in the distraction task, and this results in longer DT than were registered in the basic four-choice task. The extra time is necessary for dealing with the conflict, i.e. for making a final choice where to go. It seems then, that head-injured patients need more time than controls to deal with response interference. In other words, the experiment merely points out that patients show a slowing down of controlled processing, but it brought no evidence for a deficit in focused attention.

Recently Miller and Cruzat (1981) investigated the effect of distracting stimuli on speed of card sorting in head-injured subjects. The test was presented to a 'mild' group, with a median PTA duration of 20 minutes, and to a 'severe' group with a median PTA duration of nine days. Piles of cards had to be sorted on the occurence of the letter A or B, while a variable number of distracting letters was printed on the cards (in conditions with 0, 1, 4, or 8 irrelevant letters). It appeared that only the severely injured group was significantly slower than a control group, but there was no interaction between severity and task difficulty. In other words, an increase in the number of irrelevant letters on the cards had no specific effect on the sorting speed of these patients. Miller and Cruzat supposed that the generally slower speed of sorting in the severely injured group was explicable on the basis of slower reaction times.

Summary

So far, there is no evidence for a deficit of focused attention in people who have sustained a head injury. Nevertheless, it seems too early to make a final statement on the matter. The auditory experiments described above made use of very obvious cues for the selection of relevant information, while in addition only cases of mild head injury were tested. In the visual modality the Stroop Color Word Test likewise failed to reveal a deficit in selectivity, when presented to children with varying severity of injury and to adults with mild head injuries. Finally, a mirror-drawing task, a visual re-action time task with distracting stimuli, and a card-sorting task with dis-tracting stimuli all demonstrated that patients performed slower than con-trol subjects. However, in these experiments the control groups were hindered as well by the experimental variables. Therefore, the stronger ef-fects on the head-injury patients cannot be explained simply as proof of a deficit in selective attention. Rather, they may indicate that the patients are *slower* in dealing with interference from irrelevant stimulation that could be ignored neither by patients nor by controls. This brings us to the issue of the next paragraph: attention defined in terms of speed of processing.

SPEED OF INFORMATION PROCESSING

Theories

In the James' definition of attention, selection of certain stimuli was described more or less as an act of will: the perceiver decided to withdraw from some things in order to deal better with others. Today a more realistic view has emerged, i.e. an organism is forced to ignore most of the stimula-tion that reaches its senses by the limitations of its information processing capacity. It is simply impossible to deal with all available information, and this fact links the selectivity described in the preceding paragraph to pro-cessing capacity. Stated otherwise, the speed with which we can process in-formation will partly determine what we will notice, and how much will go unnoticed. We only have a limited amount of attention to pay, and the limitation seems to be found in the rate of controlled processing.

The reader will remember the distinction made by Shiffrin and Schneider (1977) between automatic and controlled processing, and the FAD featuring in this two-process model. In addition to this FAD, the authors also describe a DAD. This deficit is linked in particular with controlled process-ing, a mode of processing that is supposed to be capacity limited and usually serial in nature. It makes use of the results of preceding automatic process-ing, and it operates on this information by means of a strategy formed on the basis of instruction, prior learning, and context. Transformations are carried out and responses have to be selected from the behavioural reper-toire. However, the number of operations possible in a certain time unit is finite. Whenever controlled processing fails to deal with all information that should be processed for optimal task performance, a DAD occurs. The term 'divided' in this context refers to the fact that the available processing capacity must be divided over several cognitive operations required for task performance. Just like FADs these DADs are very common in daily life. Whenever we ask the way to our destination in a town we never visited before, the kind informant will give us a complicated instruction, listing the second street on our right, a public garden, a left turn, a petrol station etc.

As this instruction usually exceeds our processing capacity, we will thank our instructor with the silent intention to ask again along the road.

Although the proper choice of a control strategy may help us to deal with an overload of information, it will be clear that time is a critical factor for the occurrence of DADs, in particular time pressure. It is useful to make a distinction between extrinsic and intrinsic time pressure. *Extrinsic* time pressure may be induced by an investigator in the psychological laboratory, when he manipulates the rate of stimulus presentation, or by daily life tasks that present essential information at high speed. On the other hand, there may be an intrinsic time pressure stemming from the specific character of the task at hand. According to Kahneman (1973) intrinsic time pressure inevitably occurs in tasks involving short-term memory activity, like mental arithmetic. In such a task, the subject's rate of activity must be paced by the rate of decay of the stored elements: when calculating 3×274 the sub-total 600 that we keep in store will tend to disappear when we are working on the second part of the calculation.

In the two-process model of Shiffrin and Schneider, automatic processing is described as a reliable, effortless process proceeding to a level of abstraction determined by prior learning. On the contrary, controlled processing is described as a more vulnerable process subject to FADs and DADs. It will be clear that an analysis of attentional deficits after closed head injury must ask at least two questions: is automatic processing still efficient and effortless after head injury, and is controlled processing disturbed to an abnormal degree by DADs and FADs? In the preceding paragraph it turned out that there is no strong evidence for differences in vulnerability to FADs (or reduced focusing ability) in patients. We will now review what is known about speed of information processing in people who have sustained head injuries. As the concept of DADs relies not only on speed but as well on control strategies, we will keep an eye on possible differences in strategies used by patients and control subjects.

Pathology

'Mental slowness' of people with head injuries has been reported very frequently by clinical observers, and this observation was confirmed when psychologists began to study the effects of head injury. In contrast to early statements about 'attention', the reports on slowness are less questionable. For example, Ruesch (1944*a*) reported that his patients were slow in colour naming and in reading. In a second study (Ruesch 1944*b*) he demonstrated that acute head-injury patients, tested while still in hospital, showed significantly longer reaction times than control subjects. It is probable that in both studies some of the patients in the acute groups were still in PTA. In 1961 Norman and Svahn reported on the reaction time (RT) of 22 patients who had suffered a severe cerebral concussion at least two years earlier, and who had been in coma for at least one week after the injury. In this group, a three-choice reaction to visual stimuli revealed a highly significant slowness in comparison with a control group of neurotics. A simple visual reaction revealed no difference between the groups.

Decreased speed of information processing is illustrated best by some recent studies of RT after head injury. In 1969 Miller (personal communication) was asked to assess a professional footballer from a famous British club, who had suffered a severe head injury in a road traffic accident. Following this the sportsman lost his place in the first team and was unable to hold a place in any of the club's regular sides. The reason for his poor play, according to the club's manager and trainer, was slow reactions. This led Miller (1970) to investigate visual RT in a small group of head-injury victims, comparing their performance with the behaviour of a control group matched on sex and age. His subjects had been in PTA for over a week (very severe concussion, in the Russell classification) and were tested between 3 and 12 months after injury. The apparatus used differed markedly from instruments in earlier clinical studies, mainly by the use of symbolic stimuli. The subjects were standing at a horizontal panel that showed push-buttons in a circular array, the buttons being numbered from 1 to 8. They kept the index finger of their preferred hand on a central button until a number appeared in a small visual display facing the subject. As soon as this number appeared subjects were required to release the central button and press the appropriate button in the surrounding array. In any condition, subjects were told which numbers could be expected and which push-buttons were to be used. RT was tested under four conditions, with increasing numbers of stimulus alternatives, i.e. 1, 2, 4 and 8 numbers.

The groups differed in speed of reaction, the head-injury group being slower in all conditions. Moreover, the extent of the differences increased with the complexity of the task, that is, with log2 of the number of stimulus alternatives. Analysis of variance accordingly revealed a significant interaction between groups and conditions. Miller was the first to describe clinical RT data in terms of information theory: the more bits of information to be processed, the greater the difference between groups. Miller concluded that the effect of head injury must be to slow down the decision-making and information-processing abilities of the subjects.

Gronwall and Sampson (1974) tested visual choice RT in 12 mildly concussed males, with PTA duration of less than 1 hour. Patients were tested within 24 hours of admission to the hospital, and their performance was compared with the performance of twelve Navy ratings in the same age range. Subjects were tested with 2, 4, 6, 8 and 10-choice tasks, the stimulus being a table-tennis ball falling down the alleys of a pin-ball machine. Response keys were set at the base of each alley, and numbered 1−10 from left to right. Two forms of responding were measured, characterized by the authors as non-symbolic and symbolic. In the non-symbolic form, subjects simply had to press the key of the alley in which the ball appeared. In the symbolic form, the alleys had numbers running one to ten from right to left, that is, contrary to the numbering of the keys. Subjects were now required to press the key indicated by the number of the alley in which the ball appeared. Thus, in the symbolic two-choice task, the alleys 5 and 6 in the middle of the panel were used, and subjects were expected to press key 6 when the ball entered alley 5. It turned out that the concussed patients had significantly longer RTs at the eight- and ten-choice symbolic tasks only. It will be clear that the symbolic form of this test had a low stimulus–response compatibility. Looking at the overall results of the symbolic test form there was no significant interaction between groups and numbers of choices. However, as Mann–Whitney U-tests showed that the concussed patients had significantly longer RTs in the most complex sub-tests only, the authors concluded that central processing time was significantly increased following concussion. Both in Miller's and Gronwall and Sampson's experiments the usual linear relation between information transmitted and RT was found in the control group as well as in the patient group. This makes it unlikely that the patients used a different strategy of processing.

Van Zomeren and Deelman (1976) compared simple and four-choice visual RT in 20 subjects with varying severity of injury and 20 control subjects matched on sex and age. They found a significant interaction of groups and tasks, and in a second experiment they demonstrated that the slowing down of information processing was proportional to severity of injury as expressed in duration of coma. A follow-up study covering 2 years after injury (Van Zomeren and Deelman 1978) revealed that even after almost two years the most severe group, with a coma lasting over a week, performed significantly slower than less severely injured groups on the four-choice task.

The investigations described above indicate that RT of head-injured patients is influenced disproportionately by two variables: number of stimulus alternatives, and stimulus-response compatibility. Both these variables are thought to influence the stages of response selection (Theios 1975; Sanders 1977) in information processing. In a more global sense, these RT data give evidence for a slowing down of controlled processing as described by Shiffrin and Schneider (1977). Leaving the field of RT, another study indicating a slowing down of controlled processing must be quoted. Gronwall and Sampson (1974) studied the effect of head injury with the Paced Auditory Serial Addition Task or PASAT, a task that is clearly aiming at DADs. In this test tape-recorded one-digit numbers are presented in different blocks at different rates. Subjects are required to add every pair of successive numbers and to give the answer immediately. This implies dividing attention between stimuli, stored memory elements, mental transformations, and responding. The dependent variable is the percentage of correct answers. Gronwall and Sampson presented this task to hospital

controls and concussed patients classified in two degrees of severity according to duration of PTA. Patients were significantly more influenced by rate
of presentation, and within the patient group there was an interaction of
severity and rate of presentation. Further, it was unlikely that patients used
a qualitatively different control strategy in the light of the following
findings:

1. The nature of errors did not discriminate patients from controls.

2. Without time pressure both patients and controls could do the task
almost perfectly.

3. Early processing up to the level of meaning of individual verbal stimuli
was investigated and found to be normal in these patients.

Therefore it may be concluded that decreased PASAT performance under
time pressure is probably the result of slow execution of a qualitatively normal control strategy. A decreased PASAT performance was not found by
Thomas (1977) when testing a head-injured group of comparable severity.
However, she used a lower rate of presentation, and thus her results may
well indicate that speed of processing is indeed the critical factor. On the
basis of patterns of correlations between performances on various tests she
stated: 'The speed component seems to be more important in the head-
injured group than the controls, also, since the tests involving speed correlate together only in the head-injured group.'

It seems, then, that there is convincing evidence for a slowing down of
controlled processing of information after head injury. But apart from this
central slowness there are also some suggestions of decreased perceptual
speed. Both Dencker and Löfving (1958) and Ruesch (1944*b*) reported that
head-injured patients needed longer exposure times than control subjects
before they could name familiar objects or words presented in a tachistoscope.

These findings suggest that automatic processing may as well be influenced by head injury, if we assume that recognition of familiar objects
and words automatically results from the proper physical input. The
tachistoscope experiments at least indicate that early stages of processing
deserve a further experimental analysis in head-injured subjects. Further, it
has been mentioned that movement times can be prolonged, and thus it is
obviously not justified to interpret a slow performance on any task in terms
of controlled processing only.

Summary

To summarize this section: early clinical observations of mental slowness
have been objectified and confirmed by psychological studies. This
slowness is mainly explained by a decreased rate of controlled processing,
although there is some evidence for a slowing down of perceptual and
motor stages as well. The slowing down of information processing must

result in attentional deficits, as the patients can no longer deal with the information that is necessary for optimal task performance. Stated otherwise, the head-injury patient has less attention to pay than the healthy individual.

ALERTNESS

Theory

Human performance is not constant over time. There are both phasic and tonic shifts in the efficiency or quality of behaviour that are best explained in terms of fluctuations of 'alertness'. This is the third sense in which the word attention is used. According to Posner (1975) alertness refers to a hypothetical state of the central nervous system which affects general receptivity to stimulation. This state may vary from a very low level in sleep to a high level in wakefulness. Changes in alertness affect performance on many tasks and are accompanied by changes in electrophysiological indices. Therefore the study of alertness has been the domain of psychophysiologists in particular. Although it is beyond the scope of this chapter to discuss theoretical views in great detail, a distinction has to be made between phasic and tonic changes in alertness.

Phasic changes in alertness occur rapidly, and depend on a subject's interests and intentions. The best example would be the effect of a warning signal (WS) on a subject's preparations for action: although he will show no overt behaviour yet, his EEG will show slow negative shifts in widespread cortical regions. This phenomenon has become known as the Contingent Negative Variation (CNV) or Expectancy Wave (Walter, Cooper, Aldridge, McCallum, and Winter 1964). Further study revealed that the CNV consists of at least two components (e.g. Gaillard 1978). An early component is related to the information present in the WS, while later components are signs of preparation for action. The early component peaks at about 600 ms after the WS, and has its maximum at frontal electrodes. A second negative component peaks just about the moment when the second (imperative) stimulus appears, and this shift is maximal at central sites. When a fast motor response to the imperative stimulus is required, there is a specific negativity superimposed on the second component. This is looked upon as a sign of specific motor preparation, and has been termed a *Bereitschafts-potential* (readiness potential) in German.

When a unimanual motor response is required, the *Bereitschaftspotential* is lateralized, i.e. stronger in the 'active' hemisphere. The CNV components described are dependent on the task relevance of the signals, and on the contingency of the WS with the imperative stimulus. In a laboratory experiment the WS will fail to evoke a CNV as soon as the experimenter tells the subject that he can ignore the warning stimulus. These phenomena have been studied by psychophysiologists in their laboratories, but they must obviously be present in daily life too. A sprinter waiting for the starting shot will show clear cortical signs of motor preparation. Or, to take a more common example: the brain of a car driver waiting for a traffic-light to change is idling, like his engine, until he notices that crossing traffic is stopping. As this is a sign that his light will turn green, it is very likely that a CNV occurs in his brain from then on. (In some countries the green light is preceded by an orange light. In the absence of such a formal WS, many drivers will compensate for it by attending to the behaviour of their fellow traffic participants.)

Tonic changes of alertness occur slowly and unvoluntarily, and are mostly explained as resulting from physiological changes in the organism. A well-known example would be the diurnal rythm: there is a gradual change in many autonomic indicants over the course of the day, and this is accompanied by a change in performance on particular tasks. This change may be negative, as is illustrated by the notorious 'post-lunch dip'. On the other hand, the effect may be positive in simple tasks, as was demonstrated by Broadbent (1971) who found an increase in the ability to discriminate signals over the day. A specific kind of change in tonic alertness is the one that can be observed within half an hour when subjects are expected to stay alert in a monotonous, low event rate watch-keeping situation. As mentioned in the Introduction, it was noted under war-time conditions that people tend to miss more signals the longer they are on duty. Studies in the psychological laboratory (Mackworth 1950) confirmed that 'vigilance' decreases rapidly in such situations, resulting in a decrease of signal detection. The 'classical' theoretical explanation of this phenomenon is in terms of decreased collateral sensory inputs into the brainstem reticular formation (Broadbent 1971).

Tonic alertness may be described as a continuing receptivity to stimulation, covering minutes or hours. It has been investigated in two ways mostly, that is, with vigilance tasks and continuous reaction time tasks. In vigilance tasks typically the efficiency of signal detection is tested, in this case in a low event rate situation that presents positive and negative signals differing slightly in intensity. In normal subjects a decrement of signal detection occurs within half an hour, and this is accompanied by an increase of drowsiness signs in the EEG. However, while there is a good deal of evidence that the decrement of signal detection is correlated with the decrease in EEG arousal, the exact nature of this relationship is as yet unclear (Townsend and Johnson 1979). The usual finding in the 'eyes closed' condition is that alpha power gradually decreases, and relative theta power increases over the session. When the EEG just before misses is compared with the EEG just before hits, analogous results are found: relatively little alpha and more theta before missed signals (O'Hanlon and Beatty 1977, Groll 1966, Williams, Granada, Jones, Lubin, and Armington 1962). Another psychophysiological variable thought to be a sensitive index of alertness is heart rate variability (HRV). At low levels of tonic altertness the heart beats slower and less regularly than at higher levels of alertness (for an explanation in terms of the baroreceptor reflex mechanism see Williams, *et al*. 1962, and Brouwer and Mulder 1977).

In continuous reaction time tasks (Sanders and Hoogenboom 1970) the stimuli are presented either paced or self-paced. In the paced condition the stimuli succeed each other at a rate determined by the experimenter. In the self-paced condition, the next stimulus will appear as soon as the subject has reacted to the preceding one. Thus, in the latter condition the subject himself determines the rate of presentation. Both versions are sensitive to time-on-task effects under stressing conditions of various sorts. In the case of sleep deprivation, which is supposed to induce a lowered level of tonic alertness, the self-paced version is the best choice (Broadbent 1971). In this situation, relations with EEG preceding 'lapses' of attention have been demonstrated (Schacter 1977).

Pathology

First we will discuss phasic changes in alertness, in particular the process taking place in the brain of a person who is expecting a relevant stimulus in the immediate future. As stated above, a warning signal will induce a CNV and this is interpreted as reflecting a central process of preparation for action. On the behavioural level a WS is known to shorten RT, and it is likely that this is related to the preparation for action during the foreperiod.

So far, only two studies have been published on the 'expectancy wave' in head-injured patients. Rizzo *et al*. (1978) studied the central CNV in 27 patients with very severe head injuries and an average duration of coma of 15 days. As the minimum period between injury and test was 15 months, most patients must have been out of PTA. The requirement set by Rizzo *et al*. was that their neuropsychological condition should be stabilized. The WS was a light flash, and after 1500ms a 700Hz sound was presented that had to be switched off by the subject by pressing a push-button. A significant decrease of the CNV magnitude was found when the head-injured patients were compared with eighty normal subjects. The paper does not present corresponding RTs, but in the light of the available evidence on RT after head injury it seems very probable that this severely injured group must have been slower than the control group. Thus, it is likely that phasic alertness, as judged by EEG criteria, is not optimal after severe head injury. Unfortunately the limited duration of the interval between WS and imperative stimulus in this study, and the use of a single active electrode, prevent us from noticing whether any specific component of the CNV was influenced in particular. Curry (1981) studied CNV in a group of 25 patients with severity of injury ranging from mild to severe (PTA longer than one week). Testing was carried out as soon as possible after the post-traumatic amnesic period. In accordance with the findings by Rizzo *et al.* Curry noted a decreased CNV when comparing his patients with a control group. In the severely injured group even absence of a measurable CNV occurred frequently.

Tonic alertness may be related to the supposed deficit of 'sustained attention' mentioned in older studies. Conkey and Ruesch supposed that a basic deficit after head injury was an inability to sustain attention of a level required for normal performance on some of their tests.

Sustained attention was tested by Dencker and Löfving (1958) with a continuous RT task, by presenting their subjects with a ten-choice reaction task of 15 minutes' duration. As mentioned before, their patient group consisted of 28 people who had been concussed many years ago, while the control group consisted of their twin brothers or sisters. The apparatus used presented 68 visual stimuli per minute, which amounts to 1020 stimuli in a quarter of an hour. The dependent measure was the number of correct reactions in each block of 25 successive trials, and the authors were interested in particular in a decline of performance over the 15-minute interval. It turned out that the patients gave significantly fewer correct reactions, but there was no interaction of groups and time on task. In both groups no decline in the number of correct reactions over time was found. Therefore, it may be doubted whether the task indeed tapped tonic alertness or vigilance. Further, the task described here is different from the continuous reaction tasks that seem most sensitive to lapses of attention in one important sense: it is not subject paced. The stimuli in the Dencker and Löfving experiment arrived at a predetermined rate, while in most studies with non-injured subjects the next stimulus appears immediately after the subject's reaction to the preceding one (Glenville, *et al.* 1978; Schacter 1977). Thus it remains to be seen what will happen in a continuous reaction task in which head-injured patients are free to choose their own rate or working, and which is shown to be sensitive in normal subjects.

Tonic alertness is at the moment studied in our laboratory by means of an auditory vigilance task. We present a low-event-rate signal detection task of 30 minutes duration. Every 4 seconds a click is presented by means of head-phones, the standard click being 40 decibels above subjective thresholds (assessed individually). One out of five clicks, randomly distributed, is 4 decibels weaker than this standard. The subjects are instructed to give a manual response when they think a weaker click occurs. After this 30-minute session, there is an 'activating' break, and finally another 10 minutes are spent on the vigilance task. The last part is incorporated in order to be able to distinguish between state-dependent effects and effects of learning or expectancy (Broadbent 1971). During the experiment subjects keep their eyes closed. Besides stimuli and responses, bilateral monopolar occipital EEG and heart rate are stored on magnetic tape.

In 16 sessions with normal male subjects we found clear performance

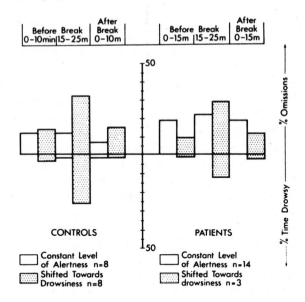

Fig. 5.3.

Drowsiness and omissions in three stages of a vigilance task in control subjects and patients.

decrements during the second half of the 30-minute sessions. Statistical analysis of EEG data and performance revealed significant relations: the EEG of subjects who missed many signals almost invariably showed many signs of drowsiness. Secondly, significant differences between the EEG preceding hits and the EEG preceding misses were found only in those sub-jects who had a drowsy background EEG (Fig. 5.3).

  In the nine patients with severe head injury we have tested so far, these relations between EEG and performance were *not* found. In fact they showed persistently alert EEGs during the task, while their heart rates were higher than those of the control group. Furthermore, although signal detec-tion was decidedly poorer than in the control group, it was also quite stable over time (Fig. 5.4). The initial level of performance seemed to be strongly related to severity of injury, as expressed by duration of PTA. In fact, there were two patients with a PTA of more than 30 days who despite prolonged training could not reach the 70 per cent detection level that we thought necessary for taking the test. Because of the small number of patients tested, one must be cautious in interpreting these results. At first sight, however, they do not support the hypothesis that poor performance in head-injured patients is caused by a low level of alertness, as it was brought forward by Gronwall and Sampson (1974). In addition, the lack of decre-ment in performance over time fails to support the hypothesis expressed by Conkey (1938) and Ruesch (1944) which states that patients are unable to

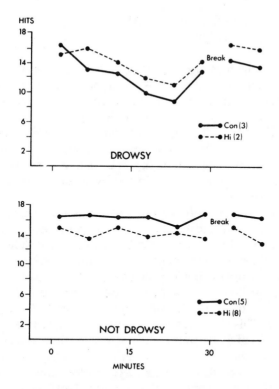

Fig. 5.4.

Signal detection performance over a 30-minute period in control subjects and patients.

sustain attention on a level required for normal performance, unless the authors meant this to be a label for a chronic condition or steady state, already present at the beginning of a task. The relevance of their statement for the present discussion is somewhat reduced by the fact that some of their patients must have been in PTA at the time of testing.

Summary

There is some evidence that phasic alertness may be non-optimal after head injury: in very severe patients a decreased magnitude of CNV was demonstrated, suggesting a deficit in preparation for action. Tonic alertness has been studied with continuous RT task and with a low-event-rate vigilance task; in both studies head-injured patients performed worse than controls, but their performance was remarkably stable over time. Thus there is no evidence for an abnormal decline of tonic alertness. On the contrary, preliminary psychophysiological data from our own laboratory suggest that head-injured patients show higher tonic levels of alertness than controls, at least in an experimental situation.

HEAD INJURY AND MENTAL EFFORT: THE COPING HYPOTHESIS

Gronwall and Wrightson (1974) reported a close correspondence between slow decision making in the PASAT task and the occurrence of post-traumatic vegetative and emotional complaints in patients returning to work. These complaints may be headache, dizziness, anxiety, chronic fatigue, and irritability. This complex of symptoms is often called 'the post-traumatic syndrome', in particular when it persists for months or years following head injury. The authors suggested that these symptoms were the result of a chronic compensatory effort to overcome the cognitive deficits present in the patients.

The notion of effort to cope with task demands and its possible negative effects had been mentioned before. Goldstein (1952) explained 'neurotic' symptoms after head injury as secondary to cognitive deficits. Hillbom (1960) stressed the point that relatively mildly injured people may be more apt to become a victim of chonic compensatory effort. In more severe cases of head injury, pathology is readily visible for everyone, and there will be no social pressure to resume former responsibilities or to perform at the premorbid level. This line of reasoning seems to be supported by the finding of Lishman (1978) of a relatively high incidence of emotional and vegetative complaints in patients with less severe injuries. Description of these complaints in terms of 'accident neurosis', a form of malingering with the aim of receiving financial compensation (Miller 1961) is completely unwarranted, as has been shown by Guthkelch (1980).

To elaborate the coping hypothesis: the head-injury patient has a decreased rate of information processing, and is very frequently hindered by a memory deficit (see Chapter 4). This implies that he cannot always deal efficiently with the demands of daily life. He will try to compensate for his deficits by spending a greater effort. When this compensatory effort becomes chronic, it may result in secondary symptoms of the type found in people who have been living under chronic stress for some time. Thus, the head-injury patient may develop symptoms that are easily classified as 'neurotic'.

Evaluation of the coping hypothesis meets obvious difficulties: it is not easy to operationalize concepts like effort and stress. We will therefore restrict ourselves to the effects of cognitive tasks on physiological measures of mental effort. It has been demonstrated in normal subjects that difficulty of mental tasks is reflected in a variety of physiological responses. Especially autonomic measures like pupil size (Kahneman 1973), heart rate, and heart rate variability are thought to be sensitive indices of mental effort (Brouwer and Mulder 1977; Mulder 1980). The coping hypothesis would be supported if such indices show an increased mental effort in head-injury patients performing cognitive tasks, in comparison with control patients.

Martinius, Hoffmann, Mayer, and Klicpera (1977) studied mental effort by means of EEG arousal in patients tested with a reaction time task of varying complexity. A monopolar occipital EEG was recorded from the right hemisphere, in two groups of head-injured children differing in severity of injury and in a normal control group matched on age and sex. The least severely injured group consisted of children with a coma duration of less than four days, the severely injured group consisted of children with a coma duration of more than five days. On the average the time between injury and test was two years. In the RT test, both reaction times and errors were recorded. When compared with normals, the least severe group showed a significantly stronger EEG-arousal although their performance was almost comparable, judged on RT and number of errors. On the other hand, in the severely injured group Martinius *et al.* found a significantly worse performance in combination with a normal EEG-arousal. Thus there was an apparent dissociation of severity of injury and EEG-arousal, and the findings in the less severely injured group lend some support to the coping hypothesis. Unfortunately, no data are given on the resting EEG, and thus it is possible that the higher EEG-arousal in the less severe cases was already present before the testing actually began. In that case higher arousal during the RT task could not be easily interpreted as an effect of task performance. Moreover the index of mental effort used in this study is not a very usual one (Rohmert and Luczac 1979).

In our laboratory we studied mental effort after head injury with more conventional means, viz. measures of heart rate variabilty (HRV) and the mean heart beat interval (HBI). We tested a group of recently concussed males within two months after the end of their PTA, and compared their performance with that of a group of healthy males of the same age. We assessed the base rate of the physiological indices before presenting a visual reaction time task. It turned out that heart activity was not comparable in both groups: the patients' hearts were beating significantly faster and were less variable than those of the controls (Mann–Whitney U-tests, $p < 0.05$). If these results had occurred during the actual test, they might have been interpreted as evidence for greater mental effort.

The task presented was a simple visual reaction task of intermediate S-R complexity (Fitts and Posner 1968). The stimuli were presented at a fixed rate of 30 stimuli per minute. Execution of the task was started within 5 minutes after the resting registration. We found that patients were significantly slower on the task, both in their decision times and their movement times ($t = 3.539$ and 4.303 respectively df $= 21$; $p < 0.001$). In the analyses of variance of HR and HRV there were significant main effects of rest versus task, and significant main effects of groups. However, there were no significant interactions of groups and tasks. Thus, the main findings of this study were the different values of HR and HRV in patients and controls, irrespective of task demands. The coping hypothesis was not supported in a strict sense: heart activity of both patients and controls was influenced in a similar manner by the presentation of the task. However, there was a significant difference in intercepts, as the patients' hearts beat faster and more regularly. (The possibility of a ceiling effect in the patients' heart activity must be kept in mind as an alternative explanation for the absence of a specific task effect in the patients; it could be that their hearts were beating at a maximal rate.) It could be, that this 'effort reaction' shown by the patients was not specific to the task situation we created. It might as well be a manifestation of chronic effort to sustain the rather demanding neuro-psychological testing situation. In this respect it is interesting that the data we collected in our vigilance experiment likewise showed a faster and more regular heart activity, while the background EEG was quite alert.

This increased level of automatic and EEG arousal in response to a testing situation may be an effect of head injury, and it is certainly reminiscent of some of the complaints that patients report. However, interpretation of these physiological effects in terms of head injury seems not yet fully justified, due to the nature of the control groups. For any normal control group a testing situation may have a quite different emotional significance than it has for patients. The former group consists of volunteers for whom the results of the test will have no consequences at all—while the latter group consists of patients who are aware of their deficits and who know that they 'are put to the test'. For this reason, we are now replicating the experiment using a patient control group consisting of mildly concussed males (PTA less than 2 hours) who are tested at a comparable interval after injury. Returning to the observed dissociation of severity and tonic nervous reactivity (Martinius *et al.* 1977) it should be noted that such a dissociation is also suggested by the findings of Rigorea and Floria-Ciocoia (1979). These authors found increased autonomic and EEG reactivity in patients with so-called 'post-traumatic neurosis' but decreased reactivity in the so-called 'post-traumatic dementia'. At the level of manifest complaints the same dissociation seems to be reflected in the aforementioned relatively high proportion of post-traumatic vegetative and emotional signs after relatively minor injuries. To quote Hillbom (1960; page 125):

Noteworthy are also the facts that these neuroses are not found in connection with the most severe, and especially not with personality deteriorating injuries, and that these injured had to make great efforts to keep up a certain level in life.

Seidel, Chadwick, and Rutter (1975), after studying children with cerebral damage, reported that psychiatric disorder was four times more common in children with moderate physical disability than in those with severe disability. One might speculate that the clue to understanding this discontinuity is once again found in the subjective perception of abilities and demands. Only when a gap is perceived, and when it is thought to be bridgeable, a patient will try to cope with the situation. If too much compensatory effort is invested for too long a period, neurotic-like symptoms may appear. It is to be hoped that future research in this area may profit from new developments in stress research in which account is taken of cognitive processes as mediators of stress and coping (Folkman, Schaefer, and Lazarus 1979).

DISCUSSION

Our major hypothesis is that attentional deficits in head-injured patients who are out of PTA are mainly the result of a slowing down in the execution of consciously controlled strategies. It is a hypothesis and not a conclusion, as our definition of controlled processing is rather loose when compared with the paradigm-specific definition given by Shiffrin and Schneider (1977).

Although the chapter is concerned with attentional deficits, it must be noted that some of these may be related to other deficits found after head injury. The slowing down of information processing would predict in general that head-injured patients will perform worse than normal on a variety of cognitive tasks in which time of processing is crucial. In our department this has been shown with timed intelligence tests as opposed to intelligence tests without a time limit (Deelman 1977). The same explanation seems to hold for the difference between verbal and performance parts of the Wechsler in head-injured patients, as demonstrated by Mandleberg (1975). More specifically, a relationship might be expected between speed of processing and the formation of memory traces. In discussing Divided Attention Deficits, we illustrated the concept with the fate of someone who is asking the way to his destination in a town that he never visited before. Due to the limitation of his processing capacity he is unable to store all the information given to him, that is, he 'forgets' the second half of the instruction. The slowing down of information processing after closed head injury thus implies that patients cannot store information in memory with the efficiency they used to have before the injury. Numerous studies have indeed documented the memory problems of head-injured patients (Chapter 4; Schacter and Crovitz 1977; Newcombe and Artiola i Fortuny 1979; Deelman, Brouwer, Van Zomeren, and Saan 1980).

In particular the free recall of supra-span word lists has been shown to be a sensitive method (Brooks 1972; Newcombe and Saan 1977; Deelman 1977; Deelman *et al.* 1980). However, so far no research has been reported that aimed directly at the influence of processing time on the formation of memory traces. In our department (Deelman 1977; Deelman, *et al.* 1980) we demonstrated that head-injured patients show a deficit in subjective organization when learning word lists that are repeatedly presented to them (multi-trial free recall task). Normal control subjects show an increase in subjective organization (as expressed in the PF-index: Sternberg and Tulving 1977) when the lists are presented again and again, while such an increase is absent or far smaller in patients. A relation between subjective organization and processing time is plausible, but has not yet been demonstrated experimentally. Of course it is not to be expected that in the end all deficits after head injury can be explained from a slowing down of information processing. On the anecdotical level, this is rendered unlikely by patients in whom we recorded perfectly normal choice reaction times in spite of an obvious amnestic deficit. Nevertheless it is clear that this factor may play a dominant role, both in laboratory experiments and in daily life.

Attempts have been made to relate the slowness of controlled processing in head-injury patients to specific cerebral structures. Gronwall and Sampson (1974) hypothesized that *brainstem dysfunctions* play a role. Anatomical evidence for damage to the brainstem in head injury is scarce, however, even in very severe cases (Adams, Mitchell, Graham, and Doyle 1977). In fact, Ommaya (1979) holds that the mid-brain is extremely well-protected against the effects of a powerful impact. This point of view seems to be confirmed by *in vivo* localization methods, like the Auditory Far Field Potentials and the registration of postural and ocular signs. These techniques have demonstrated that detectable primary brainstem dysfunction certainly isn't the rule, even in acute closed head injuries (Plum and Posner 1972; Uziel and Benezech 1978). Evidence of its presence is usually limited to patients with a bad prognosis. On the other hand, it cannot be ruled out that 'secondary' brainstem dysfunction has some relevance for the slowing down of controlled processing. Dysfunction could be the result of biochemical alterations (Minderhoud, Van Woerkom, and Van Weerden 1976) or, in a different theoretical framework, of disruption in higher order cortical and diencephalic control systems that regulate brainstem functions (Luria 1978; Ommaya 1979).

The suggestion of such a temporary brainstem dysfunction led Gronwall and Sampson (1974) to the hypothesis that reduced information processing capacity found in concussed patients who were out of PTA is caused by 'lowered arousal'. This reasoning is based on the presumed relationship between midbrain reticular formation activity and cortical alertness as described by Moruzzi and Magoun (1949). In our laboratory we have tested this hypothesis of lowered arousal by means of a vigilance task (see section on 'Alertness'). Both EEG recordings and heart activity quite unequivocally pointed into the direction of increased, rather than decreased levels of alertness in our patients. Therefore, it is rendered unlikely that decreased performance of head-injured patients on neuropsychological tests can be explained from 'lowered arousal', as even a task specifically designed to elicit it did provoke neither drowsiness, nor performance decrements over time.

Of course, these results do not prove that brainstem dysfunction is absent. If Luria (1979) and Ommaya (1979) are right, there remains the possibility of disruption in cortical–subcortical and particularly, of *cortical–diencephalon connections*. If this is the case, it is not obvious that the background state of alertness be influenced. Ommaya holds that the cortical frontotemporal zones are critically vulnerable in closed head injury. Therefore, especially reticular formation functions which are dependent on these connections might be selectively impaired. Hence, it might rather be the phasic, task-related fluctuations of alertness which are involved. Such phasic changes of alertness can be measured by means of event-related EEG potentials like the late, non-specific CNV, and the components known as the P-300 and N-100 (Donchin 1979; Hillyard and Picton 1979). The first two potentials are thought to be generated by midbrain reticular formation structures under the control of prefrontal areas (Desmedt and Debecker 1979). The N-100 component is modality-specific and may either involve the more specific thalamic reticular system, which is also thought to be controlled from a prefrontal centre (Desmedt and Debecker 1979), or alternatively a large number of synchronously active sources in the temporal and frontal lobes. The work of Rizzo and Curry can be seen as the first step in this psychophysiological approach of deficits after head injury. Their data were in line with the hypothesis of disturbed phasic alertness.

Still, the data presented by Rizzo and co-authors can also be interpreted in a slightly different theoretical framework, based on a paper by Hicks and Birren (1970). These authors reviewed the evidence on psychomotor slowing due to brain damage in general, and to ageing. They concluded that behavioural, neuroanatomical, and neurophysiological evidence indicated that the *basal ganglia* with their complex neural connections are importantly involved in the speed of initiating and executing movements. Although they admitted that most of the evidence in their review was indirect, the authors expressed the belief that damage to or dysfunction of the basal ganglia may be a basis for the psychomotor slowing observed in both human and animal subjects. In view of the evidence for a slowing down of controlled processing presented before, it is improbable that basal ganglia dysfunction is the only factor in closed head injury. However, as a secondary factor it cannot be ruled out, certainly not in tasks which are highly demanding in terms of fast motor programme selection and motor execution.

A neuropsychological text can hardly review anatomical candidates responsible for slowing down without mentioning the *cerebral cortex*. Unfortunately, the experiments reviewed above had little to say about specific localization of cortical dysfunctions. Therefore, they tended to pick up global effects of closed head injury only. The available evidence on discrete localization of brain damage by head injury is limited. Uzzell, Zimmerman, Dolinskas, and Obrist (1979) showed that only in a minority of cases a discrete lesion could be found by means of CT scans. In many cases, however, a crude localization in terms of the hemisphere most affected was possible. The authors demonstrated that the pattern of performance on

WAIS subtests was usually in accordance with a preponderance of damage in either the left or right hemisphere. If the specificity of such localizatory evidence could be improved in the future, it might be worthwhile to design a battery of process-oriented tasks (e.g. reaction time, event-related potentials) tapping specific aspects of information processing that are assumed to be related to distinct cortical areas. Small changes in processing time could well be sensitive indicators of subtle cortical dysfunction (e.g. Moscowich 1979).

Concerning brain damage in general, it has been postulated by De Renzi and Faglioni (1965) that RT is prolonged in relation to the size of a cerebral lesion. This hypothesis was based on investigation of patients with focal lesions of varying aetiologies implying that both cortical and sub-cortical pathology may have played a role in the observed slowing down of visual RT. The assumed mass effect of lesion size has been studied by means of brain scans by Boller, Howes and Patten (1970). The relation between size of lesion and RT was found in patients with right-hemisphere lesions only, but even this finding could not be confirmed in a second study using the same method (Howes and Boller 1975). Returning to patients with head injury, a correlation has been observed between diffuse EEG disturbances and prolonged visual RT (van Zomeren and Deelman 1978). As these diffuse disturbances consisted mainly of slow activity, they might indicate a connection between cortical function and speed of processing.

SUMMARY

This chapter attempted to describe attentional deficits in head-injured patients beyond the acute stage characterized by PTA, in a terminology derived from current theories of attention. The literature was reviewed under the headings of selectivity, speed of information processing, and alertness or receptivity to stimulation. In addition, a coping hypothesis was elaborated that explains 'neurotic' symptoms as a result of chronic compensatory effort.

Concerning *selectivity*, there is no evidence yet that closed head injury may result in deficits of focused attention. However, the matter is not yet completely settled: not all grades of severity have been tested, and the distinction between relevant and irrelevant stimuli was too obvious in most studies. More subtle forms of distraction might reveal a deficit in selectivity, in particular in more severe cases.

There is convincing evidence that a *slowing down of information processing* occurs, even after minor head injuries. The slowing down is found in particular in the domain of conscious processing, that is, in the stages of mental transformations, decision making and response selection. In terms of choice reaction tasks the variables of stimulus–response compatibility and number of stimulus alternatives are most suited to demonstrate deficits after head injury. In addition, there is some evidence that more peripheral stages in the chain of events between stimulus and response may be prolonged as well (perception, movement). The latter phenomena will have to be studied in more detail before any conclusive statements can be made.

There is scarce evidence on deficits of *alertness*. Only two studies on phasic alertness have been published, reporting a decreased amplitude or even absence of the Contingent Negative Variation in the EEG. This phenomenon may be interpreted as a sign of non-optimal preparation to a stimulus that is to be expected immediately. Studies of tonic alertness during sustained attention have begun only recently. The preliminary findings in both vigilance and reaction time tasks point in the direction of higher levels of arousal in patients than in controls. Therefore a straightforward explanation of decreased performance as a result of lowered arousal levels (the under-arousal hypothesis) seems untenable.

We have tried to relate cognitive deficits to the genesis of post-traumatic 'neurotic' symptoms. It was hypothesized that patients with mild and moderate severe injuries will try to meet the demands of daily life and work by spending more effort in mental tasks. This *coping hypothesis* predicts stronger physiological signs of mental effort in patients than in controls, on specific tasks. Although this was found in two experiments, interpretation of these effects in terms of task load is not yet warranted, either because significant differences were already present during rest, or because resting values were lacking in the study. Still, considering the sometimes reported dissociation of severity of injury and 'neurotic' symptoms in patients with very severe injuries, a two-factor theory for explaining such symptoms in less severe cases seems most likely. Assuming an interaction between neurological and psychological factors might be the best approach of the complicated problems presented by patients with head injuries, and might have practical consequences for rehabilitation, for the finding of suitable jobs for reconvalescents, and for medico-legal assessments.

The chapter closes with a review of cerebral structures that could play a role in the slowing down of information processing. The evidence is incomplete for all candidates, but for the time being the emphasis seems to lie on subcortical structures, broadly speaking. The under-arousal hypothesis, however, seems to become less plausible in view of recent psychophysiological studies and neuroanatomical studies of its presumed substrate, the brainstem reticular formation.

REFERENCES

Adams, J. H., Mitchell, D. E., Graham, D. I., and Doyle, D. (1977). Diffuse brain damage of immediate impact type: its relationship to 'primary brainstem damage' in head injury. *Brain* **100**, 489–502.

Boller, F., Howes, D., and Patten, D. H. (1970). A behavioural evaluation of brain-scan estimates of lesion size. *Neurol. Minneap.* **20**, 852–9.

Broadbent, D. E. (1958). *Perception and communication*, Pergamon Press, London.

——, (1971). *Decision and stress*, Academic Press, London.

Brooks, D. N. (1972). Memory and head injury. *J. nerv. ment. Dis.* **155**, 350–5.

Brouwer, W. H. and Mulder, G. (1977). Cardiovascular assessment of a sentence comprehension task. *Heymans Bull.* **77** 271.

Brunia, C. H. M. and Vingerhoets, A. J. J. M. (1980). The central and peripheral recording of motor preparation in man. *Biol. Psychol.* **11**, 181–91.

Chadwick, O. (1976). Conference notes of a meeting of the joint British-Dutch head injury workshop, Oxford. (Unpublished observations.)

Conkey, R. C. (1938). Psychological changes associated with head injuries. *Arch. Psychol.* **33**, 1–62.

Curry, S. H. (1981) Event-related potentials as indicants of structural and functional damage in closed head injury. *Progr. Brain Research* **54**, 507–15.

Deelman, B. G. (1977). Memory deficits after closed head injury. Presented at *The International Neuropsychology Society European Conference.* Oxford.

——, Brouwer, W. H., Van Zomeren, A. H., and Saan, R. J. (1980). Functiestoornissen na trauma capitis. In *Neuropsychologie in Nederland* pp. 253–81. (ed. A. Jennekens-Schinkel, J. J. Diamant, H. F. A. Diesfeldt, and R. Haaxma.) Van Loghum Slaterus, Deventer.

Dencker, S. J. and Löfving, B. (1958). A psychometric study of identical twins discordant for closed head injury. *Acta Psychiat. Neurol. Scand.*, **33**, Suppl. 122.

De Renzi, E. and Fagioni, P. (1965). The comparative efficiency of intelligence and vigilance tasks in detecting hemispheric cerebral damage. *Cortex* **1**, 410–33.

Desmedt, J. E. and Debecker, J. (1979). Wave form and neural mechanism of the decision P 350 elicited without pre-stimulus CNV or readiness potential in random sequences of near-threshold auditory clicks and finger stimuli. *Electroenceph. Clin. Neurophysiol.* **47**, 648–70.

Deutsch, J. A. and Deutsch, D. (1963). Attention: some theoretical considerations. *Psychol. Rev.* **70**, 80–90.

Donchin, E. (1979). Event-related brain potentials: a tool in the study of human information processing. In *Evoked brain potentials and behaviour* pp. 13–88. (ed. H. Begleiter) Plenum Press, New York.

Fitts, P. M. and Posner, M. I. (1973). *Human performance.* Prentice Hall, London.

Folkman, S., Schaefer, G., and Lazarus R. S. (1979). Cognitive processes as mediators of stress and coping. In *Human Stress and Cognition—an information processing approach* (ed. V. Hamilton and D. M. Warburton) Wiley, Chichester.

Gaillard, A. (1978). *Slow brain potentials preceding task performance.* Academische Pers. Amsterdam.

Glenville, M., Broughton, R., Wing, A. M., and Wilkinson, R. T. (1978). Effects of sleep deprivation on short deviation performance measures, compared to the Wilkinson Auditory Vigilance Test. *Sleep* **1**, 169–76.

Goldstein, K. (1952). The effects of brain damage on personality. *Psychiatry* **15**, 245–60.

Graham, D. I., Hume Adams, J., and Doyle, D. (1978). Ischaemic brain damage in fatal non-missile head injuries. *J. Neurol. Sci.* **39**, 213–34.

Gray, J. A. and Wedderburn, A. A. I. (1960). Grouping strategies with simultaneous stimuli. *Q. J. Exp. Psychol.* **12**, 180–4.

Groll, E. (1966). Zentralnervöse und periphere Aktivierungsvariabelen bei Vigilanz leistungen (with summary in English). *Zeitschr. Exp. Angew. Psychol.* **13**, 248–64.

Gronwall, D. M. A. and Sampson, H. (1974). *The psychological effects of concussion.* Auckland University Press.

—— and Wrightson, P. (1974). Delayed recovery of intellectual function after minor head injury. *Lancet* ii, 605–9.

Guthkelch, A. N. (1980). PTA, postconcussional symptoms and accident neurosis. *Eur. Neurol.* 19, 91–102.

Hicks, L. and Birren, J. E. (1970). Aging, brain damage and psychomotor slowing. *Psychol. Bull.* 74, 377–96.

Hillbom, E. (1960). After effects of brain injuries. *Acta Psychiat. Scand.*, Suppl. 142.

Hillyard, S. A. and Picton, T. W. (1979). Event-related brain potentials and selective information processing in man. In *Cognitive components in cerebral event-related potentials and selective attention* (ed. J. E. Desmedt) *Progress in Clinical Neurophysiology.* Karger, Basel, Vol. 6, pp. 1–52.

Howes, D. and Boller, F. (1975). Simple reaction time: evidence for focal impairment from lesions of the right hemisphere. *Brain* 98, 317–32.

James, W. (1890). *The principles of psychology* Vol. 1. Holt and Co., New York.

Kahneman, D. (1973). *Attention and effort.* Prentice Hall, Englewood Cliffs.

La Berge, D. (1973). Attention and the measurement of perceptual learning. *Mem. Cog.* 1, 268–76.

Lishman, W. A. (1978). *Organic psychiatry.* Blackwell, Oxford.

Luria, A. R. (1969). Restoration of higher cortical function following local brain damage. In *Handbook of clinical neurology* (ed. P. J. Vinken and G. W. Bruyn) Vol. 3, pp. 368–433. North–Holland, Amsterdam.

——, (1978). The human brain and conscious activity. In *Consciousness and self-regulation* pp. 1–35. (ed. G. E. Schwartz and D. Shapiro) Wiley, London.

Mackworth, N. H. (1950). *Researches in the Measurement of human performance.* M.R.C. Spec. Report 268. HMSO, London. Reprinted in H. A. Sinaiko (ed.) (1961): *Selected papers on human factors in the design and use of control systems.* pp. 174–331. Dover, London.

Mandleberg, I. A. (1975). Cognitive recovery after severe head injury. 2: Wechsler Adult Intelligence Scale during post-traumatic amnesia. *J. Neurol. Neurosurg. Psychiat.* 38, 1127–32.

Martinius, J., Hoffmann, R. Mayer, F. X., and Klicpera, K. (1977). Hirnleistungsschwäche nach Schädelhirntrauma im Kindesalter. *Mschr. Kinderheilk.* 125, 401–3.

Meyer, A. (1904). The anatomical facts and clinical varieties of traumatic insanity. *Am. J. Insanity.* 60, 373–441.

Miller, E. (1970). Simple and choice reaction time following severe head injury. *Cortex* 6, 121–7.

—— and Cruzat, A. (1981). A note on the effects of irrelevant information on task performance after mild and severe head injury. *Br. J. Soc. Clin. Psychol.* 20, 69–70.

Miller, H. (1961). Accident neurosis. *Br. Med. J.* i, 919.

Minderhoud, J. M., Van Woerkom, Th. C. A. M., and Van Weerden, T. W. (1976). On the nature of brainstem disorders in severe head-injured patients: II, A study on caloric vestibular reactions and neurotransmitter treatment. *Acta Neurochir.* 34, 32–5.

Moray, N. (1969). *Listening and attention.* Penguin, Harmondsworth.

Moruzzi, G. and Magoun, H. W. (1949). Brainstem reticular formation and activation of the EEG. *Electroenceph. Clin. Neurophysiol.* 1, 455–73.

Moscovitch, M. (1979). Information processing and the cerebral hemispheres. In *Handbook of behavioural neurobiology* (ed. M. S. Gazzaniga) Vol. 2, *Neuropsychology.* Plenum Press, New York.

Mulder, G. (1980). The heart of mental effort. Studies in the cardiovasculai psychophysiology of mental work. Dissertation. University of Groningen.

Neisser, Y. (1967). *Cognitive psychology.* Appleton-Century-Crofts, New York.

Newcombe, F. and Saan, R. J. (1977). Memory impairment after closed head injury. Presented at *The International Neuropsychological Society European Conference,* Oxford.

—— and Artiola i Fortuny, L. (1979). Problems and perspectives in the evaluation of psychological deficits after cerebral lesions. *Int. rehabil. Med.* **1,** 182–92.

Norman, B. and Svahn, E. K. (1961). A follow-up study of severe brain injuries. *Acta Psychiat. Scand.* **37,** 236–64.

Norman, D. A. (1969). *Memory and attention. An introduction to human information processing.* Wiley, New York.

O'Hanlon, J. F. and Beatty, J. (1977). Concurrence of electroencephalographic and performance changes during a simulated radar watch, and some implications for the arousal theory of vigilance. In *Vigilance: theory, operational performance, and physiological correlates* (ed. R. R. McKie) pp. 189–201. Plenum Press, New York.

Ommaya, A. K. (1979). Reintegrative action of the nervous system after trauma. In *Neural trauma—seminars in neurological surgery* (ed. A. J. Popp) pp. 00–00. Raven Press, New York.

Plum, F. and Posner, J. B. (1972). *Diagnosis of stupor and coma.* Davis, Philadelphia.

Posner, M. I. (1975). The psychobiology of attention. In *Handbook of psychobiology* (ed. M. S. Gazzaniga and C. Blakemore) pp. 441–80. Academic Press, New York.

Rigorea, R. and Florea-Ciocoiu, V. (1979). Nervous reactivity disturbances in patients with late post-traumatic encephalic syndromes. *Appl. Neurophysiol.* **42,** 224–33.

Rizzo, P. A. Amabile, G., Caporali, M., Spadaro, M., Zanasi, M., and Morocutti, C. (1978). A CNV study in a group of patients with traumatic head injuries. *Electroenceph. Clin. Neurophysiol* **45,** 281–5.

Rohmert, W. and Luczak, H. (1979). Stress, work and productivity. In *Human stress and cognition—an Information Processing Approach* (ed. V. Hamilton and D. M. Warburton) pp. 339–79. John Wiley, Chichester.

Ruesch, J. (1944*a*). Intellectual impairment in head injuries. *Am. J. Psychiat.* **100,** 480–96.

——, (1944*b*). Dark adaptation, negative after images, tachistocopic examinations and reaction time in head injuries. *J. Neurosurg.* **1,** 243–51.

Russell, W. R. (1934). The after-effects of head injury. *Edinb. Med. J.* **41,** 129.

——, (1971). *The traumatic amnesias.* Oxford University Press.

Sanders, A. F. and Hoogenboom, W. (1970). On the effects of continuous active work on performance. *Acta Psychol.* **33,** 414–31.

Sanders, A. F. (1977). Structural and functional aspects of the reaction process. In *Attention and performance* VI (ed. S. Dornic) pp. 00–00. Erlbaum, Hillsdale, N. J.

Schacter, D. L. (1977). EEG theta waves and psychological phenomena: a review and analysis. *Biol. Psychol.* **5,** 47–82.

—— and Crovitz, H. F. (1977). Memory function after closed head injury: a review of quantitative research. *Cortex* **13,** 150–76.

Schneider, W. and Shiffrin, R. M. (1977). Controlled and automatic human information processing: I. Detection, search and attention. *Psychol. Rev.* **84,** 1–66.

Seidel, U. P., Chadwick, O. F. D., and Rutter, M. (1975). Psychological disorders in crippled children: a comparative study of children with and without brain damage. *Dev. Med. Child. Neurol.* **17**, 563–73.

Shiffrin, R. M. (1975). The locus and role of attention in memory systems. In *Attention and performance*, V. (ed. P. M. A. Rabbit and S. Dornic) pp. 168–93. Academic Press, New York.

—— and Schneider, W. (1977). Controlled and automatic human information processing: II. Perceptual learning, automatic attending and a general theory. *Psychol. Rev.* **84**, 127–90.

Sternberg, R. C. and Tulving, E. (1977). The measurement of subjective organization in free recall. *Psychol. Bull.* **84**, 539–56.

Sternberg, S. (1969). The discovery of processing stages: extensions of Donders' method. *Acta Psychol.* **30**, Suppl. 2, 276.

Stroop, J. R. (1935). Studies of interference in serial verbal reactions. *J. Exp. Psychol.* **18**, 643–62.

Thackray, R. I., Bailey, J. P., and Touchstone, M. (1977). Physiological, subjective and performance correlates of reported boredom and monotony while performing a simulated radar control task. In *Vigilance: Theory, Operational Performance and Physiological Correlates* (ed. R. R. McKie). Plenum Press, New York.

Theios, J. (1975). The components of response latency in simple human information processing tasks. In *Attention and performance* (ed. P. M. A. Rabbitt and S. Dornic) Vol. V, pp. 00–00. Academic Press, New York.

Thomas, C. (1977). Deficits of memory and attention following closed head injury. M.Sc. thesis. Oxford University.

Townsend, R. F. and Johnson, L. C. (1979). Relation of frequency-analyzed EEG to monitoring behaviour. *Electroenceph. Clin. Neurophysiol.* **47**, 272–9.

Treisman, A. M. (1964). Verbal cues, language and meaning in attention. *Am. J. Psychol.* **77**, 206–19.

Uziel, A. and Benezech, J. (1978). Auditory brainstem responses in comatose patients: relationship with brainstem reflexes and levels of coma. *Electroenceph. Clin. Neurophysiol.* **45**, 515–24.

Uzzell, B. P., Zimmerman, R. A., Dolinskas, C. A., and Obrist, W. D. (1979). Lateralized psychological impairment associated with CT lesions in head-injured patients. *Cortex* **15**, 391–401.

Walter, W. G., Cooper, R., Aldridge, V. J., McCallum, W. C., and Winter, A. L. (1964). Contingent negative variation: an electric sign of sensorimotor association and expectancy in the human brain. *Nature, Lond.* **203**, 380–4.

Williams, H. L., Granda, H. M., Jones, R. C., Lubin, A., and Armington, J. C. (1962). EEG frequency and finger pulse volume as predictors and reaction time during sleep loss. *Electroenceph. Clin. Neurophysiol.* **14**, 64–70.

Van Zomeren, A. H. and Deelman, B. G. (1976). Differential effects of simple and choice reaction after closed head injury. *Clin. Neurol. Neurosurg.* **79**, 81–90.

——, ——, (1978). Long-term recovery of visual reaction time after closed head injury. *J. Neurol. Neurosurg. Psychiat.* **41**, 452–7.

6 Head injury and social adjustment

Michael Oddy

INTRODUCTION

Closed head injury does not hold the same scientific fascination as penetrating injuries of the brain because it does not result in discrete localized lesions. Rather, it produces a confusing picture of widespread diffuse lesions to cortical and subcortical structures. However, closed head injury is an extremely common occurrence whereas penetrating wounds in peace time are quite rare. Because research into brain/behaviour relationships after closed injury is more complicated than after penetrating injuries, studies of closed head injury (CHI) have by necessity been directed towards assessing more practical than theoretical problems.

The frequency, nature, and course of recovery of various sequelae of CHI have been investigated. However, there have been few attempts to answer the broader questions concerning the implications of these sequelae for a person's ability to pursue a normal life. It is to these and related questions that the present chapter will address itself.

In order to do this it is convenient to consider the different roles a person must perform in the course of his daily life. These include the ability to cope with the demands of work, leisure activities, social activities, family, and marital relationships. There have been a number of previous studies concerning the ability of people to return to work after CHI but few concerned with other aspects of normal living.

Since the effects of head injury can vary from the trivial to the fatal, the severity of the initial injury has to be taken into account in any discussion of its effects on the victim's way of life. Of all cases of CHI admitted to hospital it appears that about 97 per cent return to work. Rowbotham, McIver, Dickson, and Bousfield (1954) followed up a series of 250 consecutive adults who had sustained head injuries and had been treated in a department of neurological surgery. Postal questionnaires were returned by 236 of these patients some three to four years after injury. Of these only 10 had been unable to return to work although 19 were engaged in 'light' work and 10 had been unable to work regularly.

A similar rate of return to previous occupation was obtained by Steadman and Graham (1970) who contacted 415 out of 484 consecutive head-injury admissions to a Cardiff teaching hospital, five years after injury. Even amongst those suffering severe concussion (PTA >24 hours) it appears that 80–90 per cent are able to return to work, and this may well be a conservative estimate since it is derived from studies in which PTA was not the sole criterion for inclusion in the series. Miller and Stern (1965), for example, re-examined the 92 survivors of 100 consecutive cases they had seen for medicolegal assessment. Approximately half had depressed skull fractures and the mean PTA was 13 days. Three to 40 years after injury they found that forty-five had been able to resume their previous work, 30 had been downgraded, and ten were totally unable to work.

Adey (1967) sent questionnaires to 98 patients who had been unconscious for 24 hours or more following a CHI 5–15 years previously. None had suffered intracranial haematoma or severe multiple injuries. He received 78 replies and found that 49 had returned to their original work, ten were in alternative employment, and nine were unemployed.

Fahy, Irving, and Millac (1967) found similar rates of re-employment six years after injury amongst a small sample ($n = 26$), all of whom had PTAs exceeding three days and all of whom had been examined by means of burr holes giving direct evidence of brain damage. Carlsson, Von Essen, and Lofgren (1968) and Hpay (1971) both conducted careful studies reaching broadly similar conclusions.

Heiskanen and Sipponen (1970), however, found that only 53 per cent of their series, all of whom had been unconscious for more than 24 hours, had returned to work when followed up three to five years after injury. This study included children so the figures include those able to return to normal school.

Studies of patients unconscious for more than 3 weeks have found that between 58 per cent (Lecuire, Dechaume, and Deruty 1971) and 75 per cent (Lewin 1968; Van der Zwan 1969) have returned to work at follow-up. Both Lecuire *et al.* and Van der Zwan had samples of fewer than 30 patients, but Lewin (1959, 1968) reported on 95 patients unconscious for more than a month. Seventy-five per cent made a 'practical recovery'. This indicated return to work or housework, although in most cases there was some mental and/or physical disability. Even in this very extreme group a third were considered to have recovered physically and mentally.

MacIver, Lassman, Thomson, and McLeod (1958) described a group of very severe head injuries all of whom had been in a state of partial or complete decerebrate rigidity with tonic fits and rising temperature. Eleven of the sixteen survivors (69 per cent) had returned to work by follow-up. It is unclear how long after injury follow-up took place, but it appears that the time varied considerably and in no case was it more than three years.

It is perhaps not surprising that studies based on specialist units or rehabilitation centres show the poorest prognosis in terms of return to work.

Bruckner and Randle (1972) found that 64 per cent of their sample of 93 admissions to a rehabilitation unit had returned to work but 38 per cent of these were working at a lower socioeconomic level than prior to their injuries. Follow-up in this study was three years or more after injury. Most were re-examined personally but 24 were assessed by questionnaire.

Wilkinson (1969) found that less than half of her sample of fifty-four consecutive admissions to a neurological unit were able to return to work. However, it is unclear from this report as to when follow-up took place, if indeed the patients were re-assessed after discharge. Similar resettlement rates were obtained in three studies of patients followed up after periods in rehabilitation centres (Richardson 1971; Gerstenbrand 1969; Lundholm, Jepsen, and Thornval 1975). One study, however, found that only 30 per cent of their patients were able to return to work (Gjone, Kristiansen, and Sponheim 1972). A partial explanation of this may be the fact that more than 25 per cent of this sample were known alcoholics and these were found to have a particularly poor prognosis. Furthermore, the authors considered 45 of their patients to be fit to return to work, whereas only 28 had actually done so.

After severity of the initial injury, age appears to be the most important determinant of occupational resettlement (Carlsson, Von Essen, and Lofgren 1968; Hpay 1971; Gutterman and Shenkin 1970; Roberts 1976; Lundholme *et al.* 1975; Lecuire *et al.* 1971). Heiskanen and Sipponen found that amongst patients unconscious for 24 hours or more, 70 per cent of those under 20 were able to resume work but amongst those over 50 only 30 per cent were able to do so.

Another factor of obvious importance is time since injury. Unfortunately, there has been wide variability in the timing of follow-ups within most studies, so it is not possible to make comparisons across studies. However, Vigouroux *et al.* (1971) have directly investigated this variable and their findings suggest that patients may still return to work more than two years after injury. Indeed, Brown (1975) described the case of a man who returned to work more than four years after his injury.

Although the importance of the severity of the original injury is indisputable, the role of neurological sequelae is less clear. Lundholm *et al.* (1975) found that amongst 30 survivors of very severe injuries, most of whom had pareses, there was no relationship between the presence of neurological signs and social outcome. Similarly, Lecuire *et al.* (1971) stressed the fact that neurological sequelae including post-traumatic epilepsy, dysphasia, and hemiplegia were associated with poorer chances of returning to work, but were of less importance than cognitive complaints (e.g. impaired memory, concentration, or intellect) and behavioural changes (e.g. impaired initiative and sense of responsiblity, emotional lability, depression, and aggression).

The importance of personality and cognitive deficits is supported by a number of studies. Roberts (1976) stated that in two-thirds of his series, decline in level of employment had been due to impaired personality or intellectual function. Fahy, Irving, and Millac (1967) and Lecuire *et al.* (1971) both found that psychiatric disturbance (including cognitive deficits) was a prominent cause of impaired capacity for work. Bond (1975) and Lundholm *et al.* (1975) found that cognitive deficits were related to both work and poor social recovery in a wider sense.

The suggestion that patients' premorbid characteristics influence recovery (e.g. Symonds 1937) has not been substantiated by any evidence regarding the likelihood or speed of return to work.

In contrast to the voluminous work on the resumption of employment after CHI only three studies have concerned themselves with the effects of head injury upon leisure and social activities. Hpay (1971) found that 65 per cent of her sample were able to return to their previous social life, whilst 14 per cent became 'complete social outcasts'. However, no further details were given. Bond (1975, 1976) devised a scale which embraced various aspects of social recovery including work, family life, and leisure activities, but did not include the degree of contact with friends. He found that work and leisure activities were the most disrupted aspects of daily life.

Thomsen (1974) found that the main problem mentioned by patients one to six years after severe head injury was lack of social contact. Her series contained a high proportion (21 out of 50) of aphasics, and amongst these patients the problem was most acute, although few attributed their isolation directly to their speech problems. Most had lost contact with old friends and had little opportunity to make new friends because they spent nearly all their time at home.

What evidence there is points to the fact that leisure activities and social contact are at least as vulnerable as work capacity. For the age group most at risk of CHI, these are of great importance. Thomsen's study indicates that as far as the patients themselves are concerned, social isolation is the most devastating effect of a head injury.

There are difficulties in the interpretation and synthesis of the studies reviewed for a number of reasons. First, the different means of sampling employed make it difficult to find comparable groups. Many studies have used one of the generally recognized indices of the severity of CHI (duration of PTA or of unconsciousness) as a criterion for inclusion in this study. Nevertheless, it is remarkably difficult to find two studies using exactly similar levels of these measures as the criterion. Furthermore, most studies have not used these criteria as the sole method of selecting patients. Often the initial selection of patients depends on their being treated at a particular specialist centre, for example, a neurosurgical department (Bond 1975) a neurological unit (Wilkinson 1969), or a rehabilitation centre (Bruckner and Randle 1972): each centre tends to have an idiosyncratic admissions policy. A second stage of selection may then occur using one of the common yardsticks for severity of injury.

Yet other criteria or methods of selection have been used in some studies.

For example, Miller and Stern (1965) studied 100 patients referred for medicolegal investigations and London (1967) used length of hospitalization for head injury as the criterion for inclusion.

Another problem of comparability stems from the fact that studies differ in the age restrictions they set and in the distribution of patients within these limits. There is clear evidence that age is an important factor in recovery from CHI and therefore samples from a restricted age range or at least separate analyses would help to produce comprehensible findings.

A second source of difficulty in synthesizing the results of different studies stems from the fact that patients have been followed up at intervals varying from a month (Bond 1975) to 40 years (Miller and Stern 1965). These variations occur not only between studies but within studies as well. Since, as reported above, head-injured patients may return to work after absences of as long as four years, it is clearly not legitimate to lump together cases interviewed within a few months of injury and those seen several years afterwards.

Finally, different methods of assessment have been employed which may influence findings. For example, certain studies (e.g. Adey 1967) have relied wholly or partially upon postal questionnaires. Since in such studies it is common for a sizeable proportion not to be returned, this raises the question of how representative the findings are.

Nevertheless, a reasonably consistent picture of rates of return to work emerges from this review. Information relating to other aspects of social adjustment is almost entirely lacking. In this paper, I shall report the findings of two studies which were designed to investigate the degree of social readjustment after CHI in a wider perspective than that of work alone.

These studies, conducted by myself and colleagues Michael Humphrey and Rodger Weddell, both used similar methods of assessment and focused upon patients between the ages of 16 and 39 years. The first was a prospective study of a representative sample of 50 patients who had suffered a severe CHI (PTA >24 hours). The final assessment for this group was carried out 12 months after the injury had occurred. The second was a cross-sectional study of an even more severely injured population. All 44 patients in the second study had undergone a course of rehabilitation at the Wolfson Medical Rehabilitation Centre which specializes in neurological conditions. These patients were all reassessed two years after their accident.

In fact, the two studies provide a picture of social recovery from CHIs of three grades of severity. The subjects in the prospective study may be divided into (1) those with CHIs leading to a PTA of between one and seven days (group A, severe concussion) and (2) those with CHIs leading to a PTA of more than seven days (group B, very severe concussion). The length of PTA in the third group also exceeded seven days in every case. However, since the Wolfson Centre is the only one of its kind in a large geographical area it takes only the most severely injured survivors of CHI. The median length of time unconscious in this group was four weeks. All but three had been unconscious for more than one week and 15 had been unconscious for more than six weeks. This group will be referred to as the 'rehabilitation group' (group C).

PROCEDURE

The design and procedure followed in the two studies have been fully reported by Oddy, Humphrey, and Uttley (1978) and Weddell, Oddy, and Jenkins (1980) respectively, so I shall give only a brief description of the design here.

The prospective study

A representative sample of all patients who receive a severe closed head injury (CHI leading to a PTA of more than 24 hours) was collected.

Each of the 50 patients was identified for the purposes of this study within a few days of the accident. A close relative was contacted and interviewed within two or three weeks. This was to assess the pre-accident personality and social adjustment of the patient and to obtain a general history. Two follow-up assessments were carried out six and 12 months after injury, and on both occasions the relative was interviewed to reassess the patient's personality and social adjustment. Cognitive tests were administered to the patient.

Fifty per cent of these patients were aged between sixteen and twenty and 80 per cent were under 25. Only nine were female.

Statistical comparisons were made between the ratings of pre-accident social adjustment and the ratings made at follow-up.

The cross-sectional study

All patients who had attended the Wolfson Centre following a closed head injury during a two-year period (1.8.74–31.7.76) were contacted and asked to attend the centre in the company of a relative. Forty-four of the 48 patients invited attended the centre for assessment two years + / − three months after their injury. Each patient was given a thorough neurological examination and the results were quantified by means of the Bond Neurophysical Scale (Bond 1975, 1976). The Standard Progressive Matrices (Raven 1960) was administered as a brief screening test of intellectual ability and a semi-structured interview was conducted with the relative in order to assess the social readjustment of the patient. We compared the findings for this group with a control group matched for age, sex, and social class. For this purpose we used the pre-morbid measures of social adjustment for matched subjects from the prospective study.

Thirty-one patients in this group were male and thirteen female. The mean age was 24.4 years (standard deviation 6.2 years, range 16 to 39).

RESULTS

We examined the effects of CHI on work, social and leisure activities, and on family life.

Work

In the prospective study we found that all but seven of the 50 cases were able to return to work within 12 months (Table 6.1). Six of the seven unable to do so had been very severely concussed. The other patient was unable to resume work due to an arm amputation, not because of the head injury.

None of those who had returned to work had been downgraded or had had to take on a less demanding job, although employers had made certain adjustments. A policeman and a post-office despatch rider had been confined to office duties, a skilled welder was required to work more closely with colleagues, and a bricklayer was no longer required to work at heights. The work load of a general practitioner was lessened by sharing it out amongst his partners, a section manager in a department store was moved to a less busy and demanding section, whilst a marine engineer was no longer sent by his employers to assignments overseas.

There were a few further cases where it seemed that employers may have altered their demands on the patient although these cases were not as clear cut as those cited above. Thus it seems that employers try to reduce the work load, reduce the responsibilities, and ensure greater supervision of staff returning after a head injury. Whether this is due to an actual inability to cope or to the employer's unjustified fear that this will be the case is a question that we are unable to answer from our present data.

Furthermore, we cannot say whether or not such adjustments are temporary although there were indications that as time went by the patient's responsibilities once more increased.

We also made ratings of the degree of job satisfaction and these showed a tendency towards less job satisfaction after return to work, particularly where the demands of the job had altered.

Table 6.1 *Proportion of patients able to return to work*

	Category		
	Severe	Very severe	Rehabilitation
Back at work	25	16	16
Unable to return	1	6	25

A rather more bleak picture of occupational resettlement was obtained for the 44 cases in the rehabilitation group. Only five had been able to return to their former jobs, in all cases after absences of six or more months.

Three other patients had resumed their roles as housewives and were said, by their husbands, to cope with their daily tasks adequately.

Eleven patients were able, 6–18 months after their accidents, to begin working full time again but in a reduced capacity. Many had attempted a series of different jobs and we had no reason to suppose that they had settled in the job they held at the time of assessment. Indeed, several appeared to rely on their employer's goodwill and required a considerable amount of assistance with their work.

Twenty patients in the rehabilitation group had been unable to work at all since sustaining their injuries. Half of these were attending day centres or were still receiving treatment, but the other half spent most of their time at home. The responsibility for caring for these patients fell squarely on their families. All of these patients were markedly dependent on their relatives, requiring help with personal hygiene, preparation of food, washing clothes, handling finances, etc. A further five patients had held jobs for brief periods of time since their accident but were not working at the time of assessment.

This dependence placed inevitable stress upon relatives. Nevertheless many made great sacrifices. Often the mother and sometimes the father gave up their job in order to devote themselves to the care of their son or daughter. In three cases parents had organized their own daily treatment regimen.

In addition to the severity of the initial injury, we examined the influence of a number of variables on ability to resume work. Premorbid occupational status showed no relationship to ability to resume.

Motor and sensory deficits, sometimes resulting from additional injuries, delayed return to work in the severely and very severely concussed groups. This association between physical incapacity and delayed return to work cannot be attributed to a greater severity of the head injury itself since there was no relationship between severity of injury and presence of physical disability. Neurophysical disability was greater in those members of the rehabilitation group who were unable to return to work, although in this case we were unable to differentiate between physical disability and other sequelae of brain damage in producing this effect.

Our results suggest an interaction between severity of CHI and the effects of personality and cognitive deficits on ability to resume work. In the prospective study return to work was not significantly affected by personality changes or cognitive deficit. However, both were strongly related to delay in returning to work amongst the rehabilitation patients. This may reflect both quantitive and qualitative differences in the nature of cognitive and personality changes after CHI of varying severity.

Leisure and social acitivies

Relatives were asked about the patients' interests and leisure activities. A check-list was used to help elicit this information and we recorded the frequency with which the patient participated in a wide range of leisure activities. We then made ratings on a five-point scale. Relatives were also asked about the number of friends the patient had, the frequency of visits made and received by the patient and the number of social events in which the patient participated.

The least severely injured group (group A) were able to resume their leisure activities within the first 6 months after injury. Furthermore they retained contact with friends and acquaintances throughout their recoveries. The very severely concussed patients, however, had still not resumed all their leisure activities 12 months after the accident, even though many of these patients had returned to work.

Since these patients were all young people, we considered the possibility that detrimental effects on sporting activities might be colouring the total picture. However, our analysis revealed that although involvement in sport had declined, it had done so no more than involvement in other pursuits. It appeared rather that less involvement in sport was a reflection of a more general tendency to relinquish leisure activities.

The very severely concussed were also more socially isolated throughout this period. However, loss of social contact did not appear to be directly attributable to being less able to go out to meet people. Those patients who had been unable to return to work were no more isolated than those who had returned. Furthermore, although there was a tendency for the patients in this group to visit friends less often, this was not marked and did not reach statistical significance, but a tendency for friends to visit them less often did.

Despite these changes none of the patients in group B was left completely without friends. However, once again the plight of the rehabilitation group was more extreme. Twenty-one were reported by relatives to have no friend whom they saw as often as once a week and six were reported to have no friends or acquaintances at all. We found they seldom had friends of the opposite sex and they had few interests or hobbies.

Surprisingly, motor and sensory impairment appeared to be of little significance in preventing the resumption of leisure activities in all three groups. Social isolation was also unrelated to the presence of motor and sensory deficits. In groups A and B two personality factors measured by the Katz Adjustment Scales (Katz and Lyerly 1963) were related to social isolation. These were 'confusion' and 'verbal expansiveness'. 'Confusion' refers to a tendency to be forgetful and disoriented in time and place. 'Verbal expansiveness' is a measure of the degree to which a person is brash, outspoken and verbally aggressive. In the rehabilitation group personality change was assessed by simply asking, 'Do you feel —— has changed as a person since the accident?' Further questions were asked to clarify the reply. The relatives' opinions as to whether such a change had occurred were not strongly related to loss of social contact. However, in this group we found that although those who had suffered a personality change did not have fewer social contacts there had been a change in the nature of their friendships. Compared with those without personality changes they had maintained contact with significantly fewer friends from before the accident. Instead, they had formed new relationships, but these appeared often to be casual and superficial. A remark made by a patient on his return from holiday serves to exemplify this point: 'I made two very good friends when I was on holiday—the head waiter and the barman . . .' In many cases social contacts were restricted to those achieved by visiting the pub. In other cases patients relied upon friends of their parents who had taken a particular interest in them.

Cognitive deficits may also have particularly disruptive effects on social and leisure activities. Memory deficits as measured by objective tests (Logical Memory, Inglis Paired Associate Learning Test and a Face-Name Learning Test) were related to loss of social contact in groups A and B. In the rehabilitation group the seven patients with gross intellectual loss (Matrices IQ below 70) had fewer social contacts than other patients in this group.

Family relationships

We made ratings of various aspects of family relationships during the semi-structured interview with a relative. The frequency of arguments and disagreements (friction) between patient and parent and between patient and siblings were rated. The ability of the patient and his relatives to confide in one another was also rated (communication) as was the frequency of joint family activities and the degree of dependency of the patient on his family. For married patients, we made ratings of their marital and sexual relationship.

Single patients

We detected no significant effect of the CHI on the family lives of patients in group A during the 12 months following injury. For those in group B, family relationships were affected but this did not become apparent until the 12-month assessment. By this time there was marked friction between patients and their siblings and communication had begun to break down. Friction between patient and parents was not reported so frequently although this may have been due to the parents' unwillingness to admit personal involvement in the disruption of family relationships.

In group C there was an increase in friction between patients and parents as well as between patients and siblings. Indeed in eight cases relatives gave reports of extreme friction, with the family reaching crisis point.

For those in the rehabilitation group the pattern of family life had changed in another way as well. Patients engaged in joint activities with their parents significantly more often that the controls. Parents often took their head-injured son or daughter with them when they went to visit friends and relations or even to work. In some cases this was an attempt by parents to compensate for the reduction in social contacts but in others it was due to their reluctance to leave the patients at home unsupervised.

Although in the prospective study we lack information concerning the specific precipitants of friction, we found that where the patient was suffering more from subjective symptoms friction was greater, as indeed it was amongst the families of those said to have suffered an adverse personality change. For the rehabilitation group, personality changes in general were not related to increased friction but irritability in particular was.

Physical deficits were not associated with family friction although they did lead to greater dependence upon the family.

One intriguing finding was that amongst the concussion groups good family relationships were associated with longer periods away from work. This raises the possibility that some patients may have been held back in their recovery by parental overprotection. However, an alternative explanation is that once a patient returns to work his family no longer accords him the privileges associated with the 'sick role' (Parsons 1951) and behaviour which was previously well tolerated is seen in a new light. These two explanations are by no means mutually exclusive.

Married patients

In groups A and B there was a total of 12 married patients and in group C only eight were married. With such small numbers it was not possible to make any statistical comparisons. However, we found no signs of marital problems in group A. In group B three of the seven spouses were rated as feeling less affection for their partner and in one of these cases there was a mild sexual problem (occasional loss of erection). In group C, five spouses reported that there had been no changes in their personal or sexual relationships. In one case a husband spoke of the strain and of the patience needed, but still claimed that he felt affection for his wife. Although the sexual relationship had deteriorated greatly, this marriage did not appear in imminent danger of breaking down. In two cases, however, separation had occurred although in both cases there was continued personal contact with the spouse on a fairly regular basis.

DISCUSSION

Clearly, closed head injury has wide-ranging effects on a person's life and indeed the lives of those around him. In young adults it appears that in general, where PTA is less than a week, the ability to cope with the demands of every-day life returns within a few months. Where the injury is more severe there is the likelihood of persisting deficits and the continued interruption of various aspects of daily life. Except for the most severe cases it appears that work is more rapidly resumed than leisure or social activities. This is not to ignore the supreme importance of loss of capacity for employment when it does occur. Work is a source of a sense of personal confidence and worth, particularly for young adults amongst whom head injury is most prevalent. Furthermore, we found evidence that many of those back in their original employment had not yet returned to their previous level of competence. Return to work is thus only a crude index of vocational capacities, and even a return to one's original job does not necessarily mean that these capacities remain fully intact.

Groups B and C were engaged in markedly fewer leisure activities but this could not be attributed simply to motor and sensory disability. Apathy has frequently been said to be common after CHI and our results appear to bear this out. In group B it was more common for patients to have returned to work than to have resumed leisure activities. The incentives for returning to work are obviously great but the incentive to resume other activities may be insufficient to motivate some head-injury victims.

Social isolation was apparent in the rehabilitation group and to a lesser extent in the very severely concussed. Once again physical restrictions were not able to account for this. Those able to go to work were as affected as those who remained at home. At both 6 and 12 months the number of visits received by those in group B showed a greater degree of change than the number of visits made. In group C, neurophysical status was unrelated to degree of social contact.

Personality changes in the rehabilitation group were associated with both the extent of social contacts and with the nature of these. Those with severe personality changes not only had fewer but also had only the most superficial social encounters. Personality changes were not associated with a greater degree of disruption of social life in group B, presumably because the changes were not sufficiently marked. However, in the closer confines of the family, the changes were of importance and led to poorer family relationships. In the rehabilitation group, personality changes did not lead to greater friction in the family except where irritability was reported. These two results are not inconsistent since irritability was one of the most commonly reported personality changes in the concussion groups, and was thus a common problem faced by patients and relatives. While irritability may well have a physiological basis we need to know the extent to which it can be exacerbated or diminished by environmental factors. It appeared that the frequency and intensity of irritable behaviour diminished over time, but it was unclear as to whether this was due to relatives finding ways of avoiding such reactions, to patients learning to moderate their reactions, or to physiological recovery.

It was only in the rehabilitation group that personality changes were associated with failure to return to work. Furthermore, only in this group was intellectual status related to return to work. It is possible that there are threshold levels below which personality and cognitive changes do not affect work capacity. However, more sensitive measures of work capacity than those employed in this study are needed before one can adopt such a conclusion. Furthermore, the interactions between the demands of different forms of employment and head-injury sequelae are certain to complicate matters.

As in several previous studies cognitive and personality changes were associated with disruption of many areas of daily life. Whether or not the link is casual is difficult to determine. Certainly global measures of the severity of injury such as PTA are also closely related to social dysfunction and it may simply be that cognitive and personality changes reflect this underlying variable. However, other facets of outcome such as physical or neurophysical disability, although also related to global severity, do not appear to be strongly implicated in social reintegration. This therefore suggests that of all the many possible sequelae of CHI or at least of those measured in our studies, personality and cognitive changes are amongst the most detrimental to normal daily life. Personality and cognitive ability are broad categories and clearly further refinement within these categories is necessary before the precise mechanisms involved in producing poor social adjustment can be understood.

Nevertheless, there is sufficient substance to these findings to suggest a clear need to broaden the aims of rehabilitation. There is a strong argument for the reallocation of resources to cover mental as well as physical rehabilitation. This is the challenge for all professions involved in the care of head-injured patients.

REFERENCES

Adey, C. (1967). Long term prognosis in closed head injury. *Bristol Mediocochir. J.* **82**, 58–64.

Bond, M. R. (1975). Assessment of the psychosocial outcome after severe head injury. Outcome of severe damage to the C.N.S. *Ciba Foundation Symp.* **34**, 141–53.

——, (1976). Assessment of the psychosocial outcome of severe head injury. *Acta Neurochir.* **34**, 57–70.

Brown, J. C. (1975). Late recovery from head injury case report and review. *Psychol. Med.* **5**, 239–48.

Bruckner, F. E. and Randle, A. P. H. (1972). Return to work after severe head injuries. *Rheum. phys. Med.* **11**, 344–8.

Carlsson, C. A., Von Essen, C., and Lofgren, J. (1968). Factors affecting the clinical course of patients with severe head injuries. *J. Neurosurg.* **29**, 242–51.

Fahy, T. J., Irving, M. H., and Millac, P. (1967). Severe head injuries. *Lancet* **ii**, 475–9.

Gerstenbrand, F. (1969). Rehabilitation of the head injured. In *Late effects of head injury* (ed. A. E. Walker). Thomas, Springfield, Illinois.

Gjone, R. Kristiansen, K., and Sponheim, N. (1972). Rehabilitation in severe head injuries. *Scand. J. rehabil. Med.* **4**, 2–4.

Gutterman, K. an and Sponheim, N. (1972). Rehabilitation in severe head injuries. *Scand. J. rehabil. Med.* **4**, 2–4.

Gutterman, P. and Shenkin, H. A. (1970). Prognostic features in recovery from traumatic decerebration. *J. Neurosurg.* **32**, 330.

Heiskanen, O. and Sipponen, P. (1970). Prognosis of severe brain injury. *Acta Neurol. Scand.* **45**, 343–8.

Hpay, H. (1971). Psychosocial effects of severe head injury. In *Head injury: proceedings of an international symposium* pp. 110–19. Churchill Livingstone, Edinburgh.

Katz, M. M. and Lyerly, S. B. (1963). Methods for measuring adjustment and social behaviour in the community. *Psychol. Rep.* **13**, 503–35.

Lecuire, J., Dechaume, J. P., and Deruty, R. (1971). Long-term prognosis of the prolonged and serious traumatic comas. In *Head injury: proceedings of an international* symposium pp. 161–2. Churchill Livingstone, Edinburgh.

Lewin, W. (1968). Rehabilitation after head injury. *Br. Med. J.:* **i**, 465–70.

London, P. S. (1967). Some observations on the course of events after severe head injury. *Ann. R. Coll. Surg. Eng.* **41**, 460–79.

Lundholm, J., Jepsen, B. N., and Thornval, G. (1975). The late neurological, psychological and social aspects of severe traumatic coma. *Scand. J. rehabil. Med.* **7**, 97–100.

MacIver, I. N., Lassman, L. P., Thomson, C. W., and McLeod, I. (1958). Treatment of severe head injuries. *Lancet* **ii**, 544–50.

Miller, H. and Stern, G. (1965). The long-term prognosis of severe head injury. *Lancet* **i**, 225–9.

Oddy, M. J., Humphrey, M. E., and Uttley, D. (1978). Subjective impairment and social recovery after closed head injury. *J. Neurol. Neurosurg. Psychiat.* **41**, 611–16.

Parsons, T. (1951). *The social system.* Free Press, New York.

Raven, J. C. (1960). *Guide to the standard progressive matrices,* Lewis, London.

Richardson, J. C. (1971). The late management of industrial head injuries. In *Head injury: proceedings of an international symposium* pp. 127–31. Churchill Livingstone, Edinburgh.

Roberts, A. H. (1976). Long-term prognosis of severe accidental head injury. *Proc. R. Soc. Med.* **69**, 137–41.

Rowbotham, G. F., MacIver, I. N., Dickson, J., and Bousfield, M. E. (1954). Analysis of 1,400 cases of acute injury to the head. *Br. Med. J.* **i**, 726–30.

Steadman, J. H. and Graham, J. G. (1970). Head injury: analysis and follow-up study. *Proc. R. Soc. Med.* **63**, 23–8.

Symonds, C. P. (1937). Mental disorder following head injury. *Proc. R. Soc. Med.* **30**, 1081–92.

Thomsen, I. V. (1974). The patient with severe head injury and his family—a follow-up study of 50 patients. *Scand. J. Rehabil. Med.* **6**, 180–3.

Van Der Zwan, A. (1969). Late results from prolonged traumatic unconsciousness. In *The late effects of head injury* (ed. A. E. Walker, W. F. Caveness, and Critchley) pp. 138–41. Thomas, Springfield, Illinois.

Vigouroux, R. P., Baurand, C., Naquet, R., Chament, J. H., Choux, M., Benayoun, R., Bureau, M., Charpy, J. P., Clamens-Guey, M. J., and Guey J. (1971). A series of patients with cranio-cerebral injuries, studied neurologically psychometrically, electroencephalography and socially. In *Head injury: proceedings of an international symposium on head injuries*. Churchill Livingtone, Edinburgh.

Weddell, R., Oddy, M., and Jenkins, D. (1980). Social Adjustment after rehabilitation. *Psychol. Med.* **10**, 257–63.

Wilkinson, M. I. P. (1969). The prognosis of severe head injuries in young adults. *Proc. R. Soc. Med.* **62**, 17–18.

7 Head injury and the family

Neil Brooks

INTRODUCTION

During the last ten years, studies of psychological aspects of recovery and disability after severe closed head injury have appeared at an increasing rate. The strictly cognitive consequences of severe head injury are dealt with in Chapters 4 and 5 in this volume and will not be discussed here, although one may contrast the number of studies of cognitive disturbance with the small number of studies that have been concerned with those aspects of psychological recovery that comprise 'psychosocial' functioning. Such deficits incude the behavioural, social and emotional, as well as cognitive changes occurring in the patient, together with the changes in family health and family circumstance, which result directly or indirectly from the patient's injury. These psychosocial consequences may be a matter of major concern and distress to the patient's family, yet little is known about their nature, their frequency, or their severity.

Happily, this situation is now changing, and in the current volume there are chapters by Michael Oddy on 'Social consequences of head injury, and by Michael Bond on 'Psychiatric consequences'. This chapter is concerned with the behavioural and emotional changes in the patient, and the effect that these have upon family life, but quite naturally (and desirably) there will be some degree of overlap and considerable continuity between this chapter and those by Bond and Oddy.

The medical literature on head injury has shown an understandable preoccupation with outcome after injury, yet such outcome studies have often neglected anything other than physical deficits in the patient, and very simple indices of recovery such as return to work (Miller and Stern 1965; London 1967; Carlsson, Von Essen, C., and Lofgren 1968; Vapalahti and Troupp 1971; Jennett 1972; Brown 1975; Jennet and Bond 1975; and Becker et al. 1977). An analysis of these studies shows that with the exception of those by Jennett and London, psychosocial aspects of recovery and disability are often neglected, and the papers by Vapalahti and Troupp and by Carlsson clearly illustrate this. Vapalahti and Troupp classified their patients as 'dead', 'persistent vegetative state', and 'recovered'; Carlsson et al. classified patients as 'dead', 'persistent coma', 'persistent dementia', and 'mental recovery'. The range of deficits included in the 'recovered' and 'mental recovery' categories was very high indeed: 'mental restitution' in the Carlsson study appeared to refer mainly to patients who were not ill enough to need permanent hospitalization, and patients described as 'totally recovered' were those who were not 'vegetative wrecks'.

Both Miller and Stern (1965) and Jennett (1972) mentioned personality change as one of the consequences of severe head injury. However, Miller and Stern unlike Jennett underestimated the significance of personality change, and Jennett pointed out that despite the difficulties in measuring such changes, they are a most consistent feature after closed head injury, and he noted that 'even though the patient may have made a satisfactory recovery and good social adjustment his spouse may avow that he is not the man she married' (Jennett 1972, p. 444).

Jennett, a neurosurgeon, and London (1967), an accident and emergency surgeon, have been among the first authors to recognize explicitly the burden placed upon a family and a community by the presence of severely damaged head-injured patients. London in his 1967 paper used the graphic phrase 'lame brains', to describe the young, very severely handicapped surviving patient, and he marvelled at 'the patience and understanding shown by the relatives, and particularly the wives of some of these violent and handicapped patients'. London felt that such patients were often discharged from hospital (and all too frequently thereby removed from any further care), on the grounds of physical or physiotherapeutic status, despite the fact that the patients and their families may require long-term counselling and advice about the management of personality change and behavioural problems. The number of severely damaged surviving patients may well be small in a national context (estimated by London to be around 1000 patients in England and Wales each year), but the burden that they place upon their families is severe and long lasting.

An analysis of the few studies which have dealt with psychosocial aspects of disability shows some common concerns, and on the basis of these the chapter has been organized around a series of questions as follows:

1. What are the main features of psychosocial disability and family burden?

2. Can the severity of such disability and burden be predicted by the severity of injury?

3. Which type of family relationship is most vulnerable?

4. How satisfied are relatives with the communication and information that they have received from professionals dealing with the patient?

5. What is the role of premorbid factors in predicting post-traumatic psychosocial disability?

6. How does such disability change during the first five years after injury?

THE MAIN FEATURES OF PSYCHOSOCIAL DISABILITY

An analysis of research which has examined the psychosocial deficits in detail shows a small number of studies, but a remarkable convergence of findings. Fahy, Irving, and Millac (1967) examined 32 very severely injured patients between five and six years after injury, 23 of whom were 'gainfully employed' at the time of injury. At follow-up, seven of these had reduced earning capacity, and four were completely unable to work. When reasons for reduced working capacity were examined, there was a preponderance of 'psychiatric' and cognitive disabilities which appeared directly to have caused the reduced capacity. Symptoms such as poor memory, loss of interest, changes in temperament, and even delusions were present. The patients themselves often denied or 'lightly dismissed' any disabilities, and spontaneous complaints by patients were rare—a consistent finding in this area. However, the relatives of the patients gave a very different account, often supplying details of abnormal behaviour that had not been suspected on initial examination of the patient. Relatives reported that patients had difficulties in intellect, memory and speech, but much more disturbing to the families were the marked changes in temperament. However, not all personality changes were seen as unwelcome by relatives: occasional patients were found to have become quieter and calmer following the injury, and much easier to live with, although this is unfortunately not generally the case.

Within a few years of Fahy's report, two further clinical studies were published (Panting and Merry 1972; Thomsen 1974). These supported Fahy's results, and suggested which particular psychosocial changes most distressed and burdened relatives. Panting and Merry reported the long-term outcome (up to seven years after injury) of 30 very severely injured cases referred to a rehabilitation unit, and they described the need for social and medical support for the patient's family. They (like Miller and Stern 1965, and Fahy, Irving, and Millac 1967), found a marked tendency for physical deficits to recover, but emotional disturbance did not show this tendency, and was much more difficult for relatives to deal with. Interestingly, whereas the relatives in Panting and Merry's study were most concerned with outbursts of rage, those in Thomsen's (1974) study were often concerned not with outbursts of rage, but of pathological laughter. Panting and Merry found that 60 per cent of relatives needed some kind of supportive treatment such as tranquillizing medication or sleeping tablets (not received before the injury) due to the family situation which had resulted directly from the presence of the injured patient. Thomsen (1974), a speech pathologist, added additional information as a result of a follow-up of 50 severely injured cases and their families seen up to 70 months after injury. An important feature of Thomsen's work was that she visited patients at home in order to interview relatives, and to make a direct assessment of the home situation. Her results were similar to those of Panting and Merry. None of the relatives complained of any feeling of distress or burden due to motor disability in the patient. Neuropsychological sequelae (particularly impaired memory) were often troublesome, but of much greater worry to relatives was the change in personality in the patient which, the relatives felt, overshadowed all other changes, and Thomsen commented: 'the changes in personality created the greatest trouble in their daily living. All except the relatives of eight patients complained of changes in character'. The most common symptoms found in Thomsen's patients were irritability, temper, aspontaneity, and restlessness, and many relatives felt that the patient had become much more like a child. Like Panting and Merry's and Fahy's patients, those studied by Thomsen did not complain themselves of post-traumatic disabilities, in marked contrast to their close relatives. Some patients referred in passing to their poor memory but failed completely to realize the extent of behaviour changes, despite the fact that many were lonely and had lost contact with friends made before injury.

Bond (1975) had been particularly dissatisfied with the stress upon purely physical recovery in the study of head-injured patients, so much so that he devised the scales shown in Table 7.1 to enable him to assess social and mental disability as well as physical changes. He examined 56 very severely injured patients within two years after injury, and showed that whereas there was a signficant relationship between the degree of social and mental, and social and physical handicap in the patient, this was not found between mental and physical disability. A high degree of mental disability (memory and personality impairment) was associated with a high degree of disruption of family cohesion, loss of working capacity, and disruption of leisure pursuits; but disturbances of sexual and other social functions were not related to mental disabilities. These results therefore showed that family cohesion is unaffected by physical disability but is very vulnerable to mental disability.

Table 7.1   *Components of Bond's social and mental scales*

Social	Mental
Work status	Memory defect
Leisure activities	Personality change
Family cohesion	Mental illness
Sexual activity	
Criminality	
Alcohol abuse	

From Bond (1975).

Bond's findings should be contrasted with those of Oddy *et al.* (1978*a*, 1980) who also studied severely injured patients. All of Oddy's cases had a PTA of more than 24 hours: 24 had a PTA of between 1 and 7 days and 26 of more than 7 days. Although undoubtedly severe cases, more of Oddy's patients were in the PTA category of less than a week than in many other studies in this area. In addition, the social class distribution of the 54 cases showed a large number (31) in the Professional/Management or skilled, non-manual classes. Social recovery (return to work, social contacts, leisure activities, etc.) was assessed 6 months after injury, and in general, Oddy's results suggest relatively minor social disability as a result of closed head injury; so much so that he was led to describe his 1978 findings as 'encouraging'. Most of Oddy's cases had resumed many, if not all, of their social activities, and there was little evidence of severe family or marital friction despite the fact that many patients were reported as showing personality change. However, his results are only encouraging when patients with injuries resulting in PTAs of less than a week are considered: the results for those with PTAs of more than seven days were less encouraging: in this group marked social disruption was still present six months after injury. Social isolation was found only in his patients with PTAs of longer than a week, and these naturally were the cases who were least likely to be back at work.

Subsequently, Oddy and Humphrey (1980) reported a two-year follow-up of these patients, and although most patients had returned to work, social and leisure activities were still disrupted, particularly in the more severe cases. Family relationship, however, which had shown signs of disruption at 12 months, appeared to have settled again by two years. In addition, in a group of patients attending rehabilitation, there were marked impairments here, reaching family crisis point in some cases (see Chapter 6 for further details).

Whereas both Bond and Oddy had seen their patients within two years after injury, the report by the Israeli group led by Najenson (Rosenbaum and Najenson 1976), concerned relatives of severely injured patients who were studied at exactly one year after injury. This time was chosen because at the end of a year, there is a tendency to look back and review progress: it is in Rosenbaum and Najenson's words, 'the moment of truth', when the relatives must face the full implications of disability in the patient. Recovery has often slowed by this time, and the hopes of a complete recovery may now be diminishing, and serious problems in adjustment may be beginning. Unlike the other studies described here, the Israeli work is concerned solely with marital relationships, and again unlike other studies, patients in Najenson's work were all injured in military service, with the result that 8 out of the 10 head-injured patients whom they report in their 1976 paper had suffered penetrating rather than closed head injury. The paper does not give full details of the patients who were examined, although they were all described as having 'severe brain injury'. In addition, the results reported by Rosenbaum and Najenson are based on very small numbers of cases, all of whom had access to intensive rehabilitation facilities in the Loewenstein Hospital. It is therefore difficult to know just how far one may generalize from their results, to those obtained from civilian injuries who receive only routine rehabilitation. Despite these caveats, their work is well conceived, and interestingly described, and is worth considering in some detail.

Rosenbaum and Najenson compared the wives of severely head injured patients with wives of paraplegics who had sustained their injuries in the same war. They derived a number of hypotheses as follows:

1. Wives of brain-injured men will perceive greater change in family life than wives of paraplegic men.

2. Wives of brain-injured men will evaluate life changes as more disabling than the wives of paraplegic men.

3. Wives of brain-injured men will show more evidence of depressed mood than the wives of paraplegic men.

These were investigated using a questionnaire to assess four areas comprising: change in family life, change in husband and wife interpersonal functioning, change in the distribution of marital roles, and change in the mood of wives.

The main conclusions from Rosenbaum and Najenson's (1976) study were as follows:

1. Wives of brain-injured patients reported drastic life changes.

2. Life changes associated with depressed mood in wife.

3. Interpersonal relationships tense in head-injury families.

4. Wives of brain-injured patients felt lonely and isolated.

5. Wives of brain-injured had to assume husbands' roles.

These results show that the wives of brain damaged men when compared with the wives of paraplegics or non-injured men reported greater negative change in sexual activity, in sharing in the care of the children, in leisure, in visiting the husband's family, and in general social life. Most of these changes were associated with depression in the wife, particularly so for changes relating to reduced sharing in the care of the children. In general, when the families of brain-injured men were compared with the families of paraplegics, brain-injured husbands were much more likely to be described as self-orientated and dependent, and this their wives found difficult to accept.

Reduction in sexual functioning was not restricted to the wives of head-injured patients, as wives of paraplegics also noted such changes. However, the reason underlying the changes were quite different in the two groups: in the paraplegic group, it was due to spinal physical difficulties, whereas in head-injury marriages it was due to interpersonal distress. In the latter group, the wives felt distaste at having sexual contact with their husbands whom they saw as changed persons and therefore not the person they married—indeed wives of brain-damaged patients came to dislike any physical contact with their husbands, due to the personality change suffered by the husband. In terms of family roles, the wives of brain-injured patients found themselves increasingly handling family matters outside the home, reflecting the reduced capacity of the patient to handle such matters for himself. Many of the changes in family activity and marital interaction were related to depressed mood in the wives. The severity of their depressed mood correlated highly with the degree of reduction in marital sharing in the care of the children, and with their perception of their husbands' childlike dependency.

Recent work in Glasgow (Brooks 1979; Brooks and Aughton 1979; McKinlay, Brooks, Bond, Martinage, and Marshall 1981) has attempted to identify the main features of psychosocial burden as perceived by a relative, within the first year after injury. The conceptual background of the research was derived from Grad and Sainsbury (1963) and Hoenig and Hamilton (1969). Using Hoenig and Hamilton's approach, burden upon a family may be considered in two quite different ways, reflecting two different (although related) ways in which a family might be burdened, as follows:

(A) *Objective burden type 1*—Changes in family routine, family health, housing conditions, financial status, and social and leisure activities.

Objective burden type 2—Post-traumatic symptoms and changes to the patient's behaviour and personality.

(B) *Subjective burden*—Stress felt by the person caring for the patient, resulting from the presence of objective burden.

Type 1 burden reflects changes forced upon a family by the presence of the injured patient, and type 2 reflects changes and symptoms in the patient which have resulted directly from the injury. These may be referred to as 'objective' burdens that may be observed clearly and reliably by an independent observer. In addition, there is the 'subjective' burden or the stress actually *felt* by family members caring for the patient. An estimation of this kind of burden is less easy.

The study of the two types of burden used a questionnaire, which contains items relating to changes in family routine, etc. (type 1 burden); and items relating to changes in the patient (type 2 burden). Type 1 burden is rather similar to the area of Family Activity and Family Interaction studied by the Najenson group.

Subjective burden was assessed in a number of ways, the most direct one being to ask the relative to rate her strain or distress using the seven-point scale, shown below in Fig. 7.1.

1. The questionnaire was administered only to the relative, and the results derived from it reflect therefore only the relative's view of objective and subjective burdens, and it is accepted that this might well be distorted by stress.

The analysis of results has concentrated on type 2 burden (the changes in the patient), and the effect that these have upon the relative who has the main responsibility for caring for the patient. In order to examine this, many of the 90 type 2 questionnaire items have been grouped together into a series of component scales as shown below in Table 7.2, with each scale scored out of 10. The items in the different scales represent the different

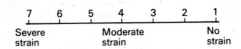

Fig. 7.1.

Assessment scale used by relative to gauge strain of subjective burden.

Table 7.2   *Main sources of type 2 objective burden*

Area of deficit	Type of change
Physical	Sensory, motor, gait disturbance, and epilepsy
Language	Dysarthria and dysphasia
Emotional	Loss of emotional control or stability
Dependence	Difficulties in self-care, and need for supervision
Subjective	Slowness, tiredness, concentration
Memory	Disorientation, omissions, repetition
Disturbed behaviour	Bizarre, puzzling, difficult conduct; includes violent and inappropriate social behaviour

Table 7.3   *Details of 55 cases studied in Glasgow*

Age (years)	Mean, 35.7; Range, 16 – 60
Sex	46 male
Marital status (at first follow up)	Married or cohabiting, 33; Single, 19; Other, 3

Post-traumatic amnesia Days:	2–7	8–14	15–28	Over 28	Not known
(No.)	12	6	14	21	2

Type of accident: Road traffic, 26; Assault, 11; Industrial, 4; Domestic, 1; Other, 13 types of change and symptoms that may be observed in head-injured patients.

The results on 55 patients (Table 7.3) are shown in Table 7.4: the patients were selected from consecutive admissions to a neurosurgical unit, and therefore represent a specific type of severely head-injured case with a high incidence of intracranial haematoma and skull fracture. No patient was seen who had been in coma (rated on the Glasgow Coma Scale—Teasdale and Jennett 1974) for less than six hours, or whose PTA was judged retrospectively to be less than two days. Within two days of admission to hospital, the main relative, who had a close knowledge of the patient (the husband or wife in 31 cases, and the parent or brother in 23), was approached and an estimate was made of the current financial and social situation in the family. The relative (and patient), was then seen again at three, six and 12 months after injury, when the questionnaire was administered, and the relative was also questioned about personality change in the patient and social functioning.

Using the classification shown in Table 7.2 an estimate may be made of the relative severity of each problem area, and this is shown in Table 7.4. The results are clear: during the first 12 months after injury, physical difficulties are perceived by the relatives as relatively infrequent. At three months, more 'emotional' and 'subjective' problems were reported than any other type, and the picture is substantially the same at six months and at 12 months.

Table 7.4 *Type 2 objective burden at 3, 6, and 12 months after injury: mean number of problems (maximum = 10) reported by relative*

	Time (months)		
	3	6	12
Physical	1.8	1.6	1.5
Subjective	4.5	4.3	4.5
Language	2.4	2.2	2.1
Emotional	4.6	5.1	5.4
Dependence	1.8	1.5	1.4
Disturbed behaviour	1.4	1.6	1.9
Memory	2.7	2.3	2.7

These results refer to broad areas of symptomatology or disability, and it is worth examining the specific symptoms reported most frequently by the relative. These are shown in Table 7.5 which illustrates the 'top 4' complaints in term of percentages, of relatives who complained of each symptom in the injured patient. At three months, the most frequent symptoms

Table 7.5 *Most frequent specific complaints made by relatives at 3, 6, and 12 months after injury: % of relatives complaining*

3 months	
Complaint	%
Slowness	86
Tiredness	82
Poor memory	73
Irritability	63

6 months	
Complaint	%
Slowness	69
Tiredness	69
Irritability	69
Tension and anxiety	64

12 months	
Complaint	%
Irritability	71
Impatience	71
Tiredness	69
Poor memory	69

From McKinlay, *et al.* (1981)

refer to tiredness, memory disturbance, and general slowness; then a group of emotional items appear, which reflect difficulties in emotional control and bad temper. At six months, the order of specific symptoms has changed only little, with slowness being slightly less important, and a drop in reports of poor memory. At 12 months the picture is very similar with irritability and impatience heading the list.

PREDICTION OF SEVERITY OF FAMILY DISABILITY

Although the burden upon the family of a severely head-injured patient can be very great, it is not an invariable consequence of head injury. Some families cope well with situations which to the outsider appear desperate in the extreme, whereas other families are crippled by apparently minor changes in the patient, and it is not easy to predict which families will show which reaction. One obvious predictor is the severity of the injury itself, and the relationship between severity of injury and severity of family disability has been a constant topic in the literature. Fahy *et al.* (1967) found that the 'psychiatric aspects' of post-traumatic change (for example increased aggression, paranoia, severe personality change, etc.) were related to severity of injury, with patients showing a more severe and persistent psychiatric disability having suffered longer PTAs. Patients in their study who showed no psychiatric disability had a mean PTA of 15 days, whereas those with moderate, or severe psychiatric disabilities had PTAs of 22 and 49 days, respectively. The correlation between PTA and psychiatric disability was +0.68 which was highly statistically significant, although still leaving just over 50 per cent of the variance in psychiatric symptomatology unexplained by severity of brain damage.

Bond (1975) also used PTA, and found significant correlations between PTA duration and severity of physical, mental, and social disabilities. He found a significant correlation between the degree of social and mental and social and physical disability, but not between mental and physical disability. Bond rightly points out that the insignificant correlations between mental and physical disability may merely reflect the fact that the physical scale he used measured neurological signs which are an index of focal rather than diffuse brain damage. This analysis was carried further by examining particular items from the mental and social sub-scales in relation to duration of PTA, and this showed that whereas the presence of a memory disability, a disorder in working capacity, and a change in leisure were all related to PTA duration, the presence of personality change, mental symptoms, changes in family cohesion, and in sexual activity were all unrelated to PTA.

The occasional contradiction in the literature between studies showing a relationship between severity of injury and severity of family distress, and those showing no such relationship, is partially resolved by Bond's work. He showed that only some of the common psychosocial changes in patient and family were related to severity, and it is likely that the differing results in the literature are a reflection of the clarity with which these changes have been defined. Tentatively, one may conclude that the changes in personality and other mental symptoms which often result from severe injury do not bear a simple relationship to the severity of the injury, although as Bond is careful to point out, once PTA is over four weeks, patients are likely to show physical, mental, and social change, and the burden upon their families is likely to be high. With injuries of a lesser severity, however, prediction of the likelihood of family burden is not easy. Patients and families may come to terms with the results of severe injury, and London (1967) while highlighting the problems facing the head-injured patient and his relatives, nevertheless is very careful to point to some of his 'success stories' showing that some very severely injured patients have made excellent recoveries, and their families have not been unduly burdened.

Some researchers have tried to identify the specific changes in the patient which are most likely to cause distress in the relatives. Thomsen (1974) noted that relatives ignored impaired language function as a source of difficulty, but complained bitterly of changes in personality in the patient; such changes 'seemed to be proportional with the severity of the trauma'.

However, Thomsen did not give figures in support of this. Relatives in Oddy's studies (Oddy, *et al.* 1978a, b; Oddy and Humphrey 1980) also complained of feeling stress as a function of change in behaviour (particularly poorly controlled behaviour) in the patient.

Work in our own laboratory in Glasgow also assessed the relationship between changes in the patient, and distress in the relative. One approach to the problem of prediction is to subdivide relatives into those with low, medium, and high burden according to their scores on the Subjective Burden analogue scale, and then to use one-way analysis of variance to compare the magnitude of scores on the various patient difficulty scales (physical, subjective, etc.). When this is done, the three burden sub-groups are found to differ significantly in the degree of subjective, emotional, and disturbed behaviour changes in the patient. Physical difficulties are never of significance here. This suggests that relatives are well able to cope with the physical consequences of the injury (unless these are very severe, or persistent, or include incontinence), but find the psychological and behavioural consequences much more burdensome.

The point that it is emotional, and not physical symptomatology in the patient that burdens a relative, was also made by Lezak (Lezak 1978; Lezak, Cosgrove, O'Brien, and Wooster 1980), who found that even at 5 years after injury, behaviour, and social disruption was common, and affected the patient's ability to get on with others. The same point was made by Thomsen (1981) in her 10–15 year follow-up.

THE SIGNIFICANCE OF THE TYPE OF FAMILY RELATIONSHIP

A number of researchers have distinguished carefully between marital, and other family relationships, and have studied burden separately within the two situations. Others, like Fahy *et al.* (1967), while implicitly commenting upon differences between the two relationships did not examine their results specifically in those terms. Fahy in summarizing the results of his study stated 'Family, *especially parental* support seemed crucial to satisfactory progress irrespective of the nature of disability . . . .' He then went on to note that in the five cases where such support was lacking, this lack was 'invariably associated with denial of progress by relatives and social withdrawal by the patient'. This statement suggests that parental support of some kind is crucial but its nature is unclear: it may be that the important support is that given by the parents of the patient to the patient's wife, rather than to the patient himself.

Panting and Merry (1972) and Thomsen (1974) both commented on the relative vulnerability of different types of family relationship, finding that in general the husband–wife relationship was less stable under the stress of a head injury than the parent–child relationship. Panting and Merry found that of ten patients married at the time of accident, three became divorced and a fourth separated. It is of course difficult to draw firm conclusions from these figures, as the relationship may have been unstable before the accident.

Thomsen, and Panting and Merry each discuss possible reasons why marital relationships should be more vulnerable, and each considered different factors. Panting and Merry noted that in all but one of their cases where patients were living with their parents, both parents were alive and this would mean that two people would be able to support each other in attempting to deal with the problems, and they could therefore share the burden imposed by the injured patient. Furthermore, while the average age of patients living with their parents was 26 years, that of patients living with their wives was 40 years. Given that the recovery in the younger patient in that study was more complete, it may have been that the wives of married patients were having to deal with a more seriously disabled patient. Thomsen, however, felt that the reasons underlying the difference in burden between marital and family relationships were much more subtle. She noted that mothers were much better able than wives to accept behaviour changes in the patient, and she pointed out that the role changes in marriage imposed by a head injury can be great. In addition, she felt that feelings of guilt in the non-injured spouse can have a deleterious effect on the relationship.

Israeli work (Rosenbaum and Najenson 1976) sheds further light on this problem. This study concentrated upon marital relationships, in which the husband had been injured in military service. The problem of guilt must be less serious in that kind of situation, while the role changes are likely to be just as marked as those in civilian injuries. The results showed that role changes within the family contributed significantly to depression in the wife, and a number of wives reported tension between themselves and their in-laws due to the over-protective attitude of the patient's parents, some of whom may have found the dependent behaviour of the patient, if not gratifying, at least acceptable. Wives, on the other hand, were totally unable to accept such dependent behaviour.

The study of Oddy *et al.* (1978*a*) also examined the burden with differing family relationships, although only 12 of their 50 head-injured cases were married, and it is therefore difficult to form firm conclusions. However, Oddy found that in only one of the 12 married cases was the marital relationship reported to be appreciably worse, and at six months after injury no spouse reported any sexual problem. Furthermore, an increase in the frequency of sexual intercourse was reported as often as a decrease. At a two-year follow-up, (Oddy and Humphrey 1980), only one of the 12 wives questioned reported any sexual difficulties. Unlike the Najenson group, Oddy did not find any increase in friction between married patients and their in-laws, nor between single patients and their parents or their siblings, although initially the most severely injured cases (those with a PTA of longer than seven days) did become more dependent upon their parents. However, married patients did not become more dependent upon either their parents or their spouses, and the parental dependency in the single patient had disappeared by 12 months. Oddy's results therefore stand in contrast to those of many of the other workers in this field, showing that family burden may be relatively mild after injury, and that marital relationships are no more vulnerable than parental relationships. However, Oddy's patients were less severely injured than those described in other series, and when he subsequently studied a considerably more seriously injured group (Weddell, Oddy, and Jenkins 1980), in three of the eight married patients there were negative changes in the patient leading to divorce or separation. Other studies which have examined relationship differences and burden after injury have produced consistent results: marital relationships are more vulnerable than parental, although the reasons for this are not clear. It may be as Panting and Merry suggested that in marital relationships the patients tend to be younger (this was obviously not the case, however, in the Oddy series of cases), or as Thomsen, and Rosenbaum and Najenson have suggested, it may be that role shifts forced upon the wife by the disabilities of her injured husband contribute largely to the family burden. In addition, Thomsen felt that feelings of guilt may have a part to play, although this is a difficult area to investigate empirically.

It is not easy to specify with any accuracy the precise behaviours which make a particular relationship more vulnerable, although there are hints from the literature that it is the child-like and dependent behaviour of the severely injured patient that the patient's wife cannot tolerate, but which the patient's parents may find less unacceptable.

COMMUNICATION BETWEEN RELATIVES AND CLINICIANS

A number of researchers have commented on difficulties in communication between the clinicians caring for the injured patient, and the patient's relatives. Some researchers have seen these difficulties arising as a result of simple failure to understand on the part of the relative (Thomsen 1974), whereas others (Romano 1974) have seen them arising as part of much more fundamental psychopathological processes such as denial.

That relatives feel aggrieved over the communication they receive cannot be disputed. Indeed the development of organizations such as Headway (Britain), The National Head Injury Foundation, and Head Trauma Support Project (USA), etc., is testimony to this fact. These organizations are set up by, and for, the relatives of patients as well as professionals dealing with the patient, and the relatives are unanimous in their complaints of poor communication and inadequate services. Many professionals would agree. Panting and Merry found that just over half of the relatives they interviewed felt that supportive services had not been adequate—and this was usually because doctors were felt not to have supplied sufficient information. Such information was felt to be particularly lacking with regard to the patient's further prognosis, and to the difficulties which might well be encountered in the future. Oddy's results are very similar (Oddy *et al.* 1978*b*); 40 per cent of the relatives in his study had some criticism to make, the most common one concerning communication between themselves and medical staff. Some relatives were dissatisfied with Social Services, with hospital after-care, and, in two cases (both with a medical background) the absence of routine neurological or psychological assessments.

Of 40 relatives interviewed in Thomsen's research (1974), 22 felt that good information had been received, but 18 were dissatisfied with the information. However, the reasons for dissatisfaction varied widely, with four relatives reporting that they did not understand what the doctor had said, three feeling that doctors never tell the truth, two feeling that the doctor was too busy and would not answer their questions, and two relatives admitting that they were either afraid and did not listen, or did not want to hear what the doctor had said.

The agreement between Panting and Merry's results and those of Thomsen and Oddy is very close, showing that around 50 per cent of relatives are dissatisfied with services or with communication. Thomsen considered that the predominantly working class relatives simply failed to understand or to remember what the doctor had said. None of the relatives who had had a higher education complained, although there were very few of these in the sample. This simple cognitive hypothesis of communication breakdown would be supported by the work of Ley (1977) on the failures of doctor–patient communication, which has shown that patients fail to understand what they are told by doctors simply because they cannot understand it, or do not remember it.

However, it is possible that in some families the failure to recall information or the feeling that none had been given is due to the defence mechanism of denial, in which hope or wish about future recovery and current status is substituted for the unacceptable reality. Evidence that this might be the case comes from statements by relatives in Thomsen's study who said that they were either afraid of what they might hear and therefore did not listen to the doctor, or simply did not want to hear what the doctor had said. Support for this comes also from a personal communication by Michael Oddy about a very intelligent relative (a mother) of an extremely severely head-injured boy. The mother emphatically stated that she did not wish to hear a gloomy prognosis, as this took away all her hope—and without hope for the future (whether rational or not) she felt lost.

The suggestion that ignorance about current status and prognosis might in itself be a defence was made explicitly by Romano (1974) who described denial in the relatives of 13 very severely injured patients. Romano's paper is not satisfactory as a research report: there is little information about the patients that she studied, or the methods that she used. Despite this, her report raises interesting speculations about how some families may deal with the problems of facing the reality of extremely handicapped survivors. Romano felt that denial was not only common *early* after injury (where it is to some extent an understandable and to be expected consequence), but it persisted long after this period, despite counselling and other help.

Her evidence for denial was based on the following features:

1. Common fantasies: 'He's only sleeping'.
2. Verbal refusals: 'His temper always was bad'.
3. Inappropriate responses: Failure to set appropriate limits.

The common fantasies that she described were quite independent of the educational and social level of the families involved, and frequently concerned the patient's conscious level. It was common to believe that the patient was merely sleeping, and this notion persisted long after it was absolutely clear to the objective observer that the patient was no longer in coma, but was awake and was to some extent, at least, responsive. Perhaps most distressing to onlookers not directly concerned with the families were the fantasies concerning the concept of will. Statements such as 'she *will* get well because after all she has three children so she *must* get well', were common. The second feature of denial concerned refusals to accept that the patient was now very different following injury. This meant that despite very clear evidence that the patient's behaviour was changed, and abnormal, relatives would make statements like 'he always did have a temper', when faced with extremely disturbed and aggressive behaviour. Finally, relatives made inappropriate responses, failing to set limits, and Romano described the parents of one perceptually and judgementally impaired boy urging him to begin driving again, as this would then prove that he was completely recovered.

Romano's report is worth following up and investigating in some detail. There is no doubt that some families have an unshakable belief in the potential for future recovery in the patient, and others misjudge, underestimate, or ignore marked negative behaviour changes. In some cases this is indeed denial, although professionals are now increasingly admitting that we have little information about the final limits on recovery in many patients. Even if relatives are seen to be denying, it is difficult for the professional to know how to manage the situation. It is naive to assume that denial is necessarily 'a bad thing'; indeed, in some families (perhaps in most early after injury) denial is highly functional, and a necessary psychological protection against an extreme situation. In others, it may be a bar to rehabilitation of the patient, and may impose extra strain and burdens on an already burdened family and patient. Without considerable clinical experience and sensitivity, it can be very difficult to decide which alternative is the case, or to decide when the first situation evolved into the second.

However, an understanding of reactions such as denial, and the part they play in recovery must be crucial for delivering adequate rehabilitation to such patients and their families.

THE ROLE OF PRE-MORBID FACTORS

There is evidence that head injured patients do not comprise a random sample of the general population. They are likely to have been drinking heavily at the time of accident (Potter 1967; Galasko and Edwards 1975; and Galbraith, Murray, Patel, and Knill-Jones 1976), and are often habitual heavy drinkers. The personality characteristics of the population are not quite so well known, but Jamieson (1971) in a brief account of 1000 consecutive head-injured admissions to a rehabilitation unit showed that many of the patients were known to the police before admission. Many of them had shown evidence of violence and antisocial behaviour, and 'were found to have unsatisfactory backgrounds, often with divorce or separation of parents, poor school records . . . poor marital stability, and a higher rate of domestic and industrial accidents than a control group of drivers'. These findings would be supported by those of Fahy *et al.* (1967) who found that 12 out of 32 cases had been 'socially maladjusted' before injury. Five had shown chronic neurotic symptoms, four had shown heavy drinking and petty crime, one had shown 'low intelligence', one had been epileptic, and one had received psychiatric treatment for chronic schizophrenia.

Panting and Merry found that attacks of emotional rage after injury were much more likely in patients who had shown pre-morbid personality instability; whereas 15 of the 22 patients judged to have been stable before injury showed emotional rage, all eight of the patients judged to have been less stable showed such rage. Unfortunately, Panting and Merry do not give clear indications of how they defined 'unstable'. Similar difficulties arise in interpreting London's (1967) report which suggested that in most cases after severe head injury, the personality and behavioural changes that occurred 'tend either to be an exaggeration of previous traits or to occur in patients that might have been expected to develop mental disorder without having had their brains damaged'.

The results in this area are not easy to interpret. There have been few serious attempts to examine pre-morbid personality status in relation to outcome and to burden following head injury, and conclusions are based often on intuition and judgement rather than on 'hard data'. However, the results such as they are do seem to suggest that the patients who have the least prepossessing personalities before injury may well show the greatest negative changes, with presumably the greatest resulting burden upon the family. However, this is not a conclusion that can be stated with any great conviction, as clinicians such as Fahy *et al.* were very careful to show that the personality changes in their patients were not always negative, and in two of their 32 cases, previously unpleasant personalities (one showing paranoid aggressive behaviour, and the other having regularly assaulted his parents) underwent a welcome change in personality, becoming good tempered and compliant.

CHANGE IN PSYCHOSOCIAL DISABILITY OVER TIME

Most studies have concentrated on a single examination of the patient and family, usually within five years after injury, and studies of the change or evolution of psychosocial deficits over time are very rare. Erculei (1961) reported a 15-year follow-up of 364 men who had been injured in the Second World War. However, these patients comprise a rather specific sample of the total head-injury population, with 241 suffering from post-traumatic epilepsy. The study was concerned mainly with 'socioeconomic' status (i.e. employment) at follow-up but a valuable feature of the study was that patients had been seen initially at between five and nine years after injury, and this did enable an analysis of very late changes to be made. Adequate data were not available on all the cases, but of those followed-up at 15 years, 121 (39 per cent) were employed or working irregularly. Eighty per cent of the patients who were unemployed blamed physical deficits for their inability to work, and 20 per cent blamed 'mental or emotional factors'. As head-injured patients often underestimate the severity of psychological change, these figures should be interpreted with caution. Features judged by Erculei to be associated with a poor long-term prognosis included increasing severity of injury, the presence of post-traumatic epilepsy, cognitive deterioration, and personality inventory scores indicating 'elevated hysterical, depressed, or hypochondriacal' features.

The Israeli group (Najenson *et al.* 1974; Groswasser *et al.* 1977) have commented on the change in disability between 6 months and 30 months after injury. Thirty-eight severely injured patients were followed up over this time, and the patients were rated on a variety of features of outcome including 'behavioural disturbance'. At the first follow-up (six months after injury), 24 out of 40 patients had shown at least some behavioural disturbances of varying degrees of severity. Of the 25 patients, 11 showed 'gross', and 14 showed 'moderate' disability. Of the 14 'moderate' cases, three were unaware of their disability, whereas 10 of the 11 'gross' cases were unaware. The gross deficits included apathy, lack of motivation, loss of affection, loss of inhibition, impulsiveness, and outbursts of aggression. Five cases showed 'regressive' behaviour disturbances, becoming self-centred, withdrawn, and unable to sustain mature relationships. The patients who showed such disturbances and who also showed lack of awareness of the disability posed very serious rehabilitation problems, despite the fact that all 11 such patients had made a full motor recovery.

By the second follow-up at 30 months after injury, the incidence of behavioural disturbance had dropped, and only 14 of 38 cases were still showing such change—five showing gross disability and nine showing a moderate disability. Of the five 'gross' patients, none showed any awareness of their disability, and of the nine 'moderate' seven failed to show awareness. When other areas of function were considered (for example, locomotor abilities, cognitive performance, communication, etc.), a marked recovery was found, although improvements, (for example, in locomotion and cognition) were often largely completed by the end of the first six months. The rate of 'late' improvement in behaviour disturbance (that is from six to 30 months after injury) was high. However, as Groswasser and his team point out, 'in all the patients where behavioural disturbances occurred concurrently with a state of unawareness, no improvement was attained at all'.

These patients had access to intensive and widely based rehabilitation facilities which were designed to deal with the full range of problems suffered by head-injured patients. Patients who left the programme were able to return at any stage for further counselling and aid, and in view of this the same improvements may not be obtained from other centres where such intensive rehabilitation may not be available.

The Israeli workers showed that 'late' recovery (that is, beyond the first weeks or months after injury) may be observed in many patients—particularly within the first 30 months after injury, but they obviously feel that the situation may continue to evolve and to change for at least three or four years after injury, and it may well be as long as that before patients are able to 'manage to exploit the potential left to them after injury'. A point made also in the long-term single case follow-up reported by Thomsen (1981).

Thomsen in a paper in preparation (quoted here with her kind permission), has added to her single case report (1981) by analyzing a 10–15-year follow-up of very severely injured patients. This shows a high frequency of marital breakdown: of the eight patients married at the time of injury, six subsequently divorced, in each case, because of loss of emotional control, and/or emotional regression. Changes in personality and behaviour were still very common, even at this late stage, being shown by 20 of the 35 cases. Other persisting changes were: sensitivity to stress (23), loss of social contact (20), tiredness (18), aspontaneity (18), slowness (17), and restlessness (14). This picture of substantial late morbidity is supported by a 5-year follow-up by Lezak *et al.* which found persisting social problems, and 'pervasive and almost universal social dislocation'. Poor emotional control, reduced social contact, and impairment in work, school and leisure were found in over 70 per cent of her 23 patients.

Other studies have concentrated on a shorter follow-up. Oddy *et al.* (1978*a,b*) and Oddy and Humphrey (1980), in London, and Brooks (1979), Brooks and Aughton (1979), and McKinlay, Brooks, Bond, Martinage and Marshall (1981), in Glasgow, each studied the change in psychological disability during recovery, but the follow-up was short, being two years in the Oddy work, and 1 year only in the Brooks studies. Oddy interviewed relatives of closed head injury patients within the first month after the accident, and then at 6, 12, and 24 months after injury, and measured the stress upon the relatives by means of a questionnaire and an interview. Very early after injury, signs of depression in the relatives were common, with 39 per cent of 46 relatives interviewed reporting depression. This proportion dropped markedly to 15 per cent at six months and 17 per cent at 12 months. The situation had obviously stabilized by six months in Oddy's study, and no further significant change took place up to the end of the first year. Neither the degree of stress upon the relative, nor the change in stress during the first year were related to severity of injury. Oddy found that 'slightly more than half' the relatives at six and 12 months reported some stress as a result of having to deal with the injured patient, and there was therefore no marked change in the relatives' feelings of stress between six and 12 months after injury. The source of the stress when it occurred was usually some aspect of the patient's condition, for example, poorly controlled behaviour.

Oddy also noted the number of relatives who had complained of an illness during the year following the patient's injury. During the first six months, four out of 48 relatives complained of physical illness, and nine of an emotional or psychosomatic condition. At 12 months, two relatives complained of physical, and ten of emotional or psychosomatic change. The proportion of relatives showing illness did not therefore change significantly during the first year, and Oddy in summarizing his results felt it important to note not only that many relatives suffered 'by stress', but also that the 'stress on the relatives showed no sign of diminishing over time'.

The Glasgow study described by Brooks (1979), Brooks and Aughton (1979), and McKinlay *et al.* (1981), was also concerned with the changes in psychosocial deficits (more specifically with family burden) within the first year after severe injury. As Tables 7.4 and 7.5 show, relatives judged that physical dependency and cognitive deficit reduced in the patient during the period between three and 12 months after injury, but behavioural and emotional deficits (reflecting loss of control and loss of emotional stability or difficult behaviour) increase, although only by a small amount. Indeed all changes during this period are slight, and the picture as judged by relatives seems to change very little during the first 12 months after injury. During that time, the same group of symptoms in the patient appeared to be reported most frequently by the relatives; slowness, tiredness, irritability, and poor memory all head the list of highly frequent symptoms, each symptom being reported by at least half the 55 relatives studied. The association between the type of symptoms shown by the patient and the burden on the relative remained substantially the same at each assessment.

The longest duration study considered here (that by Erculei) is difficult to interpret due to the specific nature of the sample of patients that he studied (many with missile wounds and many with post-traumatic epilepsy). However, Thomsen's patients seem fairly typical (except for the high proportion of females—11 out of 35, and she found continuing high degrees of morbidity at 10–15 years. But she did find a very substantial number of patients (15) living alone, compared with the situation at the first follow-up (2–5 years) when only two were living alone. At the first follow-up this had been considered impossible. Despite high morbidity, therefore, some kind of independent life may be possible for a large proportion of severely head-injured patients given adequate support. An additional point from Thomsen's work is that in several cases, relatives reported gradual behavioural improvement during the first five or six years suggesting a very prolonged, if slow, recovery period. The other studies have considered rather shorter follow-up, but even so, Najenson supported Thomsen in showing that marked improvement could be observed in behavioural disability during the first 30 months after injury. However, the patients who were unaware of disability at six months remained unaware at 30 months, and this constituted a very major obstacle to a successful outcome. The two British studies by Oddy and by Brooks suggested that there was relatively little change in psychosocial disability in the relatives during the first 6–12 months after injury, although, as might be expected, the relatives in Oddy's study showed a major reduction in depression between the very first follow-up (at 1–4 weeks after injury) and the second follow-up at six months.

Thomsen's data are very important. Currently there is all too often a feeling among professionals that the long-term outcome is always and inevitably poor. London (1967) tried to show that this was not necessarily always the case, and Thomsen's findings that some very severely injured and disabled patients nevertheless live independently (although with support from state services) is very promising indeed.

Further sequential studies are needed here, and the time-consuming and often tedious nature of such studies may be one reason for their relative neglect. Studies which demand repeated examinations of patients and families take an enormous amount of manpower and time, and it is difficult to gather a large number of cases if more than one or two repeat examinations are to be carried out. It is to be hoped that more long-term follow-ups are reported: there is the encouraging possibility that the Israeli workers may continue their follow-up, and Oddy may carry out further later follow-up studies on his patients. The Glasgow group certainly intend to continue to follow their cases for at least 5 years after injury, and the 10–15 years report by Thomsen is particularly valuable.

DISCUSSION AND CONCLUSIONS

Psychosocial deficits in patients, and burden in families have been reported in the context of a general assessment of head injury outcome, but until recently these aspects of recovery in disability were not studied in any detail. London's sobering account of the problem of 'lame brains' in 1967 remains as true now as then, showing that head injury causes serious personality change, serious emotional disability, and often childish, demanding and irritable and aggressive behaviour. These changes can impose a severe, and in some cases an intolerable, strain upon the relatives who have to deal with them, although it is not always easy to predict which families will be most burdened by the presence of an injured patient. Bond showed that the symptoms likely to cause family burden (personality change, mental symptoms, changes in family cohesion, etc.) were unrelated to PTA duration, unlike other changes in the patient (the presence of memory disability, the reduction in working capacity, etc.) which were related to severity.

Although the severity of injury may bear a tenuous relationship to the severity of family burden, a further variable does seem to be important in attempting predictions of family burden, and that is the pre-traumatic personality of the patient. The data are not available to enable unequivocal conclusions to be drawn here, but there are consistent suggestions that the patient who has shown evidence of personality abnormality before injury is more likely to show the kind of post-traumatic personality, emotional and behavioural disabilities that are recognized to be associated with family burden.

Currently, rehabilitation facilities for severely head-injured patients are often organized around the physical problems resulting from the injury, although recently this has started to change as the reports by Najenson's group in Israel, Diller's group in New York (Diller 1976; Diller and Gordon 1981), and the recent review by Rosenthal, Griffith. Bond and Miller (1983) suggest. The findings reviewed in this chapter suggest that rehabilitation services which concentrate solely on physical handicap in the patient are failing to meet the needs of the patient and his family, and rehabilitation services must now consider adopting the concept of 'the head-injured family' rather than solely the head-injured patient. Certainly when relatives are questioned about the facilities available, and the information given to them, they all too often report dissatisfaction. Whatever the reasons underlying this, it does suggest that the needs of the families are not being met.

The approach of Najenson to the rehabilitation of such patients is an interesting one. In Najenson's unit patients have access not only to the physiotherapy and other rehabilitations therapies, but also to intensive counselling, behaviour modification, and psychiatric advice. In the Diller service in New York, an attempt is being made in addition to carry out a precise psychological analysis of the deficits these patients have, and to use this analysis to construct individually tailored rehabilitation programmes aimed at measuring the extent and effects of the deficits of each patient.

This trend towards multidisciplinary approaches to the rehabilitation of the brain injured is welcome and encouraging. The use of behavioural, counselling, and other approaches in addition to conventional rehabilitation medicine, and physio-occupational and speech therapy will increase and should in time, and with careful evaluation, have a significant impact upon the problem of the brain-injured patient and family.

REFERENCES

Becker, D. P., Miller, J. D., Ward, J. D., Greenberg, R. P., Young, H. F., and Sakalas, R. (1977). The outcome from severe head injury with early diagnosis and intensive management. *J. Neurosurg.* 47, 491–502.

Bond, M. R. (1975). Assessment of the psychosocial outcome after severe head injury. In *Outcome of severe damage to the central nervous system*, CIBA Foundation Symposium 34, pp. 141–58. Elsevier, Amsterdam.

Brooks, D. N. (1979). Psychological deficits after severe blunt head injury: Their significance and rehabilitation. In *Research in psychology and medicine* (ed. D. J. Osborne, M. M. Gruneberg, and J. R. Eiser) Vol. II, pp. 469–766. Academic Press, London.

—— and Aughton, M. E. (1979). Psychological consequences of blunt head injury. *Int. rehabil. Med.*, 1, 160–5.

Brown, J. C. (1975). Late recovery from head injury: case report and review. *Psychol. Med.* 5, 239–48.

Carlsson, C. A., Von Essen, C., and Lofgren, J. (1968). Factors affecting the clinical course of patients with severe head injuries. *J. Neurosurg.* 29, 242–51.

Diller, L. (1976). A Model for retraining in rehabilitation. *Clin. Psychol.* 29, 13–15.

—— and Gordon, W. (1981). Interventions for cognitive deficits in brain-injured adults. *J. Consult. Clin. Psychol.* 49, 822–34.

Erculei, F. (1961). The socioeconomic rehabilitation of head-injured men. In *Social and economic rehabilitation: a follow-up study of head wounds in World War II* (ed. A. E. Walker, *et al.*) US Government Printing Office, Washington.

Fahy, T. J., Irving, M. H., and Millac, P. (1967). Severe head injuries: a six year follow-up. *Lancet* ii, 475–9.

Galbraith, S., Murray, W. R., Patel, A. R., and Knill-Jones, R. (1976). The relationship between alcohol and head injury and its effects on the conscious level. *B. J. Surg.* 63, 128–30.

Galasko, C. S. B., and Edwards, D. H. (1974). The causes of injuries requiring admission to hospital in the 1970s. *Injury* 6, 107–12.

Grad, J. and Sainsbury, P. (1963). Evaluating a community care service. In *Trends in the mental health services* (ed. H. Freeman and W. L. Farndale) pp. 303–17. Pergamon, London.

Groswasser, Z., Mendelson, L., Stern, M. J., Schechter, I., and Najenson, T. (1977). Re-evaluation of prognostic factors in rehabilitation after severe head injury. *Scand. J. rehabil. Med.* 9, 147.

Hoenig, G. J. and Hamilton, M. W. (1969). *Desegregation of the mentally ill.* Routledge and Kegan Paul, London.

Jamieson, K. G. (1971). Prevention of head injury. In *Head injuries: proceedings of an international symposium* pp. 12–15. Churchill Livingstone, Edinburgh.

Jennett, B. (1972). Late effects of head injuries. In *Scientific foundations of neurology* (ed. M. Critchley, B. Jennett, and J. O'Leary). Heinemann, London.

—— and Bond, M. (1975). Assessment of outcome after severe brain damage. *Lancet* **i**, 480–4.

Ley, P. (1977). Communicating with the patients. In *Introducing psychology* (ed. J. C. Colman) pp. 321–43. Routledge, London.

Lezak, M. (1978). Living with the characterologically altered brain-injured patient. *J. Clin. Psychiat.* **39**, 592–8.

——, Cosgrove, J. N., O'Brien, K., and Wooster, K. (1980). Relationship between personality disorders, social disturbances and physical disability following traumatic brain injury. Paper presented at *Eighth Annual Meeting of International Neuropsychological Society*, San Francisco. February, 1980.

London, P. S. (1967). Some observations on the course of events after severe injury of the head. *Ann. R. Coll. Surg. Eng.* **41**, 460–79.

McKinlay, W. W., Brooks, D. N., Bond, M. R., Martinage, D. P., and Marshall, M. M. (1981). The short-term outcome of severe blunt head injury as reported by the relatives of the injured person. *J. Neurol. Neurosurg. Psychiat.* **44**, 527–33.

Miller, H. and Stern, G. (1965). The long-term prognosis of severe head injury. *Lancet* **i**, 225–9.

Najenson, T., Mendelson, L., Schechter, I., David, C., Mintz, N., and Groswasser, Z. (1974). Rehabilitation after severe head injury. *Scand. J. rehabil. Med.* **6**, 5–14.

Oddy, M. and Humphrey, M. (1980). Social recovery during the year following severe head injury. *J. Neurol. Neurosurg. Psychiat.* **43**, 798–802.

——, ——, and Uttley, D. (1978*a*). Subjective impairment and social recovery after closed head injury. *J. Neurol. Neurosurg. Psychiat.* **41**, 611–16.

——, ——, —— (1978*b*). Stresses upon the relatives of head-injured patients. *Br. J. Psychiat.* **133**, 507–13.

Panting, A. and Merry, P. (1972). The long-term rehabilitation of severe head injuries with particular reference to the need for social and medical support for the patient's family. *Rehabilitation* **38**, 33–7.

Potter, J. M. (1967). Head injuries today. *Postgrad. Med. J.* **43**, 574–81.

Romano, M. D. (1974). Family response to traumatic head injury. *Scand. J. rehabil. Med.* **6**, 1–4.

Rosenbaum, M. and Najenson, T. (1976). Changes in life patterns and symptoms of low mood as reported by wives of severely brain-injured soldiers. *J. Consult. Clin. Psychol.* **44**, 881–8.

Rosenthal, M., Griffith, E. R., Bond, M. R., and Miller, J. D. (eds.) (1983). *Rehabilitation of the head injured adult.* F. A. Davis, Philadelphia.

Teasdale, G. and Jennett, B. (1974). Assessment of coma and impaired consciousness. *Lancet* **ii**, 81–4.

Thomsen, I. V. (1974). The patient with severe head injury and his family. *Scand. J. rehabil. Med.* **6**, 180–3.

——, (1981). Neuropsychological treatment and longtime follow-up in an aphasic patient with very severe head trauma. *J. Clin. Neuropsychol.* **3**, 43–51.

Vapalahiti, M. and Troupp, H. (1971). Prognosis for patients with severe brain injuries. *Br. Med. J.* **iii**, 404–7.

Weddell, R., Oddy, M., and Jenkins, D. (1980). Social adjustment after rehabilitation: a 2-year follow-up of patients with severe head injury. *Psychol. Med.* **10**, 257–63.

8 The psychiatry of closed head injury

Michael Bond

TRAUMATIC BRAIN INJURY AND MENTAL DISORDER

The majority of head injuries in civilian life are caused by abrupt acceleration or deceleration of the head, chiefly as a result of motor vehicle accidents, but also following falls, assaults, and sports' injuries (Field 1976). They may or may not be associated with skull fractures, and/or haematoma formation within the cranium. It is known that all injuries produce structural damage and in those that are severe it is widespread with foci of destruction at the area of impact and contrecoup sites. The most consistent damage occurs in the sub-frontal and anterior temporal regions of the cortex and, in the very severely injured, structural damage in the mid-brain is common. Therefore, whatever their precise nature, the mental consequences of injury depend upon a mixture of general and focal injuries in proportions that must vary considerably from person to person. In a general way the amount of brain damaged or lost is related to the mental consequences in so far as it has been shown that the greater the volume of brain tissue lost the more severe will be the mental consequences; but it is also true that certain focal lesions cause devastating effects (Lishman 1968). The results of brain injury are likely to consist of mental changes directly attributable to damage or destruction of brain tissue, especially when injuries are severe, and emotional reactions to the personal and social consequences of them. The certain primary consequences of injury are to cognition (discussed elsewhere), perception, personality, and behaviour, but whether or not they produce symptoms more often attributable to major mental illnesses (depression, mania, or schizophrenia) is less certain and remains a subject for debate (Davidson and Bagley 1969). The secondary reactions of the injured cover the spectrum of responses to stress seen in all other injured, sick or emotionally stressed people but, in addition, brain injuries appear to produce their own specific constellations of symptoms, for example as in the case of symptoms of the post-concussional syndrome.

Brain injuries are most common in youth and old age, and age is a significant factor in determining the mental outcome of injury. On the one hand, injury amongst the young occurs in individuals actively developing mentally, physically and socially, and, on the other, in the elderly who are in the phase of life in which mental faculties begin to decline and for whom structural brain damage has a disproportionately large effect, often producing dementia after an injury which would have produced less severe changes in younger individuals with greater intellectual reserves. In other words, the effects of injury depend to a certain extent upon whether the brain is still developing, has reached maturity, or is undergoing senescence.

Post-traumatic epilepsy is a possible consequence of injury with implications for the victim's mental state and the conditions for its development have been described very clearly by Jennett (1975). It is a relatively simple matter to detect typical major seizures but temporal lobe seizures which do not culminate in classical grand mal motor activity, the so-called psychomotor fits, have several forms, described later, which may present as unusual and unrecognized mental symptoms and behavioural patterns. The subtle alterations in emotion and behaviour caused may go unnoticed by the inexperienced clinician for weeks or months, often with an associated period of great difficulty for the family and inappropriate management for the patient.

The changes mentioned do not appear in a random manner. In fact, one of the significant advances in head-injury research in recent years has been to demonstrate the natural history of the physical, mental, and social consequences of injuries at all levels of severity (Bond and Brooks 1976; Bond 1979). Therefore, it is important to consider the time-scale of events in recovery in order to present both a reasonable prognosis to patients and relations and to anticipate the likely changes that lie ahead for those devising programmes of rehabilitation. This area of investigation remains active but sufficient is known of it to enable clinicians, psychologists, and therapists from other professions to design programmes of rehabilitation and to assess their impact—although the latter step has received very little scientific attention to date.

The social aspects of the mental problems of the brain-injured form the substance of other chapters in this book and the nature of the burdens placed upon families and the way in which the victim's relatives react to them are described. These are what might be called the tertiary consequences of injury. Therefore, it is sufficient to mention that the social status of the family, their pre-traumatic relations to the patient, and their resources for coping with the burdens of care are a vital matter when considering the management of recovery from the time injury occurs. This issue raises the question of the patient's own pre-morbid mental qualities and social behaviour because it is known that in several ways the brain-injured have distinct personal and social characteristics which seem to predispose them to injury (Jamieson and Kelly 1973). Whether or not it is related to pre-morbid personal qualities, to circumstances of injury, or some combination of both is not certain, but it is clear that the presence of an impending or actual claim for compensation may have a profound effect upon the injured person, even to the extent of producing severe emotional reactions which collectively form the post-traumatic syndrome, or post-traumatic neurosis. The syndrome is said to be primarily a consequence of milder injuries, though recent evidence indicates that this is not entirely true (McKinlay, Brooks, and Bond 1983).

To conclude, the mental consequences of injury depend upon several factors both personal and social summarized in Table 8.1, and they form the basis of discussion in the remainder of this chapter.

Table 8.1 *Factors which significantly influence the psychiatric consequences of severe brain injury*

Pre-traumatic factors:
  1. Personality and social competence.
  2. Personal and family material resources.

Factors relating directly to brain trauma:
  1. Age: the state of cerebral maturity or decay.
  2. Extent of injury and sites of major areas of damage. The nature of primary deficits in cognition, personality, and behaviour determined by site and severity.
  3. Epilepsy. If psychomotor is of major psychiatric significance.
  4. Secondary emotional reactions to primary physical and mental deficits.

Social factors:
  1. Post-traumatic interpersonal relations with family and friends.
  2. Post-traumatic social resources.
  3. Presence or absence of proceedings for compensation.

THE PREDISPOSITION AND CHARACTER

This topic raises three questions. First, to what extent does an individual's age, sex, and social milieu contribute to his or her predisposition to injury? Next, to what extent do the victim's pre-traumatic personal, mental, and behavioural characteristics determine predisposition to injury and, last, to what extent and in what ways do an individual's pre-traumatic intellectual and emotional constitution contribute to the primary and secondary mental consequences of injury?

The majority of head injuries are the results of accidents and those involving motor vehicles account for 50 per cent or more of the total in most published series, predominating over those occurring at work, in the home or as a result of participation in sport. In Britain assaults account for fewer injuries than accidents, other than those due to sports accidents. The majority of the injured are males who outnumber injured females in a ratio of up to five to one, with more than 50 per cent of individuals admitted to hospital being under 20 years of age (Field 1976). Cartlidge and Shaw (1981) noted that males of all ages are at increased risk except at the extremes of life where differences are marginal. Thus, being male and under 25 carries with it the greatest risk of brain injury. Moreover, it is clear that males are more likely than females to be engaged in potentially dangerous work, 'contact sports', and to drink heavily, suggesting that cultural and social characteristics increase the risk of injury in younger men. Greater levels of physical risk-taking amongst boys between 5 and 10 years of age are associated with a higher incidence of injury than girls of the same age. There are a number of sub-cultural factors which increase the risks of head injuries amongst young males. For example, excessive heavy drinking, 'primarily a cultural phenomenon' is widespread amongst young men in the West of Scotland and is closely related to injury caused by most motor accidents and assaults, especially those occurring in the lower socio-economic groups. In Australia, high-speed car driving after drinking is a frequent cause of accidents which result in serious injuries, deaths, or both amongst adolescents and young men. In both groups, it is clear that levels of criminal and civil prosecution are likely to be high and there is some evidence that young men who sustain head injuries have had more encounters with the law than others (Jamieson and Kelly 1973). A degree of immaturity of personality and behaviour is implicit in the comments made so far. However, there is no clear evidence that other specific personality characteristics can be linked to a predisposition to injury. Therefore, it would seem that the youthful and common characteristics of impulsivity and aggressiveness in men, together with a liability to take risks in a social setting which encourages such tendencies, and high levels of alcohol consumption provides a most fertile setting for brain injury. These facts lie behind the peak incidence of brain injury which occurs between 15 and 25 years.

ALTERED CONSCIOUSNESS: EARLY OUTCOME OF BRAIN DAMAGE

The broad details of the stages of recovery from severe head injury and their relation to the duration of PTA are given in Table 8.2. In stage one patients are in coma; therefore comments will be directed only towards the second and third stages (Bond 1979). Ninety-eight per cent of patients with severe injuries in Glasgow studies have PTA exceeding 2 days and in 50 per cent it exceeds 1 month (Bond 1975). During PTA, that is before full memory for day-to-day events and orientation return, one of several patterns of disturbed mental function may be observed as a patient emerges from coma. All are marked by disorientation for time, place, and perhaps person; by cognitive, perceptual, mood, and behavioural changes; and by a number of phenomena which may or may not be present. These include delusions, particularly of the paranoid type, and less often illusions or visual hallucinations.

Table 8.2 *Recovery from severe head injury*

Average duration	Neurological state	Mental state	Management priorities
Days	*Stage 1* Intense physical reactions to injury in brain Maximum neurological deficit	Unconscious	Intensive physical care
2A: 3 months	*Stage 2* Physical reaction to injury slow	Organization of mental events serving full consciousness	Continued physical care and rehabilitation
2B: 6 months	Continued recovery of processes basic to physical recovery	Full consciousness achieved. Continued rapid recovery of processes basic to higher mental functions	Introduction* of psychological and social methods of rehabilitation
3–6 months	*Stage 3* Level of physical disability established Further recovery slight and rate of recovery slow	Levels of mental disability established Further recovery occurs and is enhanced or diminished	Psychological and social rehabilitation

* Speculative

The most common pattern of mental disturbance during PTA is characterized by disorientation, impaired attention, failure of memory for day-to-day events, illusions, misidentification of the family, friends, and medical and nursing staff, perplexity and periods of restlessness during which attempts may be made to remove bandages, intravenous infusions and other pieces of equipment attached to the body. The form of this state of traumatic delirium tends to change only gradually but the content, or observed mental phenomena, vary a good deal from hour to hour and day to day. If the patient is able to walk, he or she may wander from the ward and increased periods of sleep or somnolence are quite common.

A small number of patients have marked irritability and aggressiveness which is evident almost as soon as they emerge from the deeper levels of coma, for example:

A 40-year-old labourer, suffered a severe head injury with a fracture of the frontal bones and associated frontal- and temporal-lobe contusions beneath subdural haematomas which were removed surgically. After operation he remained in coma for several days and on recovery did not appear to have any neurological deficits. However, he was noted to be extremely restless, irritable, and noisy. He attempted to climb out of bed frequently and caused considerable damage to the fittings in his room. At a slightly later stage in his recovery, when he was able to stand, and whilst still in a confused and disorientated state, he pulled a wash basin and its taps from the wall. Although heavily sedated he caused great alarm to the staff because they feared the consequences of his physical aggressiveness.

A second patient, a 20-year-old unmarried woman, became so aggressive during the first month of recovery from an injury which caused bilateral fronto-temporal damage, netting had to be placed across the top of her bed forming a cage in which, if disturbed, she would scream and scratch and bite if she was able to catch the arm or hand of an attendant nurse or doctor. As in the previous case she was free from neurological deficits and in both cases confusion and aggressiveness persisted for many weeks though eventually it became much less marked. At a later stage each patient showed disinhibition, fatuousness, and significant cognitive impairment.

By contrast with predominantly noisy, aggressive patients, some remain very quiet though confused, showing only occasional periods of restlessness. Their PTA is lengthy and its end is difficult to determine because often the patient has a marked residual disorder of cognition, including memory, lacks spontaneity and shows apathy, perhaps with mild disinhibition or euphoria. In such cases the patient has progressed from coma through a period of disorientation to a state marked by profound cognitive deficits and some personality change; in other words to a state of dementia. Prolonged incontinence is also a feature of the disorder suggesting that injury to the medial frontal area has occurred because this is one of the centres for the control of micturition; similar mental changes are seen in patients who have had a subarachnoid haemorrhage and undergone surgery for occlusion of an anterior communicating artery aneurysm.

The third and less common group of phenomena is represented by the presence of hallucinations or delusions, as illustrated by the following brief case histories.

A middle-aged business man sustained severe head injury in a road traffic accident as a result of which he was not left with any form of neurological disability but had a fracture of bones in the lower part of one leg. His period of PTA lasted approximately three weeks. During this period he developed complex hallucinations which convinced him that he was at a ski resort which he had previously visited. This stage persisted for about two weeks throughout which the patient remained quite calm though at times perplexed. Eventually he made a good recovery without a change of personality and only mild loss of intellectual function.

A second patient, an ex-sea-captain, also had hallucinations and he was convinced he was at sea on board ship and behaved accordingly by giving orders to various men he could see standing around. In both cases it was decided not to give medicines as the patients were not distressed or distressing and both recovered in approximately two to three weeks from their 'occupational delirium'. It should be noted that neither men had a history of alcoholism, a condition in which occupational delirium may occur at the time of sudden cessation of alcohol intake.

The third patient, a 30-year-old married woman, underwent surgery for the removal of a haematoma which had formed in the posterior fossa of her skull following a head injury. After surgery intracranial pressure monitoring was carried out for several days. The patient recovered consciousness within 24 hours. At first she was quiet though confused, but two days later became convinced that her thoughts were being read via the intraventricular catheter and that the information was being taken down in the ward sister's office, although she did not know why this should be necessary. She felt that she was at the centre of a conspiracy and that her mind and brain would be taken over and eventually removed from her head. Treatment with a very small dose of thioridazine (Melleril) (25 mg three times daily) was associated with the disappearance of the symptoms within 36 hours and they did not return. The patient remained in good health thereafter.

The three cases described all began during the period when each patient was in the period of PTA and experiencing disturbances of orientation, memory, and perception. The first two cases resolved spontaneously with complete recovery of consciousness and the third ended shortly after the prescription of a neuroleptic drug. This was given for only six to seven days after which full consciousness was restored and the symptoms did not return.

Prolonged states of disturbed consciousness in children may be brought to an abrupt end by discharging them home to familiar surroundings, as the following example shows.

A 10-year-old boy, suffered a severe head injury which resulted in residual hemiparesis and a period of disordered consciousness for several weeks. Towards the end of this period he was very irritable, confused, and, on occasions, was observed to bite his hand or arm. His parents were alarmed by his failure to regain full consciousness and were convinced that he would improve more rapidly at home. With some reluctance he was discharged and within 48 hours was behaving normally, he was no longer confused, and his irritability had lessened. At a later date when asked why he had bitten his hands and arms, he replied that at the time he had felt he was in a dream and wanted to see if he could waken himself from it.

Other examples of the rapid restoration of full consciousness have been observed in young children and a parallel to this may be drawn from the effects of transferring patients with prolonged confusion from intensive care units to general wards where the cues which promote orientation are far stronger and more numerous and lead quickly to a disappearance of the disturbance in many cases.

To conclude, injury to the brain leads to several patterns of disturbed mental function but initially all are preceded by disorientation and disturbances of cognitive and perceptual function which appear to be the basis for the generation of disorders of perception, perhaps with the production of hallucinations and/or delusional systems. The reason why there should be so much individual variation is not known.

THE RE-ESTABLISHMENT OF CONSCIOUSNESS: THE FIRST 2 YEARS

Investigations of the outcome of injury for patients have been based upon the net effects of the several deficits sustained; in other words, they give a picture of the overall or global outcome which has also been measured in terms of specific features in the three main areas of physical, mental, and social handicap. Comment upon global outcome is merited here because it will give the reader a general view of the levels of overall disability that occur in populations of the brain injured, of the balance of deficits contributing to overall handicap and the changes in handicap with time prior to

Table 8.3 *The Glasgow outcome scale in its original form and in extended and contracted forms*

Extended scale	Original scale	Contracted scale			
Dead	Dead	Dead	Dead or vegetative	Dead or vegetative	Dead
Vegetative	Vegetative	Dependent	Severely disabled	Conscious	Survivors
Degree of disability: 5	Severely disabled	Dependent	Severely disabled	Conscious	Survivors
4				Conscious	
3	Moderately disabled	Independent	Independent		
2		Independent	Independent		
1	Good recovery				
0					
Total categories 8	5	3		2	

a consideration of specific primary and secondary deficits or problems.

Results will be reported in terms of assessment by means of the Glasgow Outcome Scale (GOS) (Table 8.3), which is currently widely used in Europe and the United States (Jennett and Bond 1975). It is a measure of an individual's dependency and has the virtue of ease of use, good inter-rater reliability and, because its categories can be extended or collapsed, there is some flexibility in its sensitivity although, by comparison with scales designed to assess individual deficits, it is necessarily a coarser method of measurement.

Studies in Glasgow (Jennett, Snoek, Bond, and Brooks 1981) have shown that more than 90 per cent of patients reach their final level of disability within 6 months of injury (Table 8.4). Jennett and his colleagues (1981) also observed that of 82 patients who had severe head injuries and were followed up over 18 months, only 5 per cent improved sufficiently after 12 months to reach a better category of recovery. They also noted that it was exceptional for a person who is severely disabled at three months after the injury ever to reach the category of good recovery.

Table 8.4   *Attainment of final outcome category*

Outcome 1 year after injury	No. of patients	Already in this category by (%): 3 months	6 months
Moderate disability	118	62	92
Good recovery	236	69	90

If examined in more detail, their results reveal that only a quarter of their patients were free from neurological deficits although in many cases such deficits were not severe. They were most common amongst those who had had an intracranial haematoma—a condition which has a very high correlation with focal neurological deficits during recovery. In addition, the time taken for establishment of the pattern of deficits due to neurological damage was in keeping with the figures quoted above for the time taken to reach final levels of overall disability. The number of patients with physical and mental deficits (cognitive and personality change), although sometimes mild, was high; they were present in 97 per cent of the 150 patients in the study. Two-thirds had a change in personality. However, mild changes in personality or cognitive function, although present in approximately 60 per cent of the patients, were compatible with a good outcome (Table 8.5).

From the table it is clear that the majority of patients with moderate

Table 8.5 *Frequency of deficits in each outcome category**

		Good recovery (n = 29)	Moderate disability (n = 23)	Severe disability (n = 9)
Physical	Mild	29	23	6
(as a whole)	Severe	0	0	2
Personality	Mild	12	15	1
	Severe	0	3	7
Cognitive	Mild	29	21	2
(as a whole)	Severe	0	2	7
Verbal IQ	Mild	3	9	2
	Severe	0	0	4
Performance	Mild	13	13	1
IQ	Severe	0	1	8
Verbal	Mild	11	12	1
Memory	Severe	1	5	8
Non-verbal	Mild	16	11	2
memory	Severe	0	5	7

*This table refers to 61 of the 150 patients in the study. From Jennett, *et al.* (1981).

disability had mild changes in mental function but amongst the severely disabled most had marked alterations in either personality, cognitive function or both. Marked changes in personality are virtually always associated with a cognitive impairment but the converse is found less often. Despite numerical prominence of physical over mental handicaps in this series, it is well known that emotional consequences of injury provoke far greater difficulties for patients and their relatives than do physical ones. (Thomsen 1974; Bond 1975; Oddy, Humphrey, and Uttley 1978; Brooks and Aughton 1979; McKinlay *et al.* 1981).

Of the cognitive deficits reported, disorders of learning and memory and of performance intelligence seemed to be the most persistent and most disabling. Changes in personality marked by aggression, irresponsibility, childishness, and inconsiderate behaviour produce significant burdens upon the relatives (McKinley, *et al.* 1981) but if coupled with lack of insight leave the patient relatively unmoved.

The relation of the initial severity of injury to outcome whether measured in terms of coma duration using the Glasgow Coma Scale (Teasdale and Jennett 1974), or the duration of PTA (Newcombe and Fortuny 1979; Levin, O'Donnell, and Crossman 1979), is at its highest within three months of injury and falls thereafter until by one year from injury there is only a small degree of correlation between the two forms of measurement in most respects. However, there are several factors which relate the initial severity of injury to its long-term consequences. First, those who are very severely injured and in prolonged coma from which they eventually regain consciousness (after three months or more) will have permanent serious deficits of mental and physical nature with associated impairment of social functioning (Mandleberg and Brooks 1974). Second, the duration of PTA, which is closely related to the function of memory and orientation, bears a firm relation to later memory capacity. Last, relatively short periods of loss of consciousness (up to 2 weeks) followed by several weeks of confusion may be associated with marked alterations of personality in adults. Thus there are relatively few clues in the very early stages of recovery that relate to later difficulties and especially the social capacity of the injured person. Certain basic deficits of personality and intellect do become obvious at an early stage but, especially if mild to moderate and where elements of pretraumatic personality are well preserved, the individual's reaction to injury and ability to cope make for the considerable differences observed between those who have had injuries of comparable severity and who have similar primary mental and physical deficits.

THE RE-ESTABLISHMENT OF CONSCIOUSNESS: SPECIFIC FEATURES

The end of the period of PTA marks the restoration of full memory for day-to-day events and of orientation. It marks the beginning of the second half of the second stage of recovery also (see Table 8.2), but not the end of the period of rapid improvement of basic neurological and mental functions which is reached sometime within 6–12 months of injury. Once full consciousness has been restored, the nature of the patient's mental state changes with the emergence of the main features of future disabilities, reactions to them, and certain specific but transient mental disorders. As primary deficits of intellect, perception, and personality appear they are coloured by the development of adaptive and/or maladaptive behaviours. The latter incorporate and are shaped in part by pre-traumatic personality characteristics and coping behaviour, and by external pressures due to a combination of personal, family, and social interactions.

Certain general features are common to most patients in this phase of recovery including gradual restoration of normal sleep patterns, reduction of fatigue to a variable extent, and some improvement of attention and concentration. Speed of mental activity increases but seldom to pre-traumatic levels and remains as one of the major basic cognitive handicaps of almost all patients, the other being impairment of memory which tends to improve a little with time. In association with the cognitive changes mentioned some patients also show high levels of orderliness in thinking and daily activity, resembling the symptoms of psychiatric patients with obsessional neurosis;

this is known as 'organic orderliness'. It is said that the development of this pattern of behaviour arises out of a need to retain a sense of control over thinking and events which seems a reasonable view bearing in mind the patient's imperfections of perception and cognition, his mental slowness and the anxiety generated by uncertainty and reflected in lack of confidence. Changes of mood also show certain similarities in many patients during their recovery. Of these, the most noticeable are increases in irritability and impatience with lowered tolerance for frustration and an increased likelihood of outbursts of temper. In association with this change suspiciousness and even paranoid delusions may develop. Levels of anxiety tend to rise, and depression of mood fluctuates, perhaps in association with periodic insight into the significance of residual disabilities. Insight usually alternates with periods of denial of disability in many patients — a process which is often shared with their relatives and which represents the operation of a mental defence mechanism designed to abolish anxiety about matters which are potentially overwhelming emotionally.

These general potential changes have been grouped by Lezak (1978a):

1. *An impaired capacity for social perceptiveness* in which former powers of self-criticism are diminished or lost with associated development of egocentricity and loss of empathy.

2. *Impaired capacity for control and self-regulation* producing impatience, impulsivity and restlessness.

3. *Stimulus-bound behaviour* which implies loss of personal ability to initiate and plan activities of daily life with a consequent increase in dependency.

4. *Emotional change* — The common changes possible include silliness, irritability, lability, apathy, and increase, decrease, or absence of sexual drive.

5. *Inability to learn from social experience* meaning relative or incomplete ability to learn from social experience leading to conceptual and behavioural rigidity which, in their turn, lead to difficulties of the type in categories 2 and 3.

Although stated earlier, it is worth repeating that the greater part of all forms of primary disability are established as early as six months after injury in adults. However, improvements do occur until much later, especially in personality and behaviour, but for the most part improvements represent patients' adaptation to their primary deficits and development of techniques for overcoming, in part, lost abilities.

AFFECTIVE DISORDERS

Apart from the general changes described, a number of specific mental syndromes emerge during this period of recovery. First, at a very early stage and often around the time at which the period of PTA ends, a state of hypomania, or 'organic excitement', may make a brief appearance. Second, also at a comparable stage in recovery, a state marked by the appearance of paranoid delusions may develop. Third, disorders of behaviour marked by sustained, or periodic, high levels of aggressiveness make their appearance and seem to originate either as a result of a significant lowering of a person's ability to control aggressiveness, or primary changes in the brain producing epilepsy. Fourth, various symptom combinations which form the frontal lobe syndrome may appear heralding a permanent and fundamental change in the mental state. Finally, if cognitive and personality changes are very great a second and permanent, severe state of mental disability, dementia, becomes evident.

The origins of the state of organic excitement or hypomania are uncertain. In the author's experience its development always occurs in patients emerging from PTA, or when a secondary organic lesion develops; perhaps undetected at first. The following case histories illustrate these points.

A 65-year-old man developed a subdural haematoma in the left parietal region after a fall. The haematoma was removed surgically and the patient regained full consciousness within 36 hours. As he did so, he became increasingly restless and developed pressure of talk though dysphasic. He had grandiose delusions and was disinhibited. In addition, he exhibited what appeared to be flights of ideas. He was treated with a phenothiazine and the disorder subsided over a period of 3–4 days. There was no history of previous mental illness and the condition did not recur. This patient's history indicates an association of hypomania with recent traumatic brain injury, but other cases show that the disorder may occur as a result of cerebral damage caused by other lesions.

A 50-year-old man developed hypomania after an attack of status epilepticus. Ten years prior to this episode he had had surgical treatment for an intracerebral abscess in the left temporo-parietal area and shortly afterwards developed epilepsy. This was successfully controlled with phenobarbitone for many years and, as a result, the man was able to work in a professional capacity. Within 6 months of his first attack of hypomania and without evidence of further epilepsy, he again developed hypomania and within 24 hours had become manic. His mental state and behaviour were marked by considerable disinhibition and aggressiveness and, as a result, he was admitted to hospital where he was successfully treated with haloperidol. Six months later, having discontinued treatment with this drug, a further attack of mania occurred (again in the absence of epilepsy) and control was gained as before with haloperidol and then maintained successfully thereafter for several years with lithium. As in the case of the previous patient, this patient did not have a personal or family history of mental illness.

Finally, a 22-year-old nurse suffered a closed head injury with greatest damage to the left hemisphere. She also sustained severe fractures of the pelvis and lower limbs. Six months after discharge from hospital and almost a year after injury, she returned to work where it was noticed that her personality had changed and her intellectual powers were diminished. Whereas previously she had been a pleasant, reliable, and hard-working girl, she had become irresponsible and lacking in volition and judgement. She could not cope with nursing responsibilities except at a very low level and she failed her nursing examinations. Shortly after her academic failure an episode occurred in which she claimed she was sexually assaulted. About that time, she became overactive, over-talkative, over-familiar, and inconsiderate in her habits. She dressed in bright clothes and began to wear heavy make-up. Her need for sleep lessened dramatically and she played pop music loudly well into the night, disturbing and annoying her family and neighbours. She was admitted to hospital and it was clear she was hypomanic. Treatment with haloperidol brought a marked improvement. Three months later the patient had become very subdued, lacked spontaneity, seemed confused, and was declared depressed. She was admitted to hospital where neurological examination revealed drowsiness, disorientation, and papilloedema. In fact, she had evidence of an intracranial lesion and proved to have a chronic subdural haematoma which was removed by surgical drainage. On recovery she again became hypomanic but after treatment with haloperidol her symptoms disappeared and several years later, although not having had treatment for a considerable time, she was free from symptoms of this disorder but had returned to the impaired emotional and cognitive state that preceded her hypomanic symptoms.

The three patients described had two factors in common; all had evidence of disturbances of emotions related to brain trauma with lesions involving the left hemisphere. Only one developed a persistent mental disorder and none developed depression. Prior to her attack of hypomania the young nurse's personality had been marked by fascile behaviour and mild disinhibition, whereas, in contrast, the man who had a brain abscess had been a rather irritable and querulous man. An association between affective and other forms of psychoses in a series of 50 patients with epilepsy was described by Flor-Henry (1969) and of the group nine were diagnosed as manic–depressive. Interestingly, and unlike the patient reported here, the author demonstrated that patients in his sub-group had foci which were mostly in the non-dominant hemisphere, and that fits were relatively infrequent and usually grand mal rather than psychomotor in type. Gregoriades, Fragos, Kapslakis, and Mandouvalos (1971) made similar observations regarding lateralization of foci in patients with affective disorders. Both authors reported that most patients with schizophrenia and paranoid disorders also had foci in their dominant hemispheres. Finally, it is interesting that whether hypomanic or manic both patients described in this test had premorbid personality characteristics which were the dominating features of their disturbed mental states.

The association of major psychiatric disorders with brain damage has been the subject of several studies and those dealing with schizophrenic and schizophreniform psychoses are mentioned later (see p. 163). The development of depressive psychoses after brain injury was reviewed by Lishman (1978) who concluded that affective disorders occur after injuries of all severity and may be marked after minor ones. Achté, Hillbom, and Aalberg (1967) reported that depression is more common than mania but did not draw distinction between the features of the immediate post-traumatic state in which consciousness may be disordered and later phases of recovery. Experience suggests that feelings of depression are common, usually transient and occur from 3–6 months onwards after severe head injuries. Almost always they are related to growing awareness of the physical, mental, and social consequences of injury. Early violent fluctuations of mood are sustained in only a small number of patients and there is a strong suspicion that in such patients sudden mood changes are organically determined, representing the loss of mood control mechanisms. By contrast with depression, hypomania appears to be more common in the early stages of recovery, especially about the time patients are in the final stages of PTA when the integration of information by the brain has reached an advanced level but is not complete. Interestingly, there are similarites between the state of hypomania and certain aspects of the 'frontal syndrome' described later; the most obvious are disinhibition with loss of social control. Variable levels of preservation of insight and/or a magnification of premorbid characteristics occurs in some cases. The latter is not, however, an invariable development as demonstrated in the case of the young woman described earlier (see p. 160).

The second of the major transient post-traumatic syndromes that occurs late in PTA and, or, early in the newly acquired phase of full consciousness centres upon the presence of paranoid ideas or frank delusions. They are common during disturbed consciousness and almost always seem to originate during that phase of recovery, usually being preceded by a delusional mood marked by intense suspicions of the actions and motives of others. 40 years ago Cameron (1941) explained this development as the product of a person's inability to construct an intelligible whole out of his fragmented experience. Add to this the effects of illusions and/or hallucinations which fuel the patient's anxiety and enhance perceptual and ideational distortion, and it is easy to see how feelings of fear and suspicion become projected to the environment leading to the development of a paranoid state (Lipowski 1967). It is of interest to note that such states, which Lishman (1978) regarded as one of several forms of acute post-traumatic psychosis, are more often reported after moderate and severe injuries than after mild injuries. However, they do occur as a result of minor trauma when the injured person's period of PTA is less than 24 hours in duration suggesting that perhaps the ease with which individuals develop paranoid delusions in association with disturbed consciousness due to traumatic injury varies, presumably as result of differences in constitutional susceptibility. Similar observations have been made amongst those developing disturbances of consciousness or delirium as a result of alteration in brain functions and secondary to metabolic disorders.

The following case histories illustrate these points in relation to head injury.

A 40-year-old man was assaulted and sustained a severe brain injury primarily involving his left cerebral hemisphere, producing a weakness of his right arm and leg and dysphasia. Within 48 hours of injury and in a state of agitation and irritability, he discharged himself from hospital although his period of PTA was eventually determined as two to three weeks in duration. During this period, he was subject to terrifying nightmares, developed attacts of acute anxiety, and features of paranoid state. For example, on one occasion he accused his solicitor of wrongly spending his money. However, he did not appear to develop an extensive and elaborate delusional system. Elements of this state persisted beyond the end of PTA probably being reinforced and maintained by his marked loss of memory, high levels of anxiety, and language difficulties which may also have involved some reduction in his comprehension. Although he was severely disabled the patient's levels of anxiety gradually decreased and his paranoid state disappeared. His speech improved, his self-confidence returned to some extent but his memory remained poor and he was impotent.

A young man of 20 struck his head forcibly against a goalpost during a game of football and was unconscious for several minutes. His period of PTA was judged to be approximately six hours. It was noticed that within 24 hours he would not leave his home because he felt he would be watched but did not know why. In other words, a delusional mood state had developed. Within a matter of days he had become very anxious and was convinced that his house was being watched and would only leave it if accompanied by his father. On one occasion he was taken to visit his workmates in the hope that he would be able to accept his beliefs were untrue but he felt acutely distressed as he believed they were talking about him out of his hearing, laughing at him, and watching every movement he made. He also believed they were involved in plans to keep a watch on his home. Eventually, after several weeks during which his anxieties and delusions strengthened and became more systematized, he was seen by a psychiatrist who treated him with a phenothiazine. Within 2 weeks his delusional system had weakened and all trace of it had disappeared within a month of commencement of treatment, with the duration of his symptoms having been about 3 months in total.

Lishman (1979) comments that ideas of persecution and marital infidelity figure prominently in post-traumatic paranoid states which he links to dementia or personality disturbance. He also quotes Achté *et al.* (1967) who detected frank paranoid psychoses in 2.1 per cent of a large group of brain-injured men (3552) injured in the Second World War. However, the authors were referring to disorders which developed many years after injury in individuals who had evidence of premorbid instability and serious difficulties in their lives, especially marital conflicts. The latter were related to conspicuous jealousy which was present in half the cases and a quarter of the men were impotent. Clearly the psychoses were not directly linked to brain injury but arose much later, though it was presumed that the consequences of brain injuries in terms of their effects upon personality and thus upon interpersonal relations were linked to the late paranoid development. Reports dealing with the contribution made by brain injury to psychotic states, (Feuchtwanger and Mayer-Gross 1938; Hillbom 1951 and Achté *et al.* 1967; Achté, Hillbom, and Aalberg 1969) produced evidence that the incidence of schizophrenia, including paranoid schizophrenia, is above the expected incidence of 1 per cent of the general population. Achté *et al.*

(1967, 1969) quote 2.6 per cent for psychoses resembling schizophrenia, but only 0.4 per cent for frank schizophrenia. Thus separation was drawn by these authors between schizophreniform states of the type frequently seen early after injury and 'process' schizophrenia. Davidson and Bagley (1969) drew all available evidence together and concluded that the incidence of schizophrenic-like psychoses is above the expectation for the population as a whole and that trauma is a direct precipitating factor. They found that genetic and constitutional factors were less important than amongst patients who develop naturally occurring schizophrenia and that the psychoses were related to the severity of diffuse brain injury with evidence suggesting that temporal lobes may well be the origin of the abnormal mental state. However, bearing in mind the almost universal involvement of the fronto-temporal regions in severe injuries, it is clear that there is an ample organic basis for the development of the psychosis but the proportion of patients who do so is very small therefore some other factor must be involved and constitutional ones are those most likely.

The third and last of the acute transient post-traumatic mental disturbances concerns the development of marked aggressive behaviour. As stated, restless irritability is a common feature of the early phase of recovery preceding the return of full consciousness and, in some, very aggressive and violent behaviour occurs (see cases already described). Even at that stage, premorbid personality characteristics may be acting as a basis for aggression and the reduction of self-control caused by injury releases such pre-existing tendencies. Aggressiveness continues beyond and into full consciousness although it tends to lessen in time in most patients, presumably as ability to control emotions returns during the first year after injury. However, some loss of self-control may exist for many months or even years acting as a source of considerable difficulty for the patient and his family. Patients discharged from hospital within 6 months of injury may take alcohol with alarming results if violence and aggressiveness are released by relatively trivial provocation. Moreover, the amount of alcohol needed to produce this effect may be quite small and substantially less than the amount the individual was in the habit of consuming before his injury. In other words, a lowered tolerance for alcohol combined with lowered control of aggressiveness makes an extremely dangerous combination. Episodes of marked aggressiveness or rage perhaps associated with violence to others may be related to medial temporal lobe dysfunction. Between attacks the individual concerned usually behaves normally except that as the day of the attack approaches, increased restlessness and irritability appear. This form of temporal lobe epilepsy may go unnoticed, especially if the patient was formerly aggressive and remains irritable between attacks. However, treatment with specific anticonvulsants (e.g. Tegretol (carbamazepine) not only prevents further episodes developing but often leads to a general reduction in irritability.

The following history illustrates the nature of periodic aggressiveness associated with a temporal lobe abnormality.

A 36-year-old married woman schoolteacher was severely injured in a road traffic accident which left her with diplopia, a mild right-sided hemipareisis, and minimal dysphasia. She also suffered some cognitive impairment, especially a reduction in powers of memory, but was able to teach part-time at a school for the mentally handicapped. During the first 3 months after injury, the woman was often very irritable and between 3 and 6 months began to have attacks of rage lasting two to three minutes in which she would strike out with her stick at anything or anyone near her. Sometimes these attacks occurred at home leading to damage to household objects but, on several occasions, they took place when she was away from home, and in one instance, when she was in a crowded store. On the day of the attacks, she always awoke feeling very irritable and after the attack was unable to remember what happened. The episodes would leave her feeling exhausted and extremely upset about the damage she had caused. EEG studies revealed an abnormality in the posterior left temporal region and treatment with carbamazepine (Tegretol) led to complete cessation of the attacks.

THE FRONTAL SYNDROME

Of all the permanent and primary disorders of mental state and behaviour caused by brain injury the 'frontal lobe syndrome' is the one best known to most clinicians, perhaps because of the considerable and persistent difficulties it causes for others and patients' needs for prolonged care. In turn this has led to a considerable amount of attention being given to the features of the sufferers' mental states since the first dramatic descriptions by Harlow (1848–1868) in his papers concerning Phineas Gage and the comment by Phelps (1898) that 'there seems to be a general law of a relationship between a very limited region of the brain and higher psychical phenomena'. Agreement has been established that damage to the frontal lobes leads to readily recognizable changes in emotion and behaviour and to a much more variable extent in cognition, (Lipowski 1978). The typical features mentioned by most authors include disinhibition, facile euphoria, blunting of emotional responsiveness, egocentricity, interference with the behaviour of others, irresponsibility, lack of tact and concern, and childishness. Usually patients exhibit purposeless drive and show loss of initiative and judgement and, in a proportion there is apathy and inertia, and in others marked aggressiveness.

Those who have examined patients with focal war wounds to the frontal lobes (Jarvie 1954; Lishman 1968) report that features of the disorder may occur after injury to only one lobe (Jarvie) and that the most severe effects are produced by bilateral injuries, especially those involving the orbital and frontal areas of the brain (Lishman). In patients who have had severe closed head injuries damage is so widespread that although one or other frontal lobe may show the greatest damage there will be extensive injury to its partner and also to other areas of brain, especially the anterior and inferior temporal regions; for this reason it is better to talk of the 'frontal syndrome' rather than the 'frontal lobe syndrome'.

It is clear from the literature and personal experience that symptoms of the frontal type occur in different clusters all of which are grouped under the general heading of the 'frontal syndrome'. The one characteristic common to all is the presence of disinhibition which occurs with a variety of affective and behavioural patterns and with varying levels of disturbance of intellect.

In a critical study of six patients with frontal lobe wounds caused by missiles, Jarvie (1954) chose disinhibition as the central feature of the resultant changes in mental state and argued that this mechanism is a primary release phenomena which unleashes changes in emotion, behaviour, and cognition. He pointed out that basic intellect may be spared by comparison with severe changes occurring in affect and behaviour and that patients may well retain insight into the fact that they are abnormal. The problem for the patient is that he has minimal or no control over sudden shifts in mood, basic drives and behaviour, and such control he has, if any, is short lived. Jarvie also believed that the effects of frontal injury add nothing new to the personality but, rather, revealed pre-traumatic tendencies which were previously given very limited or no public expression. Lishman (1968) also commented that the 'frontal syndrome' may accentuate or release pre-traumatic characteristics. However, he also remarked

Table 8.6 *Patterns of change in personality and other aspects of mental state in patients with the 'frontal lobe syndrome' following brain injury*

Category	Personality change	Cognitive change	No. of Patients
Fronto-limbic dementia	Frontal symptoms and irritability	Marked memory loss	50
Frontal dysmnesia	Frontal symptoms only	Memory loss	34
Dysmnesic inadequacy and phobic imbalance*	Anxiety, phobic symptoms, depression	Memory loss	22
		No memory loss	11
Traumatic dysmnesia	Few frontal symptoms	Memory loss	35
Frontal	Frontal symptoms only	Relatively little cognitive change	21
Irritable dysmnesia	Irritability	Memory loss	12

* After Roberts (1979).
Questionable inclusions within the 'frontal lobe syndrome' sub-groups.

that severe frontal-lobe injuries may have the effect of cutting across previous personalities. Roberts (1979) in his extensive retrospective study of war-wounded men, placed those with frontal lobe syndromes into six categories and the 12 dominant features in five are shown in Table 8.6. In effect he saw irritability and marked aggression (an extension of irritability), or lack of them, and disordered memory, as key changes and found that they formed different combinations with basic features of the syndrome innumerated earlier. He linked neurological disability to the symptom patterns and found that evidence of severe damage to the basal ganglia and brainstem occurred chiefly in those who were 'quietly demented'. In a sixth and older group of men disabling anxiety with phobic features was combined with a varying degree of memory loss and disturbance of balance. Roberts regarded the symptoms of this group as reactions to the basic physical disorder, thus they were not primary but secondary events.

Finally, turning to the patient who becomes apathetic, Roberts commented that injuries in the basal cortex and the brainstem are associated with apathy and memory loss and Lishman (1978) reported that Kretschmer previously described a basal syndrome in which, as a result of damage to the orbital region of the frontal lobes, hypothalamus and mid-brain, patients became apathetic and intermittently irritable with alterations in basic drives relating to appetite, drinking, sleep, and sexual activity. However, such disorders are seldom encountered even amongst the severely injured, in whom the combination of apathy, intermittent irritability, and severe cognitive disability, especially disturbances of memory and attention, are the most usual features.

The author's experience matches that of the authors quoted and it seems that the severity of the emotional, behavioural, and cognitive features of the frontal syndrome are closely related to the extent to which insight has been lost. Indeed loss of insight and disinhibition appear to be the central criteria of the severity of this particular disorder. Previous personal characteristics are accentuated in all but the most severely injured and emotion, behaviour, and the basic drives of aggressiveness and sexuality emerge frequently. Interestingly, Roberts (1979) makes relatively little comment about the difficulties caused by released sexual drive, perhaps because his review took place many years after the patients' initial injuries and at a time when concern over sexuality had diminished, or because those with disturbance of sexual behaviour, though troublesome, form a very small proportion of individuals with serious head injuries. Those who deal with the recently injured have noted that sexual disturbances, when present, cause as much distress to relatives of patients as aggressiveness.

First evidence of the emerging syndrome appears almost as soon as a severely injured person becomes conscious when extremes of mood and behaviour are most prominent. In all but the very severely injured lessening of the intensity of these features takes place over many months, suggesting that either an element of control returns spontaneously, or that the patient may be taught how to control the symptoms, or that external controls can be effectively applied. The following case illustrates ways in which a degree of control over unacceptable behaviour might be established and how symptoms change with time.

A 24-year-old married woman suffered severe brain injuries as the result of an assault. She developed symptoms of the frontal syndrome, one of the most outstanding being pathological laughter—the patient laughed uncontrollably for several minutes at frequent intervals and had the habit of banging her head with her hand to stop it. She also developed very provocative sexual behaviour when in the presence of men or teenage boys. She was distressed by the frequent bursts of laughter and later during recovery asked to be sterilized to avoid possible pregnancy.

In other words, this patient's disorder was very much in keeping with the comments made by Jarvie (1954) in so far as she had insight, attempted to control her feelings but with very limited success, and initiated a move to prevent a possible consequence of her disinhibited sexual behaviour. The patient also developed very ritualistic forms of behaviour, for example counting the exact number of steps needed to get from room to room in the home, or to the local shops. It might be argued that this also represented a facet of her attempt to gain control over activities of daily life. It was noticeable in the presence of her parents, who were very firm yet understanding, that the patient's self-control was at its best and when she was away from them at its worst. Thus control mechanisms could be increased, as in normal individuals, in the presence of an external censor.

With the passage of many months the episodes of pathological laughter lessened considerably but there was little or no change in the level of control the patient had over her sexual impulses—interestingly, prior to her injury she was known to be sexually provocative and became pregnant when in her mid-teens. In addition to the problems mentioned the patient had considerable difficulties with her memory but her level of comprehension was high. She showed some improvement over a period of two years from injury but was not able to live an independent life to that point.

The patient just described was only 21 at the time of injury and it is conceivable that the constant strict control maintained by her parents led to improvements mentioned. Experience indicates that patients who are older are far less likely to show any appreciable degree of improvement and this is in keeping with other aspects of recovery of the severely injured person.

DEMENTIA

Severe brain injuries affect all cognitive processes and yet in most patients some recovery of function takes place. Often one of the chief factors governing the use of residual intellectual capacity in everyday life resides in emotional changes produced either primarily or secondarily, and the attitudes of close relatives and friends towards the injured person. Dementia is still regarded by many as an irreversible global impairment of intellect and personality, but, as has been pointed out already, even very severe deficits are reversed to some extent by the passage of time in the brain-injured. Lipowski (1978) in a review and reformulation of organic brain syndromes, states that the diagnostic criteria of dementia are, '(1) acquired decrement in intelligence; (2) impairment of memory; (3) impairment of abstract thinking as manifested by reduced capacity for generalising, synthesizing, differentiating, logical reasoning, and concept formation; (4) impaired capacity to learn new skills and process novel and complex information; (5) change in personality style (either accentuation or alteration); (6) impaired judgement; (7) impaired expression of emotions and impulses, and (8) usually course prolonged, with either gradual resolution or permanent defects.' Thus, bearing in mind that disturbances of cognition and personality are part of complex and parallel spectra of changes ranging from dementia to minimal degrees of impairment and that the changes are dynamic, it is recommended that the term dementia, should be used sparingly and confined to the severely mentally disabled who are at least a year from their injury, who are very unlikely to recover, and who are totally dependent.

Those injured in childhood or adolescence usually show considerable improvement of intellect as recovery from injury and brain development continue after injury, and as intense efforts to promote learning and acceptable behaviour are made. In comparison, in patients of 30 or more years of age relatively little improvement occurs, although some positive gains will be made (Miller and Stern 1965), but as the years pass whatever intellect remains appears to degenerate more rapidly than usual with the advent of the later stages of ageing. In a very general and crude way the extent of cognitive recovery from brain injury is related to the duration of PTA. For example, patients with a PTA of less than a month who do not have marked primary emotional behavioural deficits (e.g. the frontal syndrome), or deficits in speech and comprehension, are capable of varying degrees of age-related cognitive recovery, but almost all patients aged over 20 years with a PTA exceeding 3 months remain severely impaired and would be regarded as irrecoverable, that is, demented.

Very occasionally patients present with features of severe mental disability reflected in impaired emotion, behaviour, and intellect, but in fact have a pseudo-dementia termed, though perhaps not always correctly, the Ganser Syndrome (Ganser 1898). The following brief case report illustrates the feature of this condition quite clearly.

A 17-year-old boy was severely injured in a motor-cycle accident and as a result had a post-traumatic amnesia of approximately 4 weeks. A diagnosis of diffuse brain injury was made and, in addition, he had a fracture of the lower part of his leg which left him with a shortened limb. In the first three months he made very good progress but intellectually and socially from six months onwards became increasingly withdrawn, lost contact with his friends, became apathetic, and complained of poor memory, concentration and depression. He was regarded as depressed and it was felt his symptoms were reactive and treatment with antidepressants was started but was not effective. Psychological tests at this time showed a marked deterioration in his intelligence. When seen 2½ years after his injury he was almost mute, remained in his own room most of the time, and showed no initiative whatsoever. Intellectual testing was attempted and revealed an apparent IQ of 50 on the WAIS. He was noted to give approximate answers to questions. For example, when asked about the weather which was cloudy he said it was sunny, the colour of a blue tie was purple, the year was 1980 (in fact it was 1981). When asked to calculate similar results were obtained. For example he could add $5 + 5$ and $8 + 2$ correctly, but not $12 + 1$. The final assessment took place one month after settlement of his claim for compensation was successful. By that time he had become alert, well orientated, recalled his previous visits, and his intelligence had increased dramatically to a level of 106 on the verbal scale and 129 on the performance scale of the WAIS. He had residual difficulty with his memory but this was slight. His social adustment remained poor at that stage but he was responding to positive attempts to provide advice and help.

The phase of relative normality at the onset of what was thought to be a post-traumatic depression, and later a dementia, the approximate answers to questions, and the prompt recovery on resolution of the claim for compensation, were the key features of the disorder and led to the diagnosis of the Ganser Syndrome. They are in keeping in part with the features described by Ganser in 1898 which were 'answering past the point', or giving approximate answers (*vorbeireden*) which are patently absurd, fluctuating levels of consciousness, and an abrupt end to the disorder. Our patient, unlike his, did not have complete amnesia for the illness, did not show evidence of hallucinations, or physical hysterical conversion symptoms. Therefore he could not be said to have the full syndrome but to have Ganser symptoms. Lishman (1979) comments that the symptoms may well be superimposed upon other psychiatric disorders. For example, they may be seen in the course of an organic dementia, depressive or schizophrenic psychosis. In fact, our patient did appear to be depressed prior to the development of the Ganser symptoms. Lishman concludes that, 'the disorder would appear to rest principally on a complex psychogenic basis in which hysterical mechanisms, or mechanisms closely allied to them, are largely responsible, though contributions due to organic brain dysfunction and psychotic thought disorder cannot be excluded in certain cases.'

PRE-MORBID CHARACTER AND RESPONSES TO INJURY

The part played by pre-morbid constitutional factors during recovery is important and complex because the emotional responses of the injured person represent the combination of primary brain damage and reactions to physical, mental, and social disability at different stages of recovery. It is clear that in all but the very severest injuries pre-traumatic personality traits are evident during recovery and influence the cause of post-traumatic disability. For example, Kozol (1946) pointed out that individuals with marked pre-traumatic neurotic tendencies are more liable to develop the three primary characteristics of the post-traumatic syndrome (headache, dizziness, and insomnia) than those of a more stable constitution. Exaggeration of pre-morbid traits after injury is common. For example, a tendency to aggressiveness, egocentric behaviour, lack of regard for others, perhaps amounting to levels indicating a psychopathic constitution may give rise to particularly difficult circumstances and totally disrupt the life of those closely involved with the injured person. This is illustrated by the following case history.

A young business man of 30 and recently married sustained a head injury in a motor vehicle accident which was not his fault. He had a period of PTA exceeding one week but was not left with any physical handicaps. On returning home, he behaved in a mildly grandiose manner, was physically and verbally aggressive towards his wife upon whom he made increased sexual demands, though impotent, and several months later she left him for another man. His intellectual abilities were only slightly impaired and he returned to work as an accountant. However, he was persistently aggrieved about the way his colleagues treated him but did not feel that he could possibly have upset them, although in reality they found him of limited capacity with regard to business, aggressive, and inconsiderate. Careful examination of his pre-morbid personality revealed that all the characteristics described had been present but to a less marked extent and had caused difficulties at home and at work. The fact that this man's wife left him is understandable in view of the recency of their marriage and previous emotional difficulties. The fact that his firm continued to employ him is not unusual either as it seems that far greater attempts are made to accommodate men with professional managerial skills, even when reduced by injury, than those who are unskilled or semi-skilled and come from a lower socioeconomic background.

In contrast, the effects of primary brain injury may lead to the moderation of previously objectionable behaviour although this one of the less common consequences of brain damage. For example, most moderate to severely brain-injured individuals discover that the injury has resulted in a significant lowering of their threshold for intoxication by alcohol. As a result, many give up their previous heavy drinking and increased sobriety together with diminished aggressiveness is regarded by the family as a definite improvement, even though a man may not be fit for work. The following case illustrates this fact.

A 62-year-old salesman suffered a severe brain injury following a fall whilst intoxicated. Prior to his accident he drank very heavily, was abusive to his wife and often returned home from his drinking bouts in an 'indescribable state'. Following the injury, he had a residual but mild left-sided hemiparesis and a severe disturbance of memory as a consequence of which he was unable to return to work. His behaviour changed completely. He gave up drinking, he was affable and cheerful to the point of being mildly disinhibited and, in fact, showed elements of what is often

termed 'the frontal syndrome'. Despite his minor physical handicap and gross disturbance of memory, his wife was 'pleased' that as a result of his injury he remained at
home, was not abusive or irritable, and had developed a good sense of humour!

This case illustrates that primary brain injury may obliterate most of the
patient's pre-traumatic personality characteristics and behaviours and that
organically determined features replace them. Therefore, it could be said
that a very severe injury may lead to the development of 'replacement
emotions and behaviours' to a varying extent and that these are not a reflection of pre-morbid characteristics and may, or, more often, may not lead to
the happy outcome just described. In fact, for the most part it is common
for the residual mental state and associated behaviours to give rise to
concern.

The two cases described give some insight into the importance of the role
of relatives and employers and the general social milieu in determining certain aspects of outcome. The first patient suffered considerably as a result
of his wife's decision to leave him for another man as it was a great blow to
his self-esteem. On the other hand, he benefited from the support given to
him by his professional colleagues. The second patient's wife, having
survived years of marital difficulties, was able to bring her considerable personal resources to bear upon the care of her seriously disabled husband. The
cases also illustrate the general observation that wives of older men are
more likely to stay with their husbands whereas young recently married
couples more often find the pressures of coping too great. Obviously it is
very difficult for a young wife to accept the prospect of many years of life
with a different person, to accept the burden of taking over the responsibilities of the house and family completely, and to accept that in many cases
the former happy loving relationship has been destroyed beyond recall
(Rosenbaum and Najenson 1976).

Considerable attention is given to exaggeration of pre-traumatic neurotic
and sociopathic personality characteristics amongst those recovering from
severe head injury. In general, they impair adjustment to the effects of
injury and/or cause havoc with interpersonal relations. In contrast, relatively little is written about important qualities that play a significant and
positive role in the recovery of some patients and which should be the focus
of positive reinforcement in their rehabilitation. This is not to say that such
characteristics do not have mixed effects upon patients' feelings,
approaches to problem solving, and adjustment to the consequences of
injury. But, coupled with the preservation of insight and comprehension,
the possession of the traits of orderliness and drive provides a powerful
springboard for a positive response to difficulties and problem solving.
Individuals with these traits before their accident tend to be punctual, tidy,
well controlled, and show both attention to detail and strong self-criticism.
When present in moderation and coupled with average or above-average

intelligence their industriousness and resourcefulness is often coupled with a successful life-style. The positive effects of these characteristics are clearly demonstrated by two case histories of talented professional women, one a 40-year-old school teacher, and the other a 43-year-old University lecturer. Both were severely injured in road traffic accidents, both had impairment of intellect, especially of memory, but not of personality, and both suffered considerable loss of self-esteem and identity, and they developed the emotions of anxiety, frustration, and anger during their early attempts to re-establish themselves professionally. Both had difficulties in word finding and the lecturer had a mild residual weakness of the left limbs together with a disturbance of balance necessitating the use of a stick. Each woman had reached the upper levels of her profession and formerly had had considerable drive and enthusiasm for work, good organizing abilities, and many external interests.

The teacher returned to work a year after her injury having convinced herself and others that she could cope. But immediately she found that her memory deficit was much greater than she had been prepared to admit. In order to teach, she and her husband spent every evening and most of each weekend preparing lessons in such a way that she would be able to teach, because her information was arranged in a careful and orderly manner. However, any interruption of her teaching routine produced great anxiety and almost total inability to recall information she had painfully learned prior to each lesson. Thus her ability to plan, organize, and her drive were preserved but almost solely devoted to the task of preparing simple school work. As a result, her husband took over control of the day-to-day running and care of the house, and her colleagues the organization and administration of the school. Eventually, after a year, the woman found the strain so great she retired from work with feelings of guilt about having failed her colleagues, her pupils, and her husband. She felt a tremendous sense of failure and loss of professional identity. However, with much tactful help from her husband, which took her through the ensuing period of deep depression, she was, within six months, more relaxed and dealing with household tasks as far as her memory difficulties would allow. Again, her husband showed great insight and tactfully shadowed her in all the tasks that she attempted to complete, but often failed. She returned to some of her social activities and a year after leaving school accepted her limitations well and had started to build a new but restricted life for herself.

The university lecturer was an even more dynamic, driving, successful, and ambitious woman in an area of academic work where the skilled use of languages was central to her life. Unfortunately, although still articulate by most standards, she had lost her high level of fluency and the verbal skills needed for her job. She retained her aggressive drive, but found great difficulty in tolerating her limitations and the insistence of others that 'she had made a marvellous recovery'. Comments of this nature touched the heart of her difficulties because she regarded her accident as a disaster and initially she would explode with anger on such occasions, or when frustrated in other ways. Later she was able to re-establish considerable control over this aspect of her emotions, partly by will and partly by learning to anticipate and retire from potentially difficult situations. She found the uncertainty over her prognosis, and the final form her intellectual and speech impairment would take, very hard to accept and ruminated frequently about her losses. In other words, she mourned the loss of part of herself, felt depressed for short periods, and projected angry feelings about her difficulties on to others. However, her drive was channelled into organizing her remaining skills; this, and her refusal to accept that problems could not be solved, at least partially—both aspects of her pre-traumatic personality — began to exert an influence leading to the rapid re-establishment of her independence although not a return to her previous employment. The competition between her former refusal to accept defeat and current necessity to accept that life could not be as it was caused great emotional pain frequently during the first year after recovery; the stage she had reached at the time this history was written.

The role of pre-morbid constitution is vital in determining the emotional reactions and behaviour of head-injured victims. But, apart from the highly specific patterns described, general reactions also occur amongst individuals without strong pre-morbid traits. These common reactions have been mentioned previously and include anxiety, depression, and irritability. All three may be present at various times representing reactions to losses and frustrations and to varying levels of feelings of insecurity. The nature and significance of each occasion causing a reaction varies as does the predominating mood and all may, as Lezak states (1978 *b*), 'mask the less readily observable problems of perplexity, distractability and fatigue'. Responses tend to be marked each time the injured person encounters a new event that in some way reflects, or brings home to him, the effects of injury and when physical or emotional or social setbacks occur. Key stages in recovery tending to cause alterations in emotion include discharge from hospital, the cessation of active rehabilitation especially when, as so often happens, the individual's expectations are not met and when he has to accept that he will not be able to pursue his former work or leisure interests. Severe depression associated with suicidal thoughts or acts is almost unknown in the early stages of recovery from injury but not at a later date. Achté and Anttinen (1963), quoted by Lishman (1978), noted a peak incidence between 15 and 19 years from injury. They reported that those involved had severe marital problems or difficulties with other relationships. A significant number had been heavy and excessive drinkers and change of character had been observed in 40 per cent of this sub-group. Overall, about half the patients investigated had personality character changes and in another study Hillbom (1960) observed that this factor made the greatest contribution to suicide in his series in which about 30 per cent of the patients had alterations in personality. Achté *et al.* (1967) reported that 41 per cent of suicides occurred during periods of depressive psychosis.

The mental mechanism of denial mentioned earlier is a protection again the potentially damaging effects upon emotional integrity of recognizing the real nature, extent, and significance of brain injuries and their aftermath. It operates in most patients with varying degrees of intensity during the first one to two years after injury and tends to promote expectations of recovery that ultimately cannot be met. Thus coming to terms with disability is a slow and painful process punctuated by periods of distress alternating with ones in which false hopes predominate. Projection of angry feelings is also common, the objects of them usually being the person or persons said to have caused the accident (e.g. the employer), relatives, or medical and allied professionals. Regression, a reaction so common in physical illness, is encountered only occasionally after head injury and the following case history illustrates various aspects of this interesting phenomenon.

A 19-year-old girl injured in a road traffic accident was left with very severe physical deficits including marked dysarthria and ataxia related to damage deep in the left cerebral hemisphere, the basal ganglia and the brainstem. She did not obey commands or show any other evidence of being sentient for eight months after injury but thereafter began to recover slowly and eventually returned home. Despite her difficulties, two years after injury she was able to feed herself, manage most toilet activities, and partially dress herself. Although she had intellectual impairment, she enjoyed reading and making simple puzzles and her emotional relationship with her father and mother was good. Every week she visited the local physiotherapy and speech therapy departments where it was fully appreciated that although she had ceased to progress physically or in terms of development of her ability to speak, she continued to improve social skills and gain self-confidence. However, it was decided to discontinue both therapies and the cessation of them, coupled with an interview with an orthopaedic surgeon who gave the impression that everything possible had been done, provoked a sudden and marked change in the girl's behaviour and mood.

She became very childish, petulant, and demanding, swore frequently at her parents, refused baths, to dress or feed herself, and stopped reading. Her speech became much more difficult to follow. On several occasions she attempted to get out of the family car when it was moving and these acts were later interpreted as suicidal gestures. The changes were present for several months and led to re-admission to a neurological unit. No further evidence of brain damage was detected, the girl would not co-operate with a psychologist who wished to interview and test her cognitive functions, and she was sent home unchanged. A short time later she was readmitted because she was still in a very distressed state and on this occasion it was appreciated that her difficulties were psychological. Before anything further was done, she met a young man on the ward who was also brain injured and who took a great interest in her. Within a matter of days her behaviour and speech altered dramatically and within a short time she resumed her previous way of life and her pleasant manner. It appeared that the restoration of her normal behaviour and self-esteem was directly related to the appreciation by another of her femininity, leading to the conclusion that her earlier regression was indeed related to the intense emotions of anger, frustration, and disappointment caused by the cessation of attempts to help her and, perhaps above all, the feeling that she had been abandoned and rejected by therapists and doctors alike, people who had formed the centre of her emotional life outside the home for many months.

Anxiety reactions with or without phobic symptoms, neurosthenic reactions lasting months or years and characterized by tiredness, weakness, loss of energy, and a presence of hypochondriacal concern, and hysterical conversion disorders, are chiefly encountered after trivial brain injuries (Lishman 1978), although occasionally patients with severe injuries do have symptoms of this type. Mild to moderate injuries are not the concern of this chapter, but it is important to note that they produce significant effects upon cognition which appear to contribute to a delay in return to work in a significant number of patients (Ota 1969; Gronwall and Wrightson 1974; Rimel, *et al.* 1981), and that in a significant number of patients with hysterical conversion disorders there are organic changes in the brain. For example, Whitlock (1967) studied 57 patients with hysterical conversion and observed that two-thirds had significant or coexisting brain disorder compared with 5 percent in a control group and that of those with conversion syndromes 21 per cent had a previous history of head injury.

CONCLUSION

Closed head injuries are associated with brain damage varying from the mild to the extremely severe. It is now appreciated that at all levels of severity, injuries produce changes, albeit transient in the majority with minor injuries, that lead to temporary, or permanent and grave, disturbances of mental and social life. The mental consequences of severe injuries should be seen as part of a dynamic continuum which begins with the return of consciousness and extends onwards for many months thereafter. Physical and mental improvements occur most rapidly over the period during which full consciousness is established and it is at this point in recovery and shortly afterwards, that is within the first six to nine months of injury, that the basic patterns of permanent changes to cognition, personality, and behaviour take place. Diminution of certain extreme mental changes and modifications of others continue to take place over many months, during which the influence of pre-morbid characteristics play an increasingly important role in moulding the feelings and behaviours of the injured person, and ultimately their adaptation to a new social role.

REFERENCES

Achté, K. A. and Anttinen, E. E. (1963) Suizide bei Hirngeschädigten des Krieges in Finland. *Fortschritte der Neurologie, Psychiatrie* **31**, 645–67.

Achté, K. A., Hillbom, E., and Aalberg, V. (1967). *Post-traumatic psychoses following war brain injuries. Reports from the Rehabilitation Institute for Brain-injured Veterans in Finland* Vol. 1. Helsinki.

——, ——, ——. (1969). Psychoses following war brain injuries. *Acta Psychiat. Scand.* **45**, 1–18.

Bond, M. R. (1975). Assessment of the psychosocial outcome after severe head injury. In *Outcome of severe damage to the central nervous system*, Amsterdam. pp.141–57. Ciba Foundation Symposium No.34 (new series). Elsevier-Excerpta Medica.

——, (1979). The stages of recovery from severe head injury with special reference to late outcome. *Int. Rehab. Med.* **1**, 155–9.

—— and Brooks, D. N. (1976). Understanding the process of recovery as a basis for the brain-injured. *Scand. J. Rehab. Med.* **8**, 127–33.

Brooks, D. N. and Aughton, M. E. (1979). Psychological consequences of blunt head injury. *Int. Rehab. Med.* **1**, 60–5.

Cameron, E. D. (1941). Studies in senile nocturnal delirium. *Psychiat. Q.* **15**, 47–53.

Cartlidge, N. E. F. and Shaw, D. A. (1981). Head injury. In *Major problems in neurology,* Vol. **10**, pp. 1–5.W. B. Saunders, London.

Davidson, K. and Bagley, C. R. (1969). Schizophrenia-like psychoses associated with organic disorders of the central nervous system; a review of the literature. In *Current Problems in Neuropsychiatry* pp.113–84. (ed. R. N. Herrington) *Br. J. Psychiat.* Special Publication No. 4.

Feuchtwanger, E. and Mayer-Gross, W. (1938). Hirnverletzung und Schizophrenie. *Schweizer Archiv. für Neurologie und Psychiatrie* **41**, 17–99.

Field, J. H. (1976) *Epidemiology of head injuries in England and Wales,* HMSO, London.

Flor-Henry, P. (1969). Psychosis and temporal lobe epilepsy: a controlled investigation. *Epilepsia* **10**, 363–95.

Ganser, S. J. M. (1898). Ueber euien eigenartigen hysterischen Daemmerzustand. *Archiv für Psychiatrie und Nervenkrankheiten,* **30**, 633–40. Translated by Schorer, C. E. (1965). *Br. J. Criminol.* **5**, 120–6.

Gregoriades, A., Fragos, E., Kapslakis, Z., and Mandouvalos, B. (1971). A correlation between mental disorders and EEG and AEG findings in temporal lobe epilepsy. Abstracts from the *5th World Congress of Psychiatry,* Mexico. p.325. La Prensa Médica Mexicana, Mexico.

Gronwall, D. and Wrightson, P. (1974). Delayed recovery of intellectual function after minor head injury. *Lancet,* **ii**, 605–9.

Harlow, J. M. (1848). *Boston Med. Surg. J.* **39**, 389.

——, (1868). *Mass. Med. Soc. Proc.* **2**, 327.

Hillbom, E. (1951). Schizophrenia-like psychoses after brain trauma. *Acta Psychiat. Scand.* Suppl. **60**, 36–47.

Jamieson, K. G. and Kelly D. (1973). Crash helmets reduce head injuries. *Med. J. Aust.* **ii**, 806.

Jarvie, N. F. (1954). Frontal lobe wounds causing disinhibition. A study of six cases. *J. Neurol. Neurosurg. Psychiat.* **17**, 14–32.

Jennett, B. (1975). *Epilepsy after non-missile head injuries,* (2nd edn.). Heinemann, London.

—— and Bond, M. R. (1975). Assessment of outcome after severe brain damage: a practical scale. *Lancet,* **i**, 480–4.

——, Snoek, J., Bond, M. R., and Brooks, D. N. (1981). Disability after severe head injury. Observations in the use of the Glasgow Outcome Scale. *J. Neurol. Neurosurg. Psychiat.* **44**, 285–93.

Kozol, H. L. (1946). Pretraumatic personality and psychiatric sequelae of head injury. *Arch. Neurol. Psychiat.* **56**, 245–57.

Levin, H. S., O'Donnell, V. M., and Grossman, R. G. (1979). The Galveston orientation and amnesia test. A practical scale to assess cognition after head injury. *J. nerv. ment. Dis.* **167**, 675–84.

Lezak, M. D. (1978a). Living with the characterologically altered brain-injured patient. *J. Clin. Psychiat.* **39**, 592–8.

——, (1978b). Subtle sequelae of brain damage. *Am. J. Phys. Med.* **57**, 9–15.

Lipowski, Z. J. (1967). Delirium, clouding of consciousness and confusion. *J. nerv. ment. Dis.* **145**, 227–55.

——, (1978). Organic brain syndromes: A reformulation. *Comp. Psychiat.* **19**, 309–21.

Lishman, W. A. (1968). Brain damage in relation to psychiatric disability after head injury. *Br. J. Psychiat.* **114**, 373–410.

——, (1973). The psychiatric sequelae of head injury: a review. *Psychol. Med.* **3**, 304–18.

——, (1978). Organic Psychiatry. In *The Psychological Consequences of Cerebral Disorder*, Blackwell Scientific Publications, Oxford, pp. 191–261.

McKinlay, W. W., Brooks, D. N., and Bond, M. R. (1983). Compensation and outcome of severe blunt head injury. (In press.)

——, ——, ——, Martinage, D. P., and Marshall, M. M. (1981). The short-term outcome of severe blunt head injury as reported by relatives of the injured person. *J. Neurol. Neurosurg. Psychiat.* **44**, 527–33.

Mandleberg, I. A. and Brooks, D. N. (1974). Cognitive recovery after severe head injury. *J. neurol. neurosurg. Psychiat.* **38**, 1121.

Miller, H. and Stern, G. (1965). The long-term prognosis of severe head injury. *Lancet* i, 225–9.

Newcombe, F. and Fortuny, L. A. I. (1979). Problems and perspectives in the evaluation of psychological deficits after cerebral lesions. *Int. rehabil. Med.* **1**, 182–92.

Oddy, M., Humphrey, M., and Uttley, D. (1978). Stresses upon the relatives of head-injured patients. *Br. J. Psychiat.* **133**, 507–13.

Ota, Y. (1969). Psychiatric studies on civilian head injuries. In *The Late Effects of Head Injury* (ed. A. E. Walker, W. F. Caveness, and M. Critchley, Thomas, Springfield, Illinois. pp. 222–35.

Phelps, C. (1898). *Traumatic injuries of the brain and its membranes.* Kimpton, London.

Rimel, R. W., Giordini, B., Barth, J. T., Boll, T. J., and Jane, J. A. (1981). Disability caused by minor head injury. *Neurosurgery* **9**, 222–35.

Roberts, A. H. (1979). *Severe accidental head injury. An assessment of long-term prognosis* pp. 55–89. Macmillan, London.

Rosenbaum, M. and Najenson, T. (1976). Changes in life patterns and symptoms of low mood as reported by wives of severely brain-injured soldiers. *J. consult. clin. Psychol.* **44**, 881–8.

Teasdale, G. and Jennett, B. (1974). Assessment of coma and impaired consciousness. *Lancet* ii, 81.

Thomsen, I. V. (1974). The patient with severe head injury and his family. *Scand. J. rehabil. Med.* **6**, 180–3.

Whitlock, F. A. (1967). The aetiology of hysteria. *Acta Psychiat. Scand.* **43**, 144–62.

9 Head injury during childhood: the psychological implications

Michael Oddy

INTRODUCTION

The study of head injury in children is both different from that in adults and more complicated, since additional developmental variables are involved.

In the first place there are differences in the ways children and adults become head injured. Although road traffic accidents are by far the most common causes in adults they represent a much smaller proportion of cases in children. Indeed, in the first three or four years of life, accidents in the home are a more common cause. Road accidents start to be a problem at three years, reaching a peak between six and seven years (Craft 1975). In pre-school children 'baby-battering' gives rise to an (unknown) proportion of head injuries. Comninos (1979) found that falls lead to 68 per cent of head injury in children under 14 years. In very young children commonly the child falls over or is dropped by a parent but in older children falls are often from a greater height (Hendrick, Harwood-Hash, and Hudson 1964).

There are also differences in the pathology of head injury in children. Compared with an adult the child's skull is flexible and the bones incompletely fused. This gives a greater resistance to the effects of head injury in that there is a cushioning effect (Cummins and Potter 1970). On the other hand, it allows a much greater deformation of the brain on impact and thus the shearing forces within the cortex are greater.

There are differences in the sites of intracranial haemorrhage with age (Jamieson and Yelland 1968), and a lower incidence of contrecoup injuries in children (Courville 1965).

The distinction between closed head injury and that caused by penetrating wounds which is so important in adult studies is of less relevance for children since so few sustain the latter form of injury, and many penetrating injuries in children result from playing with sticks and may leave only a tiny puncture wound (Jennett 1972). Although many studies fail to specify whether they have excluded penetrating injuries, the proportion of these is likely to be small and probably negligible. One study has focused on children with depressed fractures (Schaffer, Chadwick, and Rutter 1975; Thompson 1977) but most studies have given little indication of the nature of the injury involved.

In addition to the differences in the nature of head injury sustained by children and the pathological effects in children compared with adults, there appear to be differences in brain–behaviour relationships during childhood.

Certain widespread beliefs concerning the effects of lesions in childhood have come into question in recent years. The first is the notion that recovery from cortical lesions in early childhood is more complete than when the lesions are sustained in adolescence or adulthood. As St. James-Roberts (1979) has pointed out, there are two sides to this issue. One is the degree to which children recover from brain damage and the other concerns the extent of recovery in adults. Recent evidence suggests that previously the former may have been over-estimated (Benton 1974; Van Dongen and Loonen 1977) whilst the latter has been under-estimated (Geschwind 1974).

A second and related belief has been that the deficits resulting from lesions in childhood are less specific than those produced during childhood. This is usually attributed to the notion that the cortex is less specialized and/or is characterized by a greater plasticity during childhood. In other words, either localization of function has yet to take place, or if it has there is a more ready reorganization with other structures taking over the function of damaged areas. Once again evidence has mounted to oppose this view. When brain-damaged children have been compared with normal children matched for IQ, specific defects have been found in the former group (Benton 1974). Even amongst mentally handicapped children, brain damaged from birth, a variety of specific deficits have been found when they are compared with mentally handicapped children matched for mental age but showing no evidence of brain damage (Money 1963). Fedio and Mirsky (1969) have found different specific deficits associated with different forms of childhood epilepsy. In all these cases the nature of the specific deficit associated with lesions of a given location reflects, more or less, the pattern observed in adults.

Before reviewing the recovery studies, however, it is vital to examine the nature of the population which sustains head injury in childhood.

PREDISPOSITION TO HEAD INJURY IN CHILDREN

It is often suggested that children who suffer head injuries do not constitute a random sample of the population. As we have seen, not all age groups are equally at risk and boys are at far greater risk than girls. In addition, Klonoff (1971) has found that compared with matched controls those suffering head injury tend to come from more highly congested and lower income areas; their fathers are more likely to be unemployed or unskilled and their parents are more likely to be divorced, separated, or not officially married to one another. Brown and Davidson (1978) have similarly found a higher rate of accidents in children from working-class families and in children whose mothers are suffering from depression or other psychiatric disturbance.

The question of whether intellectual ability is associated with predisposition to head injury remains open. Klonoff (1971) found no such association but Chadwick, Rutter, Brown, Shaffer, and Traub (1981*b*) found that their group of relatively mildly injured children had lower IQs and poorer scholastic attainment than controls. It certainly appears that mentally handicapped children are at greater risk (Bergreen 1972).

Craft, Shaw, and Cartlidge (1972) found a considerably higher incidence of pre-morbid behaviour problems in head-injured children compared with controls.

Despite these predisposing factors neither Klonoff (1971) nor Partington (1960) found their head-injured children to have had a higher frequency of accidental injury in the past than controls.

THE EFFECTS OF HEAD INJURY IN CHILDREN

The effects of head injury are multifaceted and it is convenient to consider recovery of different functions separately.

Motor and sensory recovery

This is not the main focus of this chapter and a comprehensive review will not be given. However, it is necessary to provide at least the context for other aspects of recovery.

One of the most rigorously conducted studies in this area is that by Black, Blumer, Wellner, and Walker (1971). This was a 5-year prospective study of children aged less than 14 years. The authors found that there was recovery from neurological deficits for three months following injury but thereafter these remained stable. Amongst this series which included mild (coma of any duration) as well as severe cases, 15 per cent had residual neurological deficits. There was a longer period of potential recovery for seizures and after a year only 3 per cent were still suffering uncontrolled fits.

In a study of much more severely injured children, aged 2–18, all unconscious for more than a week, Brink, Garrett, Hale, Woo-Sam, and Nickel (1970) predictably found a much greater incidence of residual handicap. Ninety-three per cent showed some degree of spasticity at follow-up 1–7 years after injury and in half of these it was judged to be moderate or severe. Those unconscious for more than four weeks were much more likely to suffer from a more severe degree of spasticity.

Cognitive recovery

There have been relatively few studies of this aspect of recovery although recently a few carefully conducted studies have been reported. A number of questions have been investigated and these include the following: what proportion of head-injured children suffer a cognitive deficit? Is the likelihood of sustaining such a deficit directly related to the severity of head injury? Is there a threshold of severity that can be ascertained below which no permanent deficit occurs? For how long does recovery continue and what levels are attained? Are there specific cognitive abilities which are more likely to be affected? Are children of different ages likely to sustain different deficits or to recover at different rates or to different levels?

There is now quite strong evidence for a direct relationship between severity of injury and cognitive deficit (Brink *et al.* 1970; Levin and Eisenberg 1979; Chadwick *et al.* 1981*b*) although several studies have found that deficits may occur after apparently mild injuries (Klonoff, Low, and Clark 1977). Given this relationship, the proportion of children in a series suffering cognitive impairment will obviously depend on the severity of injury in the sample. In the most severely injured series reported Brink *et al.* (1970) found that amongst those unconscious for more than a week (and with a mean coma duration of four weeks) only a third were still functioning within the normal IQ range. A further third were functioning within the borderline retardation level and 15 per cent were moderately or severely retarded. However, even in a series containing mildly injured children, Klonoff *et al.* (1977) were able to demonstrate impaired cognitive performance in 23 per cent 5 years after injury.

Chadwick *et al.* (1981*b*) have addressed themselves to the question of whether there exists a threshold of severity for intellectual impairment. They found that even transient deficits are extremely unlikely after injuries leading to a PTA of less than a day. In those with PTAs of two or three weeks, cognitive deficits are usually short-lived and permanent deficits are rare with injuries leading to PTAs of less than three weeks. Levin and Eisenberg (1979) employed the Glasgow Coma Scale rather than PTA as a measure of severity. They found cognitive deficits of a transient nature in children who had been unconscious for less than 24 hours and persistent intellectual deficits (lasting a year or more) only amongst those who had been comatose for longer.

The question of the length of time over which recovery takes place demands a prospective, controlled study with a long follow-up in order to be answered. Two such studies have recently been reported. Klonoff *et al.* (1977) suggest that recovery can still take place five years after injury. Their finding is based on the fact that there were fewer differences between their head injured and control groups five years, as compared with four years, after injury. Chadwick *et al.* (1981*b*) were only able to follow their series for two years and three months. However, they examined the course of recovery in two groups of differing severity (PTA one hour to seven days and PTA more than one week). In both groups there was evidence of continuing recovery in the second year, although at a slower rate than in the first year. The rate of recovery appeared to slow down earlier in the less severely injured group.

Few studies have had sufficiently large series to investigate cognitive recovery in children of different ages. Woo Sam *et al.* (1970) had two moderately sized groups, one aged eight years and under, the other 10 years and above. They found that despite the fact that the younger children were less severely injured (in terms of coma duration) they suffered more severe intellectual deterioration.

Chadwick *et al.* (1981*b*) divided their children into those above and below the age of 10. Although there were few differences in course or extent of recovery such indications as there were suggested the younger group had made the more rapid recovery.

In a study of children who had suffered depressed fractures and hence more localized lesions, Thompson (1977) found little age effect although younger children tended to have slightly lower IQs.

Where studies report the numbers of boys versus girls in their sample there has invariably been a preponderance of boys, but only Chadwick *et al.* (1981*b*) have analyzed their cognitive test results for sex differences. They found no difference in the Wechsler Intelligence Scale for Childen (WISC) performance scores of boys and girls either at the initial assessment or in rate of recovery. However, in view of the evidence for sex differences in cognitive development, this appears a neglected area. Differential sex effects of head injury might be expected for particular cognitive skills, such as linguistic or visuospatial skills and at particular ages.

Most of the studies cited above have used the WISC as the basis of their cognitive assessment. This test, for children aged 5-16 is similar in format to the Wechsler Adult Intelligience Scale (WAIS). It consists of five 'verbal' sub-tests and five predominantly non-verbal or 'performance' sub-tests, each of which corresponds closely to the sub-tests of the WAIS. Chadwick, Rutter, and Shaffer (1981*a*) have confirmed the wisdom of this choice. Their study included more specialized neuropsychological tests in addition to the WISC and found only a small number of deficits not identified by the WISC. In a sub-group of children who showed no deficits on the WISC, tests of speed of visuomotor or visuospatial functioning were able to pick up specific deficits. Levin and Eisenberg (1979) found memory deficits to be the most common cognitive deficit in adolescents; a finding which is consistent with adult studies (Conkey 1938; Norrman and Svahn 1961; Brooks, Aughton, Bond, Jones, and Rizvi 1980). These authors did not examine memory in younger children but found motor speed, visuospatial and language deficits in more than a third of their subjects.

In conclusion, there appears to be clear evidence of an increasing likelihood of cognitive deficit with more severe injuries and there also appears to be a relationship between severity of deficit and severity of injury (judged by PTA or coma duration). It appears that persistent deficits are rare in injuries leading to a PTA of less than three weeks although transient cognitive impairment may be found in injuries leading to a PTA of 24 hours or more.

Recovery has been shown to take place throughout the period of follow-up in prospective studies. The longest period to date is five years but clearly studies over greater periods are needed to test the limits of recovery.

The question of the influence of age on intellectual recovery has rarely been investigated and the findings have been conflicting. Woo Sam *et al.* (1970) found younger children to recover less well whereas Chadwick *et al.* (1981*a*) found this group recovered more rapidly. Several explanations are possible. First, Woo Sam *et al.* (1970) reassessed their children at intervals ranging from 1 to 7 years after injury, whereas Chadwick *et al.* (1981*a*) saw all their children after 2¼ years. It may be that although younger children recover more rapidly, they do so less completely. Two other differences between the studies provide possible though perhaps less likely explanations of the different findings. Woo Sam *et al.* (1970) divided their groups into those above and below eight years whilst Chadwick *et al.* (1981 *a*) used 10 years as the criterion. Woo Sam *et al.* (1970) were studying more severely injured children and there may be an interaction between age effects and severity.

As yet no clear definition of the typical pattern of deficits after closed head injury in children has been reached but the indications are that this may not be markedly different from the adult pattern.

Personality change and psychiatric disturbance after head injury in children

There are many allusions to psychiatric disturbances following head injury in children in the literature but fewer adequately controlled studies of the role of head injury in the development of disturbed behaviour. For example, Blau (1936) described a number of cases seen in psychiatric practice where a history of head injury immediately preceded the onset of disturbance. In certain cases this was of a psychotic nature, occurred immediately after recovery of consciousness and subsided within a few weeks. In other cases there were more lasting behavioural changes involving hyperkinetic, asocial, and disinhibited behaviour.

Certainly, some degree of behavioural disturbance immediately following a period of coma is almost universal. However, in relation to later disturbance, studies such as Blau's (1936) beg many questions. It is possible that head injury plays no part whatsoever in the aetiology of the observed disturbance. Psychiatric disturbances are reasonably common in the absence of head injury and we have already discussed evidence suggesting that those who sustain head injuries in childhood are more likely to exhibit signs of psychiatric disorder prior to injury.

There is also the possibility that head injury may play an indirect role in the causation of personality change or psychiatric disturbance, possibly of a distinctive kind.

Before investigating these issues it is of interest to examine the nature of the behavioural disturbances that have been observed following the acute stages of recovery from head injury.

Black *et al.* (1969, 1971) conducted a prospective study of an unselected group of 105 children aged up to 14 years. Amongst this group, which naturally included a preponderance of relatively mildly injured children, they found four types of behavioural disturbance to be most common. These were: headache, eating problems (both overeating and poor appetite) hyperactivity and impaired attention. Anger control problems (irritability and temper outbursts), sleep disturbance, hypokinesis, and discipline problems also appeared for the first time in a number of the children. Thus the authors conclude that whereas in adults the post-traumatic syndrome is characterized by predominantly somatic symptoms, in children the symptoms tend to be behavioural. However, the authors emphasize that the majority of children showed no such changes, with only 20 per cent showing behavioural disturbances for the first time following head injury.

All these symptoms, of course, are commonly found in child psychiatric practice amongst those with no history of head injury. Indeed, many studies have emphasized the degree to which post-traumatic psychiatric sequelae resemble general child psychiatric disorders although some authors have referred to the 'post-traumatic syndrome in children' (Black *et al.* 1969). Brown *et al.* (1981) compared a control group with a group of head-injured children in whom it appeared likely that psychiatric disturbance was due to brain damage. The criteria for attributing disorder to brain damage were: (i) the period of PTA exceeded seven days; (ii) the disorder arose after the head injury; and (iii) it arose in children who did not exhibit psychiatric disorder before the injury. The comparison group included (i) children who had suffered psychiatric disturbance either before or after orthopaedic injury, but not injury to the head; (ii) children with severe head injury who had suffered psychiatric disorders before the accident; and (iii) children with mild head injuries whose disorders either preceded the accident or were observed for the first time at the 1-year follow-up.

Amongst the 'disorders attributable to brain injury' the authors found five cases diagnosed as 'disinhibited state'. None of the comparison group attracted this diagnosis. This involved 'marked socially disinhibited behaviour . . . with undue outspokenness without regard to social convention, the frequent making of personal remarks or asking of embarrassing questions, or getting undressed in social situations in which this would usually be regarded as unacceptable behaviour'.

Surprisingly, the only three cases of the hyperkinetic syndrome occurred in those where the disorder was not attributable to brain damage.

As far as emotional disorders, conduct disorders, and psychotic states were concerned, these appeared with more or less equal frequency in the two groups. When individual symptoms rather than diagnoses were examined, overeating, overtalkativeness, bed wetting, general slowness, and stuttering were all more frequent in the brain-damaged group but not significantly so. Restlessness was more common amongst controls.

It should be noted that in addition to a characteristic pattern attributable to brain damage associated with head injury there may also be a pattern which although not due to brain injury *per se* may be equally specific to head injury. For example, after mild head injury in adults the pattern known as 'post-traumatic neurosis' or the 'post-traumatic syndrome' may occur and it is commonly believed that this cannot be directly attributed to brain damage, but more to the particular sorts of emotional stresses, the motivation to pursue compensation, and the minor and transient sensory and intellectual deficits that may follow head injury.

The frequency with which personality changes or psychiatric sequelae develop is difficult to determine since much depends on the composition of the sample under scrutiny in terms of severity of injury, pre-morbid psychiatric disturbance, psychosocial adversity, and the stage at which a psychiatric assessment is made. Rune (1970) found only 10 per cent of his sample of head-injured children cared for at home to be mentally disturbed but these children had presumably very minor head injuries since none was admitted to hospital. Black *et al.* (1969) found 22 per cent of their sample of mildly and severely injured children to be suffering from a behavioural disturbance one year after injury. Klonoff and Paris (1974) reported that 30 per cent of their more severely injured children were suffering personality changes although this diminished to less than 20 per cent after two years. In this study personality change was the most common residual symptom both one and two years after injury. Brown *et al.* (1981) found that one year after head injury 54 per cent of their severely head-injured group were considered to have a psychiatric disorder compared with 24 per cent of the mildly injured and 22 per cent of the controls. When only those disorders which had arisen after the accident were considered, the contrast between groups is even more marked. Fifty-two per cent of severely head-injured children suffered a new psychiatric disturbance one year after injury compared with 16 per cent of mildly head injured and 14 per cent of controls. At a later assessment $2\frac{1}{4}$ years after injury the percentage remained the same for the severely injured but had risen to 32 per cent of the mildly injured and 18 per cent of the controls.

In a study of children with localized lesions following head injury (unilateral compound depressed fractures with associated dural tear) Shaffer *et al.* (1975) found 62 per cent with psychiatric disorder. No lateralization nor localization effects were found although an interaction effect revealed a particularly low incidence of disorder in those with right parieto-occipital lesions. This, however, appeared to be due to a lower incidence of adverse psychosocial circumstances amongst this sub-group and not to cortical effects.

Black *et al.* (1971) investigated prospectively the course of recovery from 'negative behavioural traits' over five years following head injury. They found a clear-cut increase in hyperkinesis during the first few months after injury followed by a steady decline that levelled off between three and five years after injury, more or less to pre-injury levels. Impaired control of affect (mood swings, crying, and screaming) and hyperkinesis showed similar patterns; an initial rise followed by a decline over 2-3 years, but neither quite returned to pre-morbid levels. Severe behaviour problems (destructiveness, stealing, and fighting) showed an initial rise followed by a decline for the next three years and then increased again four and five years after injury. Bowman, Blau, and Reich (1974) warn that psychiatric disturbance may not become obvious until several years after a head injury when the child reaches a different stage of development with different intellectual and emotional demands on him.

Let us now return to the question of the role of brain damage in the development of behavioural and emotional problems following head injury. Few studies have presented evidence which has a bearing on this issue. One type of evidence which, it has been argued, would militate in favour of brain damage being causally implicated is evidence of a positive correlation between severity of injury and incidence of psychiatric disorder. Shaffer *et al.* (1975) found no such relationship in their study of children with localized lesions. Brown *et al.* (1980) did find such a relationship but only at the upper extreme of PTA. These authors also found a higher rate of psychiatric disorder amongst those with neurological abnormality but noted that severely head-injured children without such abnormality still showed a rate of psychiatric disturbance considerably greater than that in the control group.

It therefore seems that there may well be an association between brain damage as a result of head injury and an increased likelihood of developing a psychiatric disorder but at present the balance of evidence suggests that the link is indirect. Brain damage puts the child under stress, perhaps as a result of cognitive deficits, or other neurological sequelae, and this in turn leads to a greater chance of psychiatric disturbance.

Pre-traumatic disturbance seems likely to predict susceptibility to psychiatric disorder following head injury. However, Black *et al.* (1969) found the rate of new psychiatric disorder to be no greater in those with a previous history of disturbance. Contradictory findings have recently been obtained by Brown *et al.* (1980), suggesting that 60 per cent of those with a previous history developed new psychiatric disorders one year after injury compared with less than a third of those with no history.

Harrington and Letemendia (1958) approached this question by comparing a group of children previously tested for head injury in a surgical hospital ward with a group of head-injured children who were referred to a child psychiatry unit. The groups were matched on various indices of severity of head injury but differed in that the psychiatric group showed a greater incidence of adverse pre-morbid personality and family characteristics.

In summary it appears that the form of behavioural or psychiatric problem that follows head injury in childhood is normally of a kind that commonly occurs in child psychiatric practice in the absence of brain damage. However, in certain severely injured cases, there may be a form of socially disinhibited behaviour that is not found amongst non-injured children.

With this notable exception, the increased frequency of psychiatric disorder found amongst children following head injury appears to be a function of pre-morbid characteristics and the stresses associated with head injury rather than of brain damage *per se*.

Estimates of the frequency of behavioural disturbance after head injury vary widely as a function of the severity of the injury and probably the sensitivity of the assessment. However, they are clearly common, if not the most common of the longer lasting sequelae. Recovery appears to continue for up to three years, although there is a suggestion that the problems can recur at later stages of development.

SOCIAL ADJUSTMENT

We have reviewed the various consequences of head injury of a physical, cognitive, and behavioural kind, but what effect do these have on the child's ability to pursue a normal life? How far do these deficits disrupt his schooling, his family life, his friendships, and his interests and hobbies? Few studies have investigated these crucial issues.

Since all children go to school and succeed or fail on similar tasks, assessing the social effects of head injury is much easier than in adults where one is contrasting and comparing the ability of people to return to work of varying kinds and where there are very different demands on the person, both at work and in personal and social relationships. Scholastic work is, of course, closely bound up with intellectual capacity and it would hardly be surprising if deficits of a cognitive kind proved crucial in this respect.

Even amongst children with relatively mild head injuries Chadwick *et al.* (1981 *a*) discovered a high rate of reading backwardness. However, since this was present throughout a two-year follow-up and since there was no recovery pattern the authors concluded that this was not a result of head injury but related to the nature of the population at risk. However, the same authors found that amongst cases with a PTA of more than three weeks, there was reading impairment followed by subsequent recovery. Residual impairment was found only amongst those who also showed persistent intellectual impairment. The final follow-up in this study was only two years and three months after injury and the authors make the important point that scholastic measures may not show immediate effects. This child may no longer progress at a normal rate and retarded attainments may not become obvious until later. Indeed in a group which included mildly injured cases Klonoff *et al.* (1977) found that only 74.3 per cent of younger children (less than nine years old) and 66.7 per cent of older children were making normal progress in school five years after injury. Flach and Malmros (1972) also found that amongst their group with simple fractures or concussion, two-thirds were able to perform normally in school during the eight to ten years after injury. Surprisingly, a similar proportion was found to be achieving normally at school in their more severely injured group with verified brain contusions. Where the brainstem was affected, however, only half were making normal scholastic progress. The significance of brainstem damage is unlikely to be due to a direct and specific effect of brain damage on scholastic performance but rather to the fact that brainstem damage is normally associated with a greater degree of cortical damage (Ommaya and Gennarelli 1974).

Chadwick *et al.* (1981 *a*) found that seven children (all with PTAs exceeding three weeks) were rated by teachers as experiencing difficulties in their school work or had been placed in special schools. Heiskanen and Kaste (1974) found that if a child had been unconscious for more than two weeks he was rarely able to make normal progress at school. Of 34 children unconscious for 24 hours or more the authors found eight who were unable to remain in a normal school and a further nine whose school performance was poor. The remaining seventeen were coping fairly normally.

Brink *et al.* (1970) studied an even more severely injured population; children who had been unconscious for more than a week following head injury. Of the 46 survivors, 12 were unable to resume any form of schooling, 26 were in special schools, and only eight were in normal schools. Even amongst the eight some were coping poorly with school.

Little information exists in the literature concerning other aspects of social re-adjustment in head-injured children. Flach and Malmros (1972) rated the social position of their subjects by comparison with a sibling or parent. Amongst the 53 patients who had suffered concussion or a simple fracture, a quarter (13) were judged to be maladjusted by this criterion. A similar finding was obtained from their sub-group with complicated skull fractures or brain contusion but more than half of those with brainstem involvement were rated as socially maladjusted.

Klonoff and Paris (1974) looked at relationships at school, at home, and with peers amongst their group of unselected children with head injury. The time when relationships at home were most likely to be disrupted was one year after trauma and this occurred in about 10 per cent of their sample.

After two years only 5 per cent of children were judged to have disturbed relationships with peers. None of the slight differences between boys or girls or age groups was statistically significant.

An interesting study of the family and head injury in childhood has been carried out but not as yet published by Brown and colleagues. These authors found that changes in parental handling of head-injured children were common during the two years after injury. Usually this was towards an under- rather than an over-use of discipline. For example, at the one year follow-up more than 20 per cent of parents of severely head-injured children were rated as using too little discipline, whereas none of the parents of control or mildly injured children were so rated. This was particularly common when the child was on anti-convulsive medication. Furthermore, changes in parental handling were associated with the presence of psychiatric disorder in the child. In discussing the direction of causality in this association the authors cite two further findings. Firstly, parents reported 'injury' characteristics rather than the behaviour of the child to account for their anxiety. Secondly, parental handling did not differ according to the type of disturbance (e.g. behavioural *v.* emotional). From these two findings Brown and colleagues conclude that the parent's behaviour is not reactive to the child's disturbance but may in fact increase the risk of disturbance developing in the child.

Brown and colleagues also provide some evidence concerning the stresses on the parents of head-injured children. More than 20 per cent of those with severely injured children were rated as having suffered adverse changes in their marriage during the follow-up period. The authors delineated four ways in which different families reacted to the anxieties. Overprotection was the most common reaction. In addition to a decreased use of discipline, parents were more likely to do things for the child, to appease him and to be overly restrictive. Denial that the child had changed was the next most common reaction. The authors found one family where the child had been scapegoated and one where the parents had reacted by devising a self-help programme for their child.

DISCUSSION

Perhaps the most surprising finding in this review is the lack of information concerning age effects on head injury sustained during childhood. This is doubly surprising when one considers the firm evidence concerning age effects within adult victims (e.g. Carlsson, Von Essen, and Lofgren 1968, Heiskanen and Sipponen 1970). In contrast to the relative stability of adulthood, childhood is a continuously evolving state. The developmental stage at which the head injury is sustained is likely to be a crucial determinant of the course of recovery. Few studies have even considered this variable and those that have, have simply divided their subjects into two groups. There is confusing evidence on the effects of age on recovery from cognitive deficit and virtually no evidence concerning age and psychiatric or personality problems. Nor is there information concerning the effects of head injury on social adjustment of children of different ages.

The notion of delayed effects of the injury is an interesting one, and warrants further study. This is suggested by Bowman *et al.* (1974) in relation to personality changes and by Chadwick *et al.* (1981*a*) in connection with scholastic attainments and takes two somewhat different forms. Chadwick *et al.* (1981*a*) simply suggest that impaired cognitive performance may have a cumulative effect on new learning such that the child's level of attainment gradually falls further behind. Bowman *et al.* (1974), however, have suggested that as the child grows older the demands on him become greater and the residual intellectual and personality disorders prevent these demands from being met. Once again one can see a clear need for a developmental perspective when considering head injury in children.

A related issue concerns the concept of age-appropriate behaviour. It has been suggested that some post-traumatic personality changes may be better tolerated by the family when the victim is a child rather than an adult. However, as the child grows towards adulthood, without further recovery, the problems associated with disinhibited behaviour, poor memory and so on are likely to grow rather than diminish. Indeed the study by Black *et al.* (1971) has produced empirical evidence on just this point. Their findings suggest that behaviour problems such as stealing, fighting, and destructiveness show a rise after head injury followed by recovery, followed by a further rise four or five years after injury.

There is clearly a need for studies with even longer follow-up periods with children than with adults. It is also important for those concerned with the rehabilitation of children after head injury to be aware of this pattern.

Although individual subjects in studies have been assessed later, the longest period of follow-up for a group of children is five years after head injury. Klonoff *et al.* (1977) have found that cognitive recovery can continue throughout this period. This is a longer period of recovery than has so far been demonstrated in adults and clearly further research is needed to examine the nature of this recovery as well as its limits.

There are some interesting though tentative pointers from studies which have investigated behavioural disorders in children and family patterns. There is the suggestion that anxiety leads parents to use discipline more sparingly after a child suffers a head injury and that this in turn leads to a higher chance of personality disturbance in the child. Clearly this needs further confirmation, but certainly it appears to have important ramifications for the rehabilitation of such children. Indeed, it is tempting to speculate that firm behavioural management of adult patients may be even more hard for relatives to achieve and may contribute to the personality problems exhibited by some patients.

The problem of rehabilitation of children after head injury appears to have received little attention. Specialized, medical facilities for rehabilitation after the acute phase of recovery are apparently lacking. In the United Kingdom it is common for permanently disabled children to be placed in special facilities provided by the education service. In the most severe cases this may be supplemented by residential care in a hospital for the mentally handicapped. The question of whether neurological rehabilitation centres are needed for children is a difficult one. Clearly a young child's primary need is to avoid separation from parents whenever possible. Even day patient facilities catering for this specialized group would have to be organized on a regional basis and the distances involved might well rule out daily travel. Perhaps the best solution would be peripatetic remedial specialists who could travel to schools, or even families, attempting to rehabilitate a head-injured child. Their role would be to provide advice and guidance in the appropriate measures that may be taken by parents and teachers. In addition to speech and physiotherapy there would seem to be a place for behavioural and cognitive therapies (McAuley and McAuley 1977; Meichenbaum 1977) to help overcome behaviour disturbances and anger control problems. There is also a need for counselling and advice on the parents' use of disciplinary measures and to counteract the tendency to over-protect the child.

In conclusion, children who suffer head injuries, like adult patients, may suffer a range of physical, sensory, cognitive, and behavioural disturbances, the extent of which depend on the severity of the injury, pre-morbid characteristics of the child, family coping abilities, and possibly other environmental influences following injury. Further clarification is needed of the range of cognitive deficits that may occur, the nature and period of recovery from these, and the effects of the child's stage of development at the time of injury. Investigation and trials of specific rehabilitative measures are needed.

ACKNOWLEDGEMENTS

I wish to thank Professor M. Rutter, Dr O. Chadwick and Mrs Gill Brown, who allowed me to read four of their papers prior to publication. I also thank them for making available to me a paper not yet submitted for publication and allowing me to quote from it.

REFERENCES

Benton, A. L. (1974). Clinical Neuropsychology of childhood: an overview. In *Clinical neuropsychology: current status and applications* (ed. R. M. Reitan and L. A. Davison), pp.47–52. Wiley, London.

Bergreen, S. M. (1972). Accidents and surgical emergencies in a population of mentally retarded children. *Acta Paediat. Scand.* **62**, 289–96.

——, Blumer, D., Wellner, A. M., and Walker A. E. (1971). The head-injured child: time-course of recovery with implications for rehabilitation. In *Head injury: proceedings of an international symposium.* pp.131–7. Churchill Livingstone, Edinburgh.

Black, P., Jeffries, J. J., Blumer, D., Wellner, A., and Walker, A. E. (1969). The post-traumatic syndrome in children. In *The late effects of head injury.* (ed. A. E. Walker, E. F. Caveness, and M. Critchley,

Blau, A. (1936). Mental changes following head trauma in children. *Arch. Psychiatr. Neurol.* **35**, 723.

Bowman, K. M., Blau, A., and Reich, R. (1974). Psychiatric state after head injury in adults and children. In *Brock's injuries of the brain and spinal cord and their coverings* (ed. E. H. Feiring) pp. 570 – 613. Springer, New York.

Brink, J. D., Garrett, A. L., Hale, W. R., Woo-Sam, J., and Nickel, V. L. (1970). Recovery of motor and intellectual function in children sustaining severe head injuries. *Devel. Med. Child. Neurol.* **12**, 565–71.

Brooks, D. N., Aughton, M. E., Bond, M. R., Jones, P., and Rizvi, S. (1980). Cognitive sequelae in relationship to early indices of severity of brain damage after severe blunt head injury. *J. Neurol. Neurosurg. Psychiatr.* **43**, 529–34.

Brown, G. W., and Davidson, S. (1978). Social class, psychiatric disorder of mother and accidents to children. *Lancet* **i**, 378–81.

——, Chadwick, O., Shaffer, D., Rutter, M., and Traub, M. (1981). A prospective study of children with head injuries, III Psychiatric sequelae. *Psychol. Med.* **11**, 63–78.

Carlsson, C. A., Von Essen, C., and Lofgren, J. (1968). Factors affecting the clinical course of patients with severe head injuries. *J. Neurosurg.* **29**, 242–51.

Chadwick, O., Rutter,, M., and Shaffer, D. (1981*a*). A prospective study of children with head injuries: IV Specific Cognitive deficit. *Psychol. Med.* (In press.)

——, Rutter, M., Brown, G., Shaffer, D., and Traub, M. (1981*b*). A prospective study of children with head injuries: II Cognitive sequelae. *Psychol. Med.* **11**, 49–62.

Comninos, S. C. (1979). Early prognosis of severe head injuries in children. *Acta Neur. Suppl.* **28**, 144–7.

Conkey, R. C. (1938). Psychological changes associated with head injury. *Arch. Psychol.* No. 2, 3, 2.

Courville, C. B. (1965). Contrecoup injuries of the brain in infancy. *Arch. Surg.* **90**, 157–65.

Craft, A. W. (1975). Head injury in children. In *Handbook of clinical neurology* Vol.23 (ed. P. Vinken and A. Bruyn) pp.101–20. Elsevier, Oxford.

——, Shaw, D. A., and Cartlidge, N. E. F. (1972). Head injury in children. *Br. Med. J.* **IV**, 200–3.

Cummins, B. H. and Potter, J. M. (1970). Head injury due to falls from heights. *Injury* **2**, 61.

Fedio, P. and Mirsky, A. F. (1969). Selective intellectual deficits in children with temporal lobe of centrencephalic epilepsy. *Neuropsychologia* **7**, 287–300.

Flach, J. and Malmros, R. (1972). A long-term follow-up study of children with severe head injury. *Scand. J. Rehabil. Med.* **4**, 9–15.

Geschwind, N. (1974). Late changes in the nervous system: an overview. In *Plasticity and Recovery of Function in the central nervous system* (ed. D. G. Stein, J. J. Rosen, and N. Butters) pp. 467–508. Academic Press, New York.

Harrington, J. A. and Letemendia, A. B. (1958). Persistent psychiatric disorders after head injuries in children. *J. Ment. Sci.* **104**, 1205–18.

Heiskanen, O. and Kaste, M. (1974). Late prognosis of severe brain injury in children. *Dev. Med. Child. Neurol.* **16**, 11–14.

—— and Sipponen, P. (1970). Prognosis of severe brain injury. *Acta Neurol. Scand.* **46**, 343–8.

Hendrick, E. B., Harwood-Hash, D. C. F., and Hudson, A. R. (1964). Head injury in children: survey of 4465 consecutive cases at the hospital for sick children. *Clin. Neurosurg.* **11**, 46–65.

Jamieson, D. L. and Kaye, H. H. (1974). Accidental head injury in childhood. *Arch. Dis. Child.* **49**, 376–81.

—— and Yelland, J. D. N. (1968). Extradural haematoma: a report of 167 cases. *J. Neurosurg.* **29**, 13–23.

Jennett, B. (1972). Head injuries in children. *Dev. Med. Child Neurol.* **14**, 137–47.

Klonoff, H. (1971). Head injuries in children: predisposing factors. *Am. J. Publ. Hlth.* **61**, 2405–17.

——, H., Low, M. D., and Clark, C. (1977). Head injuries in children: a prospective five-year follow-up. *J. Neurol. Neurosurg. Psychiatr.* **40**, 1211–19.

—— and Paris, R. (1974). Immediate, short-term and residual effects of acute head injuries in children. Neuropsychological and neurological correlates. In *Clinical Neuropsychology: current status and applications.* (ed. R. M. Reitan and L. A. Davison) pp.179–210. Wiley, Washington.

Levin, H. S. and Eisenberg, H. M. (1979). Neuropsychological outcome of closed head injury. *Child Brain* **5**, 281–92.

McAuley, R. and McAuley, P. (1977). *Child behavioural problems,* Macmillan, London.

Meichenbaum, D. (1977). *Cognitive behaviour modification,* Plenum Press, New York.

Money, J. (1963). Two cytogenic syndromes: Psychologic Comparisons. I Intelligence and specific factor quotients. *J. Psychiatr. Res.* **2**, 223–31.

Norrman, B. and Svahn, K. (1961). A follow-up study of severe brain injuries. *Acta Psychiatr. Scand.* **37**, 236–64.

Ommaya, A. K. and Gennarelli, T. A. (1974). Cerebal concussion and traumatic unconsciousness. *Brain,* **97**, 633–54.

Partington, M. W. (1960). The importance of accident proneness in the aetiology of head injuries in children. *Arch. Dis. Child.* **35**, 215–23.

Rune, V. (1970). Acute head injuries in children. *Acta Paediatr. Scand.* Supplement 209.

St. James Roberts, I. (1979). Neurological plasticity, recovery from brain insult and child development. In *Advances in child development and behaviour* (ed. H. W. Reese and L. P. Lipsitt) Vol.14, pp.254–319. Academic Press, New York.

Schaffer, D., Chadwick, O., and Rutter, M. (1975). Psychiatric outcome of localised head injury in children. In *Outcome of Severe Damage to the Central Nervous System.* pp.191–213. Ciba Symposium, No.74. Elsevier, London.

Thompson, J. A. (1977). Cognitive effects of cortical lesions sustained in childhood. PhD. Thesis, University of London.

Van Dongen, H. R. and Loonen, M. C. (1977). Factors related to prognosis in aphasia. *Cortex* **13**, 131–6.

Woo Sam, J., Zimmerman, T. L., Brink, J. D., Uyehara, K., and Miller, A. R. (1970). Socio-economic status and post-trauma intelligence in children with severe head injuries. *Psychol. Rep.* **27**, 147–53.

10 Behaviour disorders following severe brain injury: their presentation and psychological management

R. L. Wood

INTRODUCTION

Recent studies have commented on the irony that improved medical management in the acute phase following serious head injury increases the number of survivors and, *pari passu*, the number of severely handicapped individuals, many of whom will become a burden to their families and rehabilitation or social services (Bond and Brooks 1976; Brooks and Aughton 1979; McKinlay *et al.* 1981; Jennett et al. 1981). The social outcome of such injuries is now receiving closer attention, with the result that many studies suggest that emotional or other psychosocial changes are more disturbing for relatives and more difficult for the community to accept than the various forms of physical handicap (Thompsen 1974; Rosenbaum and Najenson 1976; Lezak 1978; Oddy, Humphrey, and Uttley 1978; and McKinlay *et al.* 1981).

One of the characteristics of psychosocial change is a less stable pattern of behaviour. This may include reduced tolerance of stress, increased emotional lability, verbally threatening or even physically aggressive behaviour, and a coarsening or blunting of many social skills, with the result that the person may often behave inappropriately, without concern for the feelings of others. Such behaviour changes may lead to problems in the re-settlement of the head injured within the community, and may affect the earlier stages of clinical rehabilitation, when such behaviours may be seen by therapists as threatening or likely to interfere with the process of rehabilitation.

So far, few studies have concerned themselves with the nature of disordered or disturbed behaviour after serious head injury, and even fewer with the control of such behaviour. Fahy, Irving, and Millac (1967) described the high incidence of psychiatric symptoms in such patients, while Lishman (1973, 1978) described a number of specific behaviour problems that have followed serious head injury and which accompany intellectual impairment. Earlier studies (Tennent 1937; Shapiro 1939; Hillbom 1951) were concerned principally with psychotic reactions and their aetiology but it is only recently that attention has been paid to the control of behaviour disturbances within the context of a systematic psychological framework called behaviour management (Goodkin 1966; Wall 1969; Hollon 1973; Wood and Eames 1981).

Methods of behaviour management demand that one pays close attention to the kind of problem behaviour that needs to be changed and also to the clinical or environmental variables involved in the initiation, maintenance, and direction of such behaviour. This has led to the development of a taxonomy of such behaviour disorders which, although not complete, does improve our understanding of the nature of such behaviour and ways of bringing it under control. This broad taxonomy distinguishes between positive, negative, and dissociative problems as follows.

BEHAVIOUR DISORDERS FOLLOWING SEVERE BRAIN INJURY

Positive behaviour disorders

These actively interfere with the rehabilitation process or the social acceptability of the patient. They are largely anti-social behaviours and at least three kinds of this behaviour disorder can be described.

Aggressive behaviours

Aggression is not a unitary form of behaviour, and can be seen in different forms, each having a different aetiology. One form is characterized by a sudden, spontaneous outburst of possibly violent aggression which is unprovoked, poorly controlled and usually short lived. This form of aggression is basically epileptic in nature and has been attributed to damage within the medial part of the temporal lobes (Sweets, Ervin, and Mark 1969; Lishman 1978).

It is important to distinguish between post-traumatic epileptogenic behaviours and the syndrome of temporal lobe epilepsy. In the latter, aggressive behaviours are associated with a more widespread disturbance of personality, which is not necessarily the case in head-injured patients who show impulsive aggressive disorders. Another important difference is that aggression following head injury is not necessarily associated with the lack of remorse often found in patients suffering from temporal lobe epilepsy of a non-traumatic origin. Indeed, patients with post-traumatic epileptic aggression frequently show a great deal of remorse for an episode of aggressive or destructive behaviour over which they appear to have no control. Often, this is quite out of character with pre-morbid personality and is not a feature of their behaviour between attacks.

A similar phenomenon of aggressive behaviour can occur following head injury, which is not a result of epilepsy but of 'reduced control' (Lishman 1978). Typically the patient is subject, under minor provocation, to violent behaviour quite out of proportion to the eliciting event. Sometimes such aggression is an exaggeration of pre-morbid personality traits which have become less controlled and more susceptible to the effects of stress, alcohol, or frustration. In other cases, however, the phenomenon might be a new and disturbing feature. This kind of aggressive behaviour is probably a consequence of damage to frontal lobe structures and the loss of learned inhibitory controls. This may be part of a more global frontal lobe syndrome which includes a blunting of various social skills and a tendency towards coarse behaviour.

It is not my intention to imply that aggressive behaviour is either a feature of focal temporal lobe injury or a loss of learned inhibitory controls following frontal lobe injury. Aggression is often the result of more diffuse damage which involves both of these structures, or can even be part of a general state of irritability which Lishman regards as one of the most common of the emotional responses following head injury. In such cases, aggression is not usually extreme but is a more enduring feature of short temper, non-cooperation, abusive language, and generally threatening or difficult behaviour. Lishman states that this kind of 'organic irritability' rarely persists longer than 12 months after injury. It can, however, survive as a *learned* reaction to stress and be maintained as a generalized response to other psychosocial sequelae of head injury e.g. anxiety, financial or social problems, or depression (Lishman 1968).

Sexual behaviour

Inappropriate or uncontrolled sexual behaviour can be as distressing or threatening to others as aggression. It varies considerably in its nature and intensity and includes tactless attempts at intimacy, conversation loaded with sexual innuendo, inappropriate touching, lewd remarks, and in the more severe cases indecent exposure and public masturbation. Unfortunately, clinical experience suggests that many disinhibited sexual behaviours are associated with frontal lobe injury: the patient is therefore relatively insightless and has little appreciation of the social effect such behaviour has on other individuals. This lack of perception, combined with reduced control over responses to basic drives, makes this behaviour difficult to control and offers a poor prognosis to treatment.

Attention seeking

Extreme forms of attention seeking are not a frequent legacy of head injury but when they occur, they cause management problems and staff reactions which may be quite disproportionate to the problem behaviour itself. The reason for this is that often the behaviour appears to be bizarre, involving self-injury, window smashing, screaming for no apparent reason, or head-banging. This creates, in many relatives or rehabilitation staff not experienced in psychiatry, a feeling of helplessness, or of being out of control in a situation which the patient himself seems to manipulate and command.

This kind of behaviour is largely the result of a subtle conditioning procedure whereby patients learn a new form of behaviour which enables them to avoid the effects of stressful or demanding situations. It may, however, reflect a pre-morbid personality characteristic which has been allowed to emerge, along with other disinhibited behaviours, following injury. Unlike these other behaviours, the learned component in attention seeking is often so great that a good response can be expected in the face of stricter personal and environmental controls.

Negative behaviour disorders

These are mainly disorders of drive and motivation and include the effects of organically imposed apathy and lethargy. Patients who demonstrate this kind of behaviour problem generally produce much less behaviour in a situation that would elicit interest and exploratory behaviour in most normal individuals. Although there is bound to be some overlap, negative behaviours may be divided into two types. These can be described as arousal disorders and motivational disorders.

Arousal disorders

This is an extreme form of negative behaviour in which patients will exhibit a complete indifference to or total lack of interest in their environment. They give the impression of being drowsy, lethargic, retarded in thought, and passive in the face of changing stimuli. Such behaviour may be seen in connection with severe brainstem injuries and may be assumed to result from a lack of cortical arousal which reduces ability to respond to stimuli generally. These patients are often oblivious of the need for reward of any kind, so that if left to their own devices they will progressively deteriorate and make little or no effort to remedy their plight by seeking food or comfort. Obviously, this represents the most severe kind of arousal disorder which is found in those patients who have sustained the most serious head injuries.

Motivational disorders

A more frequent and problematic form of negative behaviour is seen in patients who are often physically intact and without severe cognitive impairment. Such patients may *describe* an interest in some activity but, if given the opportunity, fail to *show* any such interest. Unlike arousal disorders, this particular problem is more an inability to translate interest (a cognitive component) into the physical activity necessary to partake of such interest (the drive component). As such, the disturbance of behaviour may be regarded as a problem of motivation.

Motivation is central to rehabilitation and in head-injury rehabilitation it poses a major problem (Belmont 1969; Field 1976). Depending upon the nature of injury, motivation can be effected in two ways:

1. *Reduction of arousal and drive* — In the normal individual, drive strength is related to need on the one hand and the attractiveness of the stimulus (reward) on the other (Hull 1943). With this category of patient, however, one cannot manipulate the attractiveness of reward and its need strengths because such patients have little *incentive* to achieve reward (whatever it is) and will therefore not direct any *effort* into the behaviour required to obtain such reward.

2. *Lack of hedonic responses* — Behaviour which is directed towards achieving some reward may be referred to as 'hedonic responsiveness' (Wood and Eames 1981). This appears to be an essential pre-requisite for motivation, as the amount of effort a person with a given level of drive is prepared to exert in order to obtain a given goal depends directly on the extent that the patient sees the goal as rewarding. If the patient is anhedonic (having no, or at least a diminished sense of reward), it may be that no degree of effort is likely to be made to achieve any reward.

Dissociative disorders

Dissociation had been recently described as a process whereby, in an attempt to control an unpleasant emotional response, a group of mental processes is split off from the main stream of consciousness, during which behaviour loses its relationship with the rest of personality (Davidson and Neale 1974). The concept of dissociation is much older than this, however, being originally introduced by Janet (1907). Like Charcot before him, Janet emphasized the neurological–physiological aspects of thinking. He believed that thought (and therefore behaviour) was the result of a synthesis of the multiple and varied experiences to which we are exposed daily. He used the term 'dissociation' as the pathological condition brought about by a breakdown in this synthesis. Factors which lead to dissociation are partly hereditary and partly the result of some kind of physical or psychological 'shock'. In this way Janet associated psychopathological reactions with physiological states.

Hysterical symptoms have figured prominently in some quite recent references to head injury (Whitlock 1967; Lishman 1978). Lishman describes a range of dissociative states which may occur following head-injury, e.g. fits, fugues, amnesias, Ganser states, motor paralysis, anaesthesias, and sensory disturbances. He describes the onset as usually occurring soon after injury, although later developments may occur in association with depression or when complex neurotic states emerge in relation to compensation issues. Whitlock's study found that of a total of 56 patients admitted to hospital with hysterical states, nearly two-thirds had suffered significant preceding or co-existing brain damage. Twenty-one per cent of these patients had sustained head injury. In reviewing this evidence, Lishman concludes that, 'It would seem that head injury may be a more frequent antecedent of the clinical picture of hysteria than is commonly supposed.'

The reason for placing dissociative behaviour within the context of hysteria is because patients can be seen to have some motivation for the symptoms they exhibit, which show a lack of genuineness, a degree of dramatization, and exaggeration. This may include unusual and bizarre body postures or disturbances of speech function which have no neurological foundation or neuropsychological similarities. Even more usual is the problem of a patient being unable, or unwilling, to produce a particular physical or behavioural response to command, when such responses are known to be produced spontaneously. One cannot help but feel that such patients have much more potential for recovery and are much less cognitively or physically handicapped than their overt presentation suggests.

Such behaviour has a devastating effect on any rehabilitation programme because of patients' active refusal to participate in any meaningful or constructive way. They will attempt to manipulate staff involved in the treatment programme and on more than one occasion have been known to sabotage attempts at rehabilitation by injuring themselves in some way (e.g. holding a foot against a hot water pipe until the skin blisters) in an attempt to prevent a specific rehabilitation programme (in this case a walking programme) continuing.

This phenomenon was recently referred to by Wood and Eames. It is in many ways associated with a lack of hedonic responsiveness, similar to that described in the category of negative behaviour disorders but more severe and bizarre. Patients with dissociative disorders not only fail to work for some reward, appearing indifferent to the value of reinforcement, but also appear immune to the effect of pain because they will refuse to make any effort that will lead to the avoidance of punishment.

MANAGING BEHAVIOUR

A method which controls inappropriate behaviour, or otherwise stimulates behaviour in patients with drive or motivational problems, is important if an organized programme of rehabilitation is to proceed. Such a method does exist and has been applied over many years in a variety of clinical situations. This is the procedure of behaviour management or behaviour modification.

This method has already been applied to individuals with brain injury (Goodkin 1966; Wall 1969; Hollon 1972). These studies describe individual behaviour programmes carried out within the context of general and conventional rehabilitation units, for the purpose of eliminating disruptive and unmanageable behaviour, improving occupational therapy skills and wheelchair mobility, and producing understandable and appropriate speech.

The only reported application of behavioural methods to *groups* of brain-damaged patients has been by Wood and Eames (1981). This described how behavioural methods were used during a multidisciplinary rehabilitation programme, on patients who were effectively denied rehabilitation following severe brain injury, because their behaviour was regarded as too disturbed or uncooperative to allow treatment in conventional rehabilitation units. A 3-year follow-up of these patients is now in progress (Eames and Wood in preparation) and the examples described later in the chapter are of patients treated on this unit. It must be emphasized, however, that although a psychological method of treatment will be described, one must not lose sight of the many neurological and neuropsychological constraints which might interfere with behavioural learning. This means that psychological methods must co-exist with forms of medical management to produce the most successful results. This principle is most evident in the management of behaviour problems which have an epileptic basis. We have found that the impulsive, unprovoked outbursts of aggression do not respond well to either medical or behaviour management alone. If, however, behaviour management is combined with an appropriate anticonvulsant drug, one can usually expect a progressive and successful improvement in the control of such behaviour.

The most straightforward way of presenting the basic principles of behaviour management involves making the distinction between procedures that may be employed to *increase* the probability of behaviour and those employed to *decrease* its probability. Procedures that increase behaviour are used when the objective is to motivate the individual to actively participate in his own rehabilitation (Allyon and Milan 1979). Those that decrease behaviour are used for the elimination of bad habits or negative attitudes which interfere with the goals of rehabilitation.

The major technique for increasing behaviour is that of reinforcement. It is expected that individuals will be more likely to engage in certain activities or behaviour if this results in the presentation or continuation of a pleasant or desired condition or outcome. To decrease behaviour, techniques are used that inhibit inappropriate responses, e.g. presentation or continuation of something unpleasant or withdrawal of something pleasant. To summarize, we can describe the four basic conditions from which behaviour management techniques develop:

1. To increase behaviour: (i) present something desirable — positive re-

inforcement; (ii) end something undesirable—negative reinforcement.

2. To decrease behaviour: (i) present something undesirable—positive punishment; (ii) end something desirable—negative punishment.

The aims of behaviour management with the brain-injured population have already been stated by Wood and Eames. The primary use is to *control* those positive behaviour disorders that prevent rehabilitation from taking place. This in many ways is the paramount reason for behaviour modification. Until *control over* behaviour is achieved, it is not possible to effect a positive *change in* that behaviour. Once control has been achieved, the next stage involves '*shaping*' an existing behavioural response into something which is more appropriate, more adaptive and more flexible in nature. Finally there is the aim of 'evincing' behaviour in those cases in which motivational problems are the primary feature.

Management system

A convenient way of applying behaviour management in rehabilitation is the 'token economy' (Allyon and Azrin 1968). This provides a way of systematically delivering reinforcement to groups of people and structuring the environment to promote adaptive social behaviour. Three essential, yet simple, ingredients make up the token economy:

1. A medium of exchange—the token.

2. A variety of back-up reinforcers—e.g. sweets, cigarettes, drinks, or any other desirable commodity which can be obtained using the token as a form of currency.

3. A set of rules that describe the interrelationship between (i)behaviours and token earnings; (ii) between tokens and back-up reinforcers.

It can reasonably be argued that the use of tokens is simply a means of ensuring that nursing and therapy staff are alert to the need to respond to certain behaviours in a specific way. This increases staff–patient interaction, helps desirable behaviours to increase and aids the elimination of maladaptive behaviours. Tokens can be administered as 'event' based reinforcers, i.e. responding to a behaviour as soon as it occurs; or on a time basis, when the object is to maintain a particular behaviour (e.g. co-operation) over time. The first not only probably increases the frequency of a desired behaviour, it also brings the patient's attention to it and as such helps develop the spontaneous, self-controlled expression of such behaviour in patients who may otherwise remain indifferent to the nature and effects of particular environmental changes.

For tokens to have any significance at all, they must acquire some secondary value and therefore be meaningful to the patient. This means that one must be able to offer a wide range and variety of back-up reinforcers which are seen as being rewarding by the patient, not the staff, and which can be made available at reasonable intervals, or for specific purposes during the rehabilitation programme.

The structured environment offered by a token economy allows a variety of individual behaviour management programmes to be implemented, in a controlled way, with careful measurement and recording of behaviour change to evaluate an individual's response to therapy over time. Because the system necessarily involves restriction of privilege, it helps to generate effortful and co-operative behaviour (to achieve such privilege) in patients who may otherwise show little incentive to apply themselves to rehabilitative training.

Applications of behaviour modification

The methods available for behavioural learning with the brain injured are essentially no different from those used with any other clinical population. If there is a difference, it is in the way these various techniques are applied, or chosen, to accommodate the neurological and neuropsychological variables which can interfere with behavioural learning. The main neurological variable has already been described, i.e. epileptogenic behaviour disturbances which require a combination of behavioural and medical management. The main neuropsychological variable involves an impairment of attention which leads to a short attention span and distractability, which Smith and Wood (in preparation) found to be a significant impediment to some severely head-injured patients acquiring a discrimination learning response. Other neuropsychological variables include the effects of memory impairment, disorders of perception, and the overall blunting of intellectual abilities which prejudice a patient's ability to acquire a behavioural response.

The existence of such neurological or neuropsychological sequelae means that it is necessary to pay particular attention to the way reinforcement is applied, allowing optimal conditions for the patient to make the association between behaviour and reinforcement and be aware of the environmental cues that precede such reinforcement. This means that reinforcement must be administered as *immediately* as possible and in an *obvious* way to ensure that the correct associations are made. It is also desirable that reinforcement is given as *frequently* as possible over an *extended* period, to help consolidate the behavioural response, through a process of over-learning which, in turn, will help that response to *generalize* to other situations that are not so well structured or controlled. It will also help prevent extinction or even actual forgetting of such a response.

Positive reinforcement

Great emphasis must be placed on the value of positive reinforcement and rewarding opportunities in encouraging a patient to make some effort towards specific rehabilitative goals. Social reinforcement, praise, encouragement, or simply giving the patient attention, are potent forms of reward for good behaviour. Within a token economy system, the plastic token is a very convenient way of administering such reward because of its acquired secondary value in obtaining the privileges available. With more severely impaired patients, it is advisable to make the time interval between token payment and exchange of that token for a tangible reward as short as possible, or even administering reward in some tangible form in the first place e.g. giving sweets or cigarettes instead of tokens.

Fig. 10.1 shows the value of token-administered reinforcements in overcoming a positive behaviour disorder in a patient who needed to improve his independent walking ability. This patient was referred three years after sustaining a severe head injury. He had an epileptogenic aggressive disorder, a form of scanning dysarthria, and a right hemiplegia. He arrived in a wheelchair, in which he had remained for the previous three years. He was uncooperative in physiotherapy, and although he had the necessary physical ability he refused to attempt independent walking. A programme was designed whereby he was helped to walk down a long corridor which had been marked off in 10-yard sections. If he completed one section using a reasonable walking pattern (as judged by the physiotherapist), he was rewarded with one token. He could earn a maximum of 12 tokens each session (four lengths of the corridor). If he collected above a certain number of tokens he was allowed to exchange them for a reward of his choice. This was determined on a sliding scale, the patient being required to earn an in-

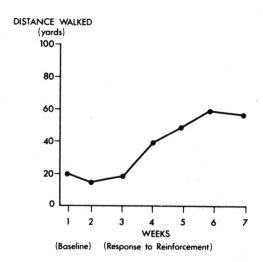

Fig. 10.1.

Positive reinforcement programme to improve independent walking.

creasing number of tokens as his walking ability and distance gradually increased. The success of this programme can be judged by the fact that when the patient was discharged he was fully mobile and was seen loading his own wheelchair (which his parents insisted they would take with them) into the boot of the family car.

Negative punishment

This describes a rather controversial system of behavioural management in which patients can be deprived of their freedom of movement, meals or other privileges that may be available within the hospital environment. It also includes the technique called 'time out' which is applied to individuals who demonstrate positive disorders, i.e. aggressive or disruptive behaviour towards staff or patients on the unit. This involves placing a patient into a locked room for a period of five minutes, or multiples of five minutes if behaviour continues to be disturbed, every time an aggressive incident occurs.

Our experience suggests that we have had to resort to negative punishment in the form of deprivation procedures more often than may be considered necessary in more conventional behaviour management programmes. This is because patients with negative behaviour disorders lack motivation and are not inclined to co-operate with, or show enthusiasm for, rehabilitative training. By linking effort to reward it is possible to obtain a reasonable degree of effort and co-operation, if not motivation. This allows patients to benefit from rehabilitative training and to improve their functional level. Fig. 10.2 demonstrates the effectiveness of a deprivation

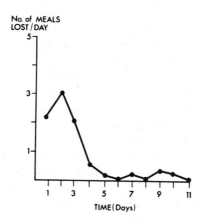

Fig. 10.2.

A negative punishment procedure; the patient was required to walk to the dining room to obtain food.

procedure on another patient who refused to walk. He had sustained a left frontal fracture and a serious brain injury during a criminal assault. He was dysphasic, apathetic, and lethargic with a residual mild right hemiplegia. For the previous eight years he had been a patient on a chronic psychiatric unit. Once it was established that he had a reasonable range of movement and adequate power, sensation and control in his right leg, he was given a walking aid and exercises by the physiotherapist to promote mobility. He made reasonable progress in sessions but would not generalize this ability to any other context. We therefore established a simple programme in which he was informed that his meal was available in the dining room but he was required to walk there to obtain it. At first he made little effort, going without many meals and receiving instead a milk-based substitute. This continued for several days but as the graph shows, his walking increased and became more spontaneous to the point where he arrived on time for nearly all his meals without receiving any prompts from the staff. More important, this walking generalized to other areas within the unit.

If a system of time out is used it is best to begin with a programme called 'time-out-on-the-spot' (TOOTS). This is a system whereby staff are required to ignore attention-seeking or disruptive behaviour. This prevents the patient benefiting from the positively reinforcing effect that attention from staff or other patients may have on many disruptive behaviours. TOOTS is a difficult procedure to administer because of one's natural tendency to give attention to, or actively interrupt, the behaviour of a patient who is being disruptive or injuring himself in some way.

If the behaviour is too disruptive, or if TOOTS does not appear to work, one has to resort to the next form of time-out procedure described *as situational* time-out. This is simply a method of separating the disruptive individual from the group, either by putting him in a side room or outside the door. If the behaviour does not respond to this procedure or if actual physical aggression towards patients, staff, or property is used, then the *time-out room* is the next necessary step.

The use of the time-out room is *not* a method of seclusion. We have found it an effective procedure in dealing with the most disruptive or aggressive forms of behaviour and one which gives therapy and nursing staff confidence in dealing with patients who are difficult or threatening in manner. If one accepts the premise that many disruptive positive behaviour disorders are maintained because of the attention they receive from other people, then it becomes easier to understand how such behaviours continue as long-term sequelae of head injuries and interfere with rehabilitation. Anybody who has observed patients recovering from coma will have seen how most attention is given by nursing staff to patients who are proving difficult in some way, i.e. being noisy, incontinent, or wandering aimlessly around the ward. If such patients are lying in bed quietly or sitting in a chair by their bed without making any noise they are generally ignored, because the nurse's attention is naturally drawn to other patients who need more care. This procedure is bound to selectively reinforce, through attention, disruptive aspects of behaviour which then increase in frequency and generalize to other situations as the patient progresses through the early stages of recovery. It is reasonable to suggest that if the appropriate reinforcement or time-out procedures were used early in the patient's recovery, many of these disruptive behaviours would be prevented from developing.

Figs. 10.3–10.5 demonstrate the effectiveness of situational time-out and the time-out room in controlling disruptive behaviour, learned aggression, and epileptogenic aggression, respectively. The absence of a graph describing a TOOTS procedure does not mean that we have shown it to be unsuccessful, simply that it is so difficult to record on a busy clinical unit (because of the frequency and often subtle way in which TOOTS is applied) that such data are not available. The absence of any baseline, by which to compare the effectiveness of such procedures, must also be understood. When a patient is demonstrating disruptive or actual aggressive behaviour, the effect on staff and the danger to other patients is so great that one cannot afford the luxury of obtaining carefully recorded baselines. One has to introduce a behavioural programme immediately the patient is admitted to the unit to achieve the maximum effect in the shortest period of time.

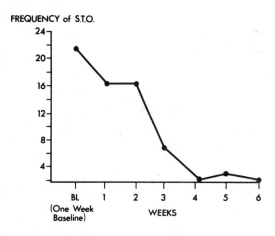

Fig. 10.3.

Reduction of disruptive behaviour using a situational time-out (STO) procedure in a patient 5 years after injury.

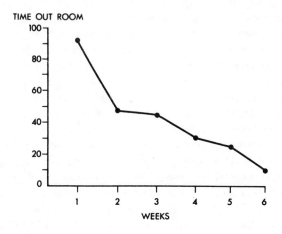

Fig. 10.4.

Control of learned aggression, which was preventing physiotherapy in a patient 5 years after injury.

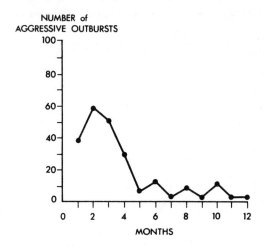

Fig. 10.5.

Control of epileptogenic aggression in a patient 3 years after injury; time-out programme and anti-convulsants were used.

Positive punishment

This is a very controversial procedure within any kind of behaviour management system. We have found it very useful, however, in programmes designed to eliminate specific behaviour problems which have (i) not responded to any other form of treatment and (ii) which prevent that patient receiving rehabilitation or admission to a long-term residential centre such as a Cheshire Home. Although it may appear to a 'last choice' therapy, its effectiveness in eliminating some behaviours—e.g. head banging, spitting, or sexual exposure—is so good that it could be used as a 'first-choice' therapy if it were not such an emotive procedure.

Traditionally, such programmes have used electric shock to administer punishment. We regard this as an excessively punitive and inefficient method. This is because it causes pain which is unpleasant for the patient, yet is not very effective because it cannot be administered at the time the problem behaviour spontaneously occurs in its natural setting. We have preferred the use of aromatic ammonia vapour. This is contained in a bottle and administered by a nurse or therapist as soon as the problem behaviour has been observed. The procedure involves passing the bottle under the patient's nose so that they inhale the vapour which acts as a noxious stimulus to disrupt the unwanted response. The patient is not restrained during this procedure and although the vapour smell is unpleasant, it is in no way harmful or damaging to the mucous membranes. Indeed, it is a very similar sensation to that experienced following inhalation of smelling salts so popular with many members of the older generation.

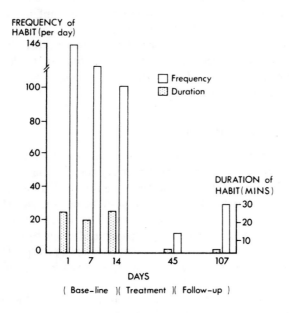

Fig. 10.6

A positive punishment procedure using anomatic ammonia vapour.

Such programmes are introduced for a limited duration and are carefully monitored to ensure that they are achieving good results. The value of this procedure may be measured by its long-term outcome. Not only is it usually successful in overcoming the specific behaviour problem but experience has shown that those patients who relapse after leaving the unit rarely relapse with respect to those behaviours that have been treated in this way.

Figure 10.6 shows the use of this procedure on a patient who was indulging in ritual throat clearing of a particularly nauseating kind. This had proved extremely distasteful to rehabilitation staff in the past and was one of several behaviours which would have prevented him from being accepted into a long-stay centre for the blind. Other behaviour methods were tried with no success but this unpleasant habit was soon eliminated following the administration of ammonia vapour.

Massed practice

This could be a very useful method for introducing reinforcement contingencies at the start of a behaviour programme. It is particularly appropriate when the patient has severe neuropsychological impairment and finds difficulty forming associations between his behaviour and the response to that behaviour. A massed practice procedure requires the patient to repeatedly produce the behaviour you want to modify, under artificial circumstances, while the reinforcement contingencies are gradually introduced under optimal conditions. This helps establish the association between behaviour and reinforcement, thus facilitating the development of the conditioned response when it occurs naturally within its usual environmental setting.

Overlearning and generalization

One of the criticisms directed at behaviour management is that behaviour is only maintained while the patient is actually on a specialized unit. This is not necessarily the case, but a lot depends on the kind of patient involved in treatment, as well as the kind of behaviour being treated. There is more chance of behaviour change being maintained if the management programme includes the procedure for *generalizing* the new behaviour response to other situations. This helps the patient develop an adaptive and flexible behaviour pattern appropriate to a variety of situations or environmental cues.

The maintenance and generalization of behaviour is further helped if the patient *overlearns* the required behavioural response. Overlearning is achieved by responding to minimal or even accidental behaviour responses that are within the same category as the 'target behaviour' under formal control, e.g. in a patient with disinhibited sexual behaviour who in-

appropriately touches female staff, one might implement a time-out programme not only for sexual touching, but for all touching, even brushing
one's shoulder while passing in a corridor. This rather harsh procedure may
seem unfair but it does impress on patients the need to monitor their
behaviour responses carefully, and leads to better behaviour control, more
socially acceptable behaviour and improves opportunities for social
reintegration or rehabilitation of a more conventional kind. Fig. 10.7
provides an example of how such a time-out procedure, which implemented
overlearnng and generalization, gained control of inappropriate sexual
touching which previously had led to the patient being discharged from a
conventional rehabilitation establishment.

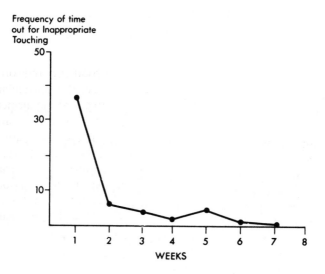

Fig. 10.7.

Elimination of inappropriate sexual behaviour during a negative punishment programme.

One of the most important aspects of the generalization procedure involves that of *weaning* the patient off the reinforcement system. This can be
done by gradually reducing the frequency of reinforcement, expecting the
patient to demonstrate more behaviour for less frequent reward, while at
the same time replacing the tangible back-up reinforcers with more social
reinforcement. This procedure was used to improve independent self-help
skills (Fig. 10.8). It was introduced as part of a morning programme which
involved a patient getting washed, dressed, and presenting herself for
breakfast in time, looking clean and tidy. This patient had proved virtually
unmanageable for the previous 4 years. She was observed to be uncooperative, slow, and disorganized in her behaviour and required a lot of

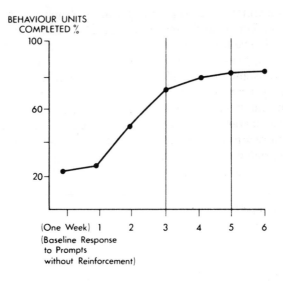

Fig. 10.8.

Improvement in self-help skills during positive reinforcement of individual units of behaviour.

nursing time to maintain personal hygiene. Improved co-operation and per-sonal care was achieved by reducing the total behavioural set to small, manageable units of behaviour e.g. 'get out of bed', 'stand by the wash basin', 'turn on the taps' etc. and a prompt given for each unit. She was re-inforced only after responding appropriately to each prompt. After week 3, the ratio of prompts to behaviour responses changed from a 1:1 to a 1:3 procedure, and after week 5 to a 1:6 procedure. This means that eventually the patient was showing six times as much spontaneous and organized behaviour than at the beginning of the programme. She later progressed to be totally independent in her morning programme and this behaviour was seen to generalize to other dressing and self-care situations.

Applications in a general rehabilitation unit

Although a behaviour management system (possibly utilizing a token economy) may be the best way to present such programmes, it is by no means a necessary condition. Depending on the nature of the problem or therapy programme, behavioural procedures can be implemented by rehabilitation staff in a variety of situations to overcome specific problems.

As an example, consider Fig. 10.9, which shows how a specific physiotherapy procedure, transfer from wheelchair to chair, can be helped by a behavioural approach. This patient had not been out of his wheelchair for 5 years following a severe head injury. He was incontinent of urine and faeces and any attempt to engage him in physiotherapy met with an aggressive response. This was dealt with independently and the outcome is shown in Fig 10.4. The behaviour programme for transfer involved breaking down the therapy task into individual units of movement. These units were then selectively and immediately reinforced with chocolate, depending upon whether they were performed correctly or not. The graph shows that compared with the baseline, which recorded progress during a non-behavioural physiotherapy approach, the patient made significant progress. Indeed, within a relatively short period of time, this patient became ambulant and independent of wheelchair or walking aid.

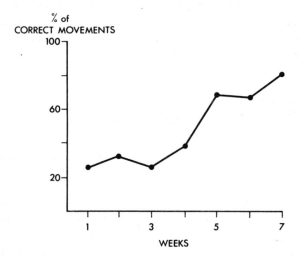

Fig. 10.9.

A positive reinforcement programme to aid transfer from wheelchair to chair during physiotherapy.

A similar application of behavioural methods in general rehabilitation was made by Goodkin (1966), who described the successful application of different behavioural approaches to patients who were not making progress in rehabilitation because they lacked co-operation, made little effort, or appeared unable to benefit from the more conventional therapy approaches currently in use. These patients were not head injured but had suffered cerebrovascular accidents, so among their major rehabilitative needs was an improvement of speech and communication skill. Goodkin describes several successful procedures used to improve performance in language-mediated activities of daily living, and also described the value of using patients' relatives to continue therapy techniques in the home, thereby improving opportunities for over-learning and generalization.

Within the context of speech and language disorders, a frequent problem following head injury is dysarthria which makes communication difficult. Fig. 10.10 demonstrates the improvement in clearly enunciated speech in a patient who demonstrated a severe scanning dysarthria 4 years after injury. He was able to produce clearly understandable speech with reasonable intonation and inflection within speech therapy sessions but would not attempt to generalize this to other situations on the unit. After attempts at positively reinforcing appropriate speech outside therapy session had failed, we resorted to a method of negative punishment, i.e. time-out room, to try to impress upon the patient the need to monitor his speech production. The procedure involved placing him in the time-out room for two minutes every time he produced unintelligible dysarthric speech. The success of this programme can be seen in the reduction of time-out penalties over a relatively short period of time. Unfortunately, this improvement did not generalize to situations outside the rehabilitation unit.

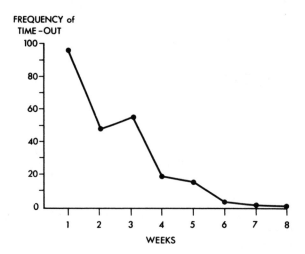

Fig. 10.10.

Reduction of dysarthric speech during a special time-out room programme.

A final example of an individual patient programme that is important to and easily implemented in a general rehabilitation unit involves attention to task training. Clearly, the amount of attention given by a patient in therapy sessions is very important to the successful outcome of rehabilitation. Patients who cannot maintain attention are distractable, difficult to work with, and slow to learn. Fig. 10.11 shows improvement in sustained concentration during selected speech and occupational therapy sessions.

The programme involved presenting token reinforcement at two-minute intervals, depending upon whether the patient was concentrating or not at the time. If the patient earned more than the minimum amount of tokens, he exchanged these for a reward at the end of the session. The improved attention response was maintained in therapy after the programme was discontinued.

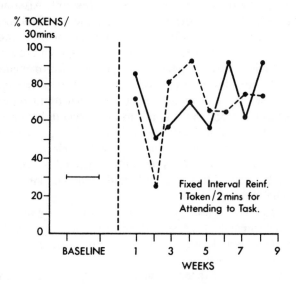

Fig. 10.11

Attention to task programme. Reinf. = Reinforcement.

SUMMARY

Behaviour management in brain injury rehabilitation is not a clinical panacea. It offers an organized procedure for controlling difficult behaviour problems, which often follow severe brain injury, and provides a system for improving existing rehabilitation procedures on conventional, non-behavioural, units. Its effectiveness, even on a specialized unit, is variable. There is no doubt that behaviour modification has proved reliable in the control of many positive behaviour disorders. The systematic procedure for dealing with aggressive or threatening behaviours gives therapy staff confidence and a feeling of personal security, allowing rehabilitation of the physical sequelae of such injuries to proceed. Behaviour modification has also been remarkably effective in providing a controlled way of administering conventional rehabilitational techniques, with the result that many patients who had been labelled 'untreatable' responded to the systematic application of reinforcement contingencies and made significant progress, at a time when any further physical recovery would have been regarded as most unlikely.

These methods are less reliable in cases where there is marked frontal lobe involvement, producing disinhibited, fatuous, and insightless behaviour. Such patients show considerable impairment of behavioural learning and, because ability for self-control is affected, when improvement does occur, it often fails to generalize to less structured settings. This does not mean, however, that behaviour modification has no value in the rehabilitation of such patients, but it does seem that more time and effort are needed to achieve control over behaviour.

Negative behaviour disorders have also proved quite difficult to treat. The apathetic and driveless character of such behaviour means that it is less influenced by a method of management which relies on manipulating and motivating behaviour through the application of rewards. Some patients do show increased drive and make greater effort on therapy tasks, but this is rarely sustained when the pressure, imposed by the behaviour management system, is removed. Obviously it is difficult to generalize about such matters: individual patients of this kind have made and maintained a very good response to rehabilitation.

The only group of patients who are definitely inappropriate for behaviour management are those with dissociative behaviour problems. Not only have we failed to make any progress with such patients, we have often made their behaviour worse.

For some time, learning theorists have felt that dissociation could be an elaborate avoidance response which serves to protect the individual from highly stressful events (Dollard and Miller 1950). Some clinical support for this comes from careful observation of such patients during a rehabilitation programme. For some time we have been aware of the paradox that although these patients are able to learn from experience, they do not show evidence of behavioural learning as a result of direct reinforcement or punishment contingencies. Knowledge that learning does occur is seen after discharge, when many of the behaviour programmes implemented within the context of rehabilitation are seen to have achieved control over problem behaviours or have improved social skills. Such objectives were part of the patient's original training programme, but no evidence of such learning occurred when the actual behaviour programme was in process. This form of 'latent learning' has been described by Eames as 'cognitive override' because of the obvious attempt by the patient to hide the fact that they are learning from, and benefiting by, the rehabilitation procedure.

Possibly, one of the most encouraging results of behaviour management in head-injury rehabilitation is that successful outcome has been achieved with a group of very severely head injured patients (PTA over 4 months) who present very difficult behaviour management problems and who, on average, are 3 years post injury. If this can be achieved with such major and chronic problems, a much faster and more meaningful outcome could be obtained in the rehabilitation of less severe brain injuries, especially if these methods were applied early in the recovery stage.

Behavioural rehabilitation is not necessarily restricted to specialist units. Methods to improve rehabilitation techniques on conventional units have been referred to above, and the earlier use of similar techniques by Goodkin in a general rehabilitation unit, supports this view. More recently, Wood (1981) described the successful application of positive reinforcement methods in improving self-care skills and reducing abusive behaviour with patients awaiting discharge from a small neurosurgical recovery unit. Similarly, Hollon (1972) showed how the application of positive reinforcement and systematic ignoring of disruptive behaviour successfully eliminated unmanageable behaviour and improved communication between patients and staff in a community rehabilitation hospital.

Behaviour methods are particularly valuable because they provide the opportunity to develop individual treatment programmes to suit the needs of particular patients, and they help the staff to concentrate their attention on specific problem behaviours. Behaviour management offers a method of carefully recording changes in behaviour so that we can evaluate the effectiveness of specific therapy techniques.

One can understand, however, that behavioural methods may not appear the most attractive treatment procedure and may be regarded by some as mechanistic, degrading, and inhuman. Their application to head-injury rehabilitation will be particularly controversial because the attitudes of many people towards handicapped victims of severe injury are that they deserve empathy and understanding, rather than the hard regimen of behaviour management, with its possible restriction of personal freedom and choice. One cannot argue with these attitudes except to say that there are different methods of behaviour management to suit different degrees of handicap and different types of problem. Only the most severe cases merit some of the extreme procedures described in this chapter. Yet, for these patients—who would otherwise receive no rehabilitation and possibly live the rest of their lives in psychiatric or subnormality units, under various degrees of sedation—behaviour management, rather than being a hard line, may offer many patients a lifeline.

REFERENCES

Allyon, T. and Azrin, N. H. (1968). *The token Economy: A motivational system for therapy and rehabilitation.* Appleton-Century-Crofts, New York.
—— and Milan, M. A. (1979). *Correctional rehabilitation and management: a psychological approach.* Wiley, New York.
Belmont, I. (1969). Effects of cerebral damage on motivation in rehabilitation. *Arch. Phys. Med. Rehabil.* **50**, 507–11.

Bond, M. R. and Brooks, D. N. (1976). Understanding the process of recovery as a basis for the investigation of rehabilitation for the brain injured. *Scand. J. Rehabil. Med.* **8**, 127–33;

Brooks, D. N. and Aughton, M. E. (1979). Psychological consequences of blunt head injury. *Int. Rehabil. Med.* **1**, 160–5.

Davidson, G. C. and Neale, J. (1974). *Abnormal psychology: an experimental clinical approach.* Wiley, New York.

Dollard, J. and Miller, N. E. (1950). *Personality and psychotherapy: an analysis in terms of learning, thinking and culture.* McGraw-Hill, New York.

Fahy, T. J., Irving, M. H., and Millac, P. (1967). Severe head injuries: a six-year follow-up. *Lancet* **ii**, 475–9.

Field, J. H. (1976). *Epidemiology of head injuries in England and Wales,* HMSO, London.

Goodkin, R. (1966). Case studies in behavioural research in rehabilitation. *Percept. Motor Skills* **23**, 171–82.

Hillbom, E. (1951). Schizophrenia-like psychosis after brain trauma. *Acta Psychiatr. Neurol. Scand.* Suppl. **60**, 36–47.

Hollon, T. H. (1972). Behaviour modification in a community hospital rehabilitation unit. *Arch. Phys. Med. Rehabil.* **54**, 65–8.

Hull, C. L. (1943). *Principles of behaviour.* Appleton, New York.

Janet, P. (1907). *The major symptoms of hysteria,* Macmillan, New York.

Jennett, B., Snoek, J., Bond, M. R., Brooks, D. N. (1981). Disability after severe head injury: observations on the use of the Glasgow Outcome Scale. *J. Neurol. Neurosurg. Psychiatr.* **44**, 285–93.

Lezak, M. D. (1978). Living with the characterologically altered brain-injured patient. *J. Clin. Psychiatr.* **39**, 592–8.

Lishman, W. A. (1968). Brain damage in relation to psychiatric disability after head injury. *Br. J. Psychiatr.* **114**, 373–410.

—— (1973). The psychiatric sequelae of head injury: a review. *Psychol. Med.* **3**, 304–18.

—— (1978). Organic psychiatry, Blackwell, Oxford.

McKinlay, W.W., Brooks, D. N., Bond, M. R., Martinage, D. P., and Marshall, M. M. (1981). The short-term outcome of severe blunt head injury, as reported by relatives of the injured persons. *J. Neurol. Neurosurg. Psychiatr.* **44**, 285–93.

Oddy, M., Humphrey, M., and Uttley, D. (1978). Subjective impairment and social recovery after closed head injury. *J. Neurol. Neurosurg. Psychiatr.* **41**, 611–16.

Rosenbaum, M. and Najenson, T. (1976). Changes in life patterns and symptoms of low mood as reported by wives of severely brain-injured soldiers. *J. Consult. Clin. Psychol.* **44**, 881–8.

Shapiro, L. B. (1939). Schizophrenia-like psychosis following head injury. *Il. Med. J.* **76**, 250–4.

Sweet, W. H., Ervin, F., and Mark, V. H. (1969). The relationship of violent behaviour to focal cerebral disease. In *Aggressive behaviour,* (ed. S. Garattini and A. Sigg). pp.336–57. Wiley, New York.

Tennent, T. (1937). Discussion on mental disorder following head injury. *Proc. R. Soc. Med.* **30**, 1092–3.

Thompsen, I. V. (1974). The patient with severe head injury and his family. *Scand. J. Rehabil. Med.* **6**, 180–3.

Wall, R. T. (1969). Behaviour modification and rehabilitation. *Rehabil. Counsel. Bull.,* December, pp.173–83.

Whitlock, F. A. (1967). The aetiology of hysteria. *Acta Psychiatr. Scand.* **43**, 144–62.

Wood, M. M. (1981). Behavioural methods in rehabilitation. In *Head Injuries an Integrated Approach* (ed. T. A. R. Dinning and J. J. Connelley). pp.66–7. Wiley, Brisbane.

Wood, R. L. and Eames, P. G. (1981). Behaviour modification in the rehabilitation of brain injury. In *Applications of conditioning theory* (ed. G. Davey) pp.81–101. Methuen, New York.

Author index

Subject index